# the Graham Kerr step-by-step cookbook

# the Graham Kerr

## step-by-step

## cookbook

### by Graham & Treena Kerr

David C. Cook Publishing Co.

ELGIN, ILLINOIS—WESTON, ONTARIO

Library of Congress Cataloging in Publication Data

Kerr, Graham.
      The Graham Kerr step-by-step cookbook.


Includes index.
1.  Cookery.   I.  Kerr, Treena, 1934-   .II.  Title.
III.  Title: Step-by-step cookbook.
TX715.K3784          641.5          82-1402
                                     AACR2

ISBN 0-89191-563-X (pbk.)

FIRST EDITION
April 1982

ISBN 0-89191-563-X

LC 82-1402

# CONTENTS

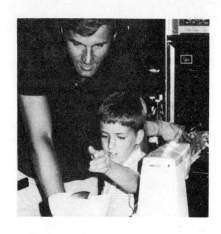

# the galloping gourmet

# CHAPTER 1

Food was my bread and butter! In all of recorded history — for a brief span of years — I became the highest paid cook in the world!

Without television, tenacity, and Treena, it wouldn't have been possible. It couldn't have lasted. And in fact, it didn't.

It all began in England on January 22, 1934, the day I was born. My father was predominantly Scottish, my mother English through and through.

I can remember little of my earliest years and some of what I feel I know is confused with tales often repeated by my parents. But I remember World War II all too well; it disrupted my relationships.

*Graham Kerr, age four, at Brighton, England.*

I was five when my father joined the army and eleven when Nazi Germany fell. When he returned, my dad was almost forty. His career interrupted, he was forced to engage in another, almost as aggressive an occupation as war.

Dad became a hotelier, or should we say hotel manager? I suspect that neither of my parents were really satisfied with their role. Their customers were "friends-of-a-sort," yet they could never forget the artificial privilege: the fact that they were paid to serve these "friends."

In the post World War II era, there was little upward mobility. The few *nouveau riche* found themselves resisted by cold shoulders in the narrow connecting corridors of the settled rich. My parents were servants to both. Yet I must admit that the gentry called them John and Marjorie with genuine affection.

I had no brothers or sisters. My singular role models were my parents, so I decided to be a hotelier like my dad — but not quite like him. I wanted to do so well that I'd leave the servant image behind. To most people a hotel manager was without skill, simply an executive barman. I decided that I would attempt to enhance the image of food, wine,

and its service so that I would gain status by association. But a long apprenticeship had to be served before I could start on that plan.

As excellent a cook as my mother is, I didn't learn to cook from her. There was no room for women in post-war chef chauvinism. My earliest influences came from Polish and French chefs who, having survived the war, were now trying hard to reestablish the traditions of haute cuisine in a land that was just emerging from food rationing.

Our customers ranged from Lord Shawcross, the chief justice of England, to Sir Winston Churchill, and on to downhome folk like J. Paul Getty. I learned to scrub floors, peel potatoes, and finally, to serve as a *commis,* the European term for a busboy.

When I was sixteen, I was given the first real advancement of my career. The headwaiter in the dining room of the Roebuck Hotel in Wychcross crooked his white, gloved finger and beckoned me to the "pulpit" from which he directed the seating. "Time to try your hand at being a waiter, Master Graham," he commanded sternly.

Lord Shawcross, then Sir Hartley Shawcross, had been seated close to the diamond-shaped, leaded windows that allowed a beautiful view across Ashdown Forest. He was my first customer.

A man of impeccable manners and excellent taste, Sir Hartley ordered a dover sole to be grilled in butter and served whole. No, he didn't want it filleted at tableside, for which I drew an almost audible sigh of relief.

Thoughts raced through my mind — giddy thoughts of the future. No longer would I simply fill water glasses and clear plates from the table. Now I would suggest entrees to our famous guests, exchanging a word or two with people I read about in the papers.

When the sole finally arrived it was fully ten inches long, weighed in just short of one pound, and glistened in *beurre maitre d'hotel.* I carefully inched the flat fish knives under the tender, buttery fish and lifted it at exactly the point of balance.

With a flourish, a natural confidence that belied my years, I served the sole...

...right onto the tablecloth. The plate that I, as a *commis,* had usually put down for the waiter was not there. Butter was slowly being absorbed by the slightly starched, white damask tablecloth.

Sir Hartley surveyed first the fish, then the advancing yellow stain, and finally lifted his eyes to mine. "May I," he asked carefully, "have a plate?"

From moments and men such as these, I began to learn that it is not only what we eat, but how we eat it, that, to a degree, reflects social status. Eight years later a casual meeting at an executive dinner party gave me the opportunity to advance far beyond even my fanciful dreams.

The Royal New Zealand Air Force had moved my wife, Treena, and me from Britain to Wellington where I was to serve as their chief catering advisor. My new position gave me the entrance to the dinner.

The meal had been a good one: a saddle of local spring lamb brought fresh from the New Zealand coastlands, early strawberries from Hawkes Bay, and some well-kept Chinese gooseberries from last season. The port had been passed, a deep ruby red that swashed about in the almost diamond brilliance of an Irish crystal decanter.

I was idly spinning a walnut at the tip of my finger, waiting to receive the hallmarked silver nutcrackers.

"I hear you were in the British Army. Which regiment?" inquired a gray-eyed young lady, whose hair was short and swept back.

*Which regiment?* I glanced down at my port. How do you respond to "Which regiment," when you served in the Army Catering Corps!

I didn't want to be known as a cook. Not in my dinner jacket, here among the established rich. The young woman's question seemed loaded with social emphasis.

Yet I answered truthfully as my thoughts tracked back to worn cement kitchen floors and the ever-present smell of grease.

"How interesting."

She didn't seem to mind. "So you are involved with food. So am I...indirectly." She smiled quickly and went on. "I work with Women's Broadcasting at the New Zealand Broadcasting Corporation...Have you ever thought of doing a radio program?"

"No, never!" I smiled. The absurdity of the idea struck me as hugely funny.

But Shirley Maddox needed someone to host a foods show. Apparently she was desperate enough to consider my hotelier, chef school, and army-catering-corps experience sufficient. After further conversation I was enlisted to write a series of radio shows.

But nine months and eight rejected scripts later, I was sure my first reaction was more accurate than hers. However the idea no longer seemed like a joke to me. Neither did the really monstrous recording sessions where I was treated to what seemed like hours of isolation in a fish-tank studio where I faltered, stammered, and began to deal with what the professionals described as the "world's most boring voice"!

Despite this handicap, Shirley's hunch proved to be right. By Christmas of 1959 she called to con-gratulate me on the success of my programs. "You see, it worked! You never believed it, did you?"

The first shows were being broadcast and they were a success. All of my cherished memories of food experiences had been used to do a series of nine-minute lectures.

"You ready to do another series?" Shirley asked almost immediately.

"Well...er...Yes, I suppose so." I could say nothing else. My wildest dreams were coming true: people were listening to me talk about food and wine and interesting places. I wasn't a cook. I was a broadcaster, a radio personality.

"Good. Then try to get them in by late January." The phone went dead. I held it away from my ear, then slowly put it down.

*September 22, 1955. The bride's parents are on the right and the groom's on the left.*

*How?* I wondered. How could a man of twenty-five have enough experiences to do more programs? I was almost angry. Treena was making sandwiches at a local milk bar for fifty cents an hour, and we were expecting our second child. Our daughter Tessa was three.

It wasn't long before I discovered the key: *The Gentlemen's Companion,* a book that was both workbook and travel guide to some nifty eateries around the world. All too easily, I became a secret armchair gourmet, broadcasting my imagined experiences as a well-seasoned traveler with ever-increasing communication skills. By the summer of 1960 Shirley was again congratulating me. "Graham, your last series was super! So much better than your first."

*Why is fiction so much better than fact?* I thought to myself. My career, once it was released from the burden of my own limited personal experience, took flight. Soon I was president of the Wine and Food Society in Wellington and chairman of the select committees on hotel training to the minister of education. By 1962 I had my own television show, where my radio recipes were given added media credibility.

Even my own fantasies had never anticipated that for the next two years I would be named "TV Personality of the Year." I retired from the air force to manage my own consulting company and display center, still maintaining my radio and television shows — and even writing a few books.

Food was not so much a personal eating experience as a script. Each dish was interwoven with words, symbols, and meanings quite beyond the value of the recipe. Gourmet cooking and elegant dining had become the status symbol I had wished for so long ago. Yet I was forced by environment — and my own desperate desire to succeed — to embellish my presentation to make it entertaining.

"The fella's too fruity to be a true mate," some Australian men complained. "'E oughta wear a apron if yer ask me!" Men didn't take kindly to my appearance on television. Largely, I suspect, because my first program replaced professional soccer at eight o'clock on a Wednesday night — risky programming to say the least!

Since I did not come complete with cauliflower ear, local accent, and mud-spattered shins, I was judged to be a potential "fruitcake." I countered this objection by adding vocabulary and humor to my show — a stunt unheard of in gastronomic circles.

I would slosh up a dish while taking a short slurp (a mouthful of wine) and generally slap the food around, rather than allow my intricate movements to be misunderstood.

It worked! All of a sudden the tiger of fame and fortune raced by. I grabbed its tail and the madness, unable to be anticipated, began. For a while I was able to run the race. But soon I became exhausted by the radical life-style changes that vast increases in money bring. By 1968, Treena and I were at a very low ebb: knee deep in difficulty, both personal, family, and financial. The tiger was about to stop, turn around, and have me for dinner!

It was at this precise moment that I was "discovered" by an American television production house in New York City. Someone had lit a fire under the tiger and with very little rhyme or reason, we were off again, this time with Treena at the helm as the show's producer. CBS chose a midday slot between two soap operas for my North American debut in January of 1969. I'm not sure that it could possibly have failed with such a placement.

Now that we earned vast amounts of money we could afford to travel continuously and locate the actual dishes described years ago in *The Gentleman's Companion.* My broadcasts were no longer gastronomic fantasies but my own experiences. Food and wine became big business, much more than my bread and butter. The "Galloping Gourmet" went worldwide, was translated into several languages, and won international awards here and there. At the impossible age of thirty-seven, I was a millionaire and possibly the best known food authority in the world — certainly the highest paid. Food and travel, all the privileges of going first-class were heaped upon us. It was pure hedonistic status.

But the list of my career successes is only matched by my personal failures. Everything had happened at such a rapid clip that I had had little time to grow as a person. In fact, Treena and I were becoming more miserable with each passing day. Our children were running wild with neglect, and our marriage was falling apart. Treena turned to a variety of mood changing drugs and alcohol to withstand the pressure of producing my tv show and keeping up with my schizophrenic life-style.

In 1970, Treena and I were at a theater watching *Lawrence of Arabia* when the manager, having recognized us as we entered, tapped me on the shoulder; we were wanted at the hospital. Our oldest daughter Tessa, then thirteen, was having her stomach pumped, because she had taken an overdose of pain killers.

We had hired the best live-in nurse we could find, but our communication with our children had often been limited to posting notices on the refrigerator door. Coming in at night long after the children were in bed, we rose after they had left for school. It had been six or seven weeks since we had spent any quality time with Tessa.

As strange as it seems, Tessa's tragic plea for help made no substantial change in our life-style. Contractual obligations had to be met. The tiger was still running and we were still hanging on desperately. So we set out on our next project. We had recorded almost five hundred international dishes on television. Now we felt it was time to circumnavigate the United States to trace how old-world dishes had been adapted by the American culture to become new classics.

We set off in a caravan of motor homes filled with cameras and equipment to make an ambitious nationwide series of over one hundred programs. At 1:00 A.M. of April 7, 1971, on U.S. Highway 101, Treena and I were almost killed in a violent accident that terminated the Galloping Gourmet then and there. My left side was partially paralyzed, and Treena was so badly traumatized, she was unable to work at all. Later she contracted tuberculosis.

We gathered up our three children, licked our wounds, and retired with our small fortune to sail about the world. As a young man I'd knocked about in fourteen-foot sailboats, but I had never, no never, in my wildest imagination considered that I would own a $496,000 yacht over five times longer.

We christened her "Treena." No man in his right mind — or wrong mind for that matter — would name a seventy-one-foot racing yacht by any other name than his wife's. In March of 1972 we set sail from England bound for the Mediterranean and then the world. Our object was to recover our strength, and see how the "other half" — those who sat in front of the tv screen — lived.

Three months later we tied our yacht up alongside a dock in Antibes in the south of France and went off to celebrate Treena's birthday by revisiting the Bonne Auberg, a famous restaurant between Cannes and Nice.

We ate exactly what we had eaten two years before when we had come to film our television series. But that night when we retired aboard the yacht to be "rocked to sleep upon the bosom of the deep," we were totally unprepared for the early morning awakening we received: with a singular lack of sophistication, Treena and I threw up our gourmet dinner!

I do not care to be sick. I am, after all, a man, and we do not suffer small illnesses well. But we had not realized how simply we had been eating on board ship. Our systems had become used to this simpler diet.

Once we realized this, we began to research and develop an alternative style of eating in earnest. Gone was the desire for the copious consumption of alcohol, butter, and cream. Oils were cut to the bone. Pastries and sugar-crusted goodies literally hit the deck along with chocolates, candies, and ice cream. We were left with lean meat, poultry, and fish, which were dry broiled or steamed. We had huge crisp salads and plenty of fresh fruit. Yogurt replaced ice cream.

The results were remarkable. No longer did we blame our "sea legs" for our stomach upsets. Instead we realized we had been awash with overrich food and wine and were literally among the walking wounded. The gentle rocking of the boat at anchor had brought our sub-physical sickness to the surface. We had chosen to change our life-style to eliminate nausea.

Good reason? You bet it was!

No matter how fancy the yacht, the human species eventually finds shipboard life arduous. After two years and 24,000 miles, we were fed up with being cut off from "normal" people. In October of 1973 we came ashore to test our decision to reside in the United States and immediately began to revert to our previous eating styles.

This time, however, the nausea returned without the need to be rocked! Our bodies were not about to revert to the elaborate foods our senses were all too eager to receive. So we switched back to a modified

*On board ship.*

boat diet and revived immediately.

Six months later I read a small book by a popular investment prophet, in which he encouraged investors to consider foundation stock. By choosing well, Treena and I might see our capital enormously increased when our selected corporation eventually went public. But the corporation we chose made a choice themselves: they went bankrupt! And we lost some $600,000.

In the ensuing weeks I learned an executive trick. When I would start to feel my heart race and my nose go numb, I reached into my briefcase to withdraw a used — but excellent quality — brown paper bag. Excusing myself I would retreat to a washroom to blow into the bag and inhale my own breath. This isn't a *Fortune* magazine tip, I realize. Yet I have found that the tensions of the twentieth century executive do lead to hyperventilation, among other more serious things, which is temporarily relieved by the paper bag trick.

I was devastated by this sudden erosion of what I had felt was a secure base, so I decided to return to television to replace the lost funds. We made a series called "Take Kerr" (I pronounce my name "care." Hence the rather neat title that nobody understood, since most people call me "cur"!)

This show was different, because it sought to reflect the lessons we had learned at sea: how to eat without self-destruction. It was short and to the point, designed to be a part of newscasts and magazine-styled local shows. The format was most successful, so we speculated that in a year or two we would recover our losses.

It has never failed to amaze me how rapidly our various economic disasters have been repealed. All it took, in each case, was for me to step in front of a camera and talk faster and faster. But then the tiger seemed capable of an exponential burst of speed each time I laid hold of its tail.

Still, I was beginning to realize that life as Treena and I were living it made little sense. This was reflected in a speech I made in Fort Lauderdale.

After this speech in February of 1975, my agent, Wilbur Freifeld, called me with a most astounding request: "A bishop who heard your speech last week wants you to do a tour of the United States speaking to his denomination...."

"Willie, you *must* be joking!"

But Wilburt was quite serious. The bishop had heard me speak about "the poor peoples of the world and their great need for food while we overfeed ourselves in our obese culture." That wasn't the kind of thing I usually said. Public relations was one thing, but preaching on poverty to an extremely affluent group simply wasn't my style.

Not long after the speech even I began to realize the monumental internal change that was taking place within me. First Treena, then I, became what is often referred to as born-again Christians.

Let me simply say that the results were radical. Close relationships shredded by our life-style were repaired and external food changes made for the purely personal motive of feeling better now took on an extraordinary new direction.

My speech in Fort Lauderdale had actually shocked me. I had been surprised by the pain I felt. As I began to practice what I had preached, the pain became stronger until one day, by careful choice, I began to emerge from my chrysalis of comfort. It was then that I began to hear the cries of the poor.

Poverty is a dark place. But when the poor are oppressed and have little recourse to justice, there is no light at all. And without light there is no hope.

Our family had been without hope, even though we were far from poor. Yet Jesus had come into our dark place to give us hope. Why then, I reasoned, couldn't this same Jesus provide light to those in poverty?

I found one small answer to this question in Paul's second letter to the church in Corinth: "...at this present time your abundance being a supply for their want, that their abundance also may become a supply for your want, that there may be equality" (2 Cor. 8:14, NASB).

I certainly had an abundant life-style — that is, more material possessions than I required for my small family's needs. Perhaps, in some small way, my family's abundance could be a supply for someone else's needs. Over the next year this thought began to grow and lead Treena and I into a very unique ministry.

We made decisions some people didn't understand: we quit television, sold our personal things of value, and began to follow Jesus. Our feelings of guidance in the next months were so absorbing, so

remarkably accurate (and inaccurate), that food seemed to become completely pedestrian, not in the least spiritual, and even the source of some fairly major heresy. After all, food had led to our extreme unhappiness.

All in all we wanted out, no more cooking for profit — ever. It was too worldly. Couldn't people just leave us alone? The "Galloping Gourmet" needed to be permanently unsaddled. He needed to die and remain buried, so we could get on with our quest to hear God, which surely must excite everyone as much as it did us!

But God's answer was quite different than we had expected. Apparently he intended to use our earlier experiences, regardless of how distasteful we felt some of them had been.

Each day my concern for the starving peoples of the world increased. The latest figures indicate that every minute fifty-seven children die of starvation. That amounts to about 30 million children a year! Almost five times as many in one year as Hitler exterminated in the full span of his "final solution" to the Jewish problem. That has something to do with food: the lack of it.

On the other hand there are nations where a person dies at the rate of one every forty-three seconds from a different kind of malnutrition: overconsuming the wrong foods.

I became a radical crusader, heralding a life-standard that stressed underconsumption. I rarely do anything halfway, so the pendulum swung $180^0$ in the opposite direction. Food and cooking had been destructive in my life; it was destructive to many peoples' bodies in the United States. The only alternative was an extreme natural foods diet.

Treena was instructed to throw away everything in our cupboard that had nitrates, food colorings, preservatives, etc. I became critical and condemnatory. If Treena or the children snuck Coke, Pepsi, or any other pop into the house, I recited a long list of statistics and chemical names in a louder-than-loud voice to prove how destructive some foods are to our bodies.

Toward the end of four years of total "abstinence," my attitudes began to mellow. I surrendered to the occasional urge to enjoy a dish of ice cream for dessert, or Treena ate a piece of ham or bacon. She even began to drink diet pop when I was around.

Now my only response to this misdemeanor would be a pleading, "Darling, I wish you wouldn't" or "Haven't you read the warning on the can?" Finally even those words became inappropriate.

The other change in our life-style was an assessment of how we used our money. At first this was relatively easy. Having earned a million taxable dollars, I had employed a tax consultant who made us record all our expenditures. At the end of each year we received a computer printout of how we had spent our money.

Treena and I carefully scrutinized this list with an eye to excess. How foolishly we had spent our money! We created a benchmark — an amount of money that was necessary for our needs — and vowed to use any excess money to provide food for those who were hungry. Each month we kept a list of everthing we spent, and then took another look at our expenditures. Even with the forced economics of our new $15,000-dollar-a-year income, we still found wasteful expenditures. This squandered money we put aside for others who needed it.

Then we carefully analyzed our food expenditures, devising a means of saving money by selecting less expensive foods and preparing them in a healthful and inexpensive way. We began to realize the wasteful portions that we in the United States consume.

Most of us only need three ounces of meat per day. But have you ever taken a good look at the amount of meat served in a restuarant? Or in your own home? If the steak doesn't cover one-fourth to one-half of the plate, we feel cheated. Treena and I found that smaller portions reduced that telltale drowsy-and-stuffed-to-the-brim feeling many of us seem to associate — pleasantly or unpleasantly — with eating.

In 1978, at a Youth-With-a-Mission training school, I felt God's call to begin a ministry that would utilize excess funds to feed the poor of Third World countries. The plan was to establish quarter-acre "microfarms" on 100 foot square plots of land, which would house, feed, and provide for a family of six. Each microfarm would include a small house, many long rows of "grow boxes" to raise various foods, a small orchard, a pond, and an animal shelter. Volunteers, trained in the United States, would build these microfarms, then train a local family to utilize certain agricultural techniques so they could run the facility themselves.

Others who heard about this idea joined with us to help raise money for our new endeavor, which became known as Project L.O.R.D. (Long Range Development for the World). We all pledged to donate our "new money" (funds that had previously been committed to meaningless or unnecessary expenditures) to the project. This was our response to God's words: Your abundance should be a supply for their want.

Even now we keep an account of what we chose *not* to buy each month; we also list savings we get from energy conservation. Then we give this amount to a third party — not one of our group — who lists what each of us gave and issues a receipt (in our case a tax exempt receipt).

In this way we have avoided being known for what we give, which seems to us to be a trap! "So when you give to the needy, do not announce it with trumpets, as the hypocrites do in the synagogues and on the streets, to be honored by men. ...Then your Father, who sees what is done in secret, will reward you" (Matt. 6:2-4, NIV).

Each month the total funds collected are shipped off in their entirety to Belize in Central America. Through God's providence this government provided Project L.O.R.D. a quarter acre of its agricultural showground, which is visited each spring by 30,000 Belizeans during their national agricultural show. A team of seven young Christians built a home on this land and began farming it. Treena and I hope that other microfarms will be established throughout Belize, Central America, and indeed throughout the hurting world of rural poverty.

In the last couple of years, God has taught us that food is no longer status; it is sacred. It is a blessing to be shared with others in our homes throughout America and our neighbors in other lands. This cookbook, which culminates my twenty years as a professional gourmet, is dedicated to eating better for less. The exotic recipes of my younger years have been revised in view of my concern for our own health and that or our brothers and sisters in other countries. Because it is a complete cookbook, recipes for preparing unusual foods (such as squid, calves brains, and raw pickled fish) are also included for those who like these dishes.

*Praise the Lord!*

My feelings about food in the last twenty three years have been a roller coaster ride: soaring high into the sky and plummeting down into the valleys. Finally the ride is over. Treena and I are on level ground. We have discovered that food can be both sustenance and celebration, a blessed part of our life here on earth. May it be as much a joy in your home as it is in ours.

# CHAPTER 2

## Color, Creativity, and Celebration

To simplify your life-style is one thing. To actually enjoy and celebrate such a change is another. Or is it?

Our great hope is that this book will provide the groundwork for a new way of living. Not another new life-style, for styles are fickle. But a new life standard because standards endure.

I do not believe God wants us to feel guilty about the thousands who are starving. Nor do I believe that he expects us to give up all we have and sleep in the streets of India. I do believe that he wants us to have compassion for those who are hungry. As Jesus said in Matthew 9: "But go and learn what this means; I desire compassion, and not sacrifice" (vs. 13).

By giving the excess of our income each month, Treena and I feel that we are showing this compassion. Rather than writing a check every year or so, we are recognizing our brotherhood with them each day. We feel that it is possible to obey the great one-liner: "Whether, then, you eat or drink or whatever you do, do all to the glory of God" (1 Cor. 10:31). And when we do this, we are free to enjoy the funds that remain.

At one time Treena and I were deeply motivated by creative advertising inducements, even though we actually helped produce many of them and knew how we manipulated status symbols of power and privilege to make self-indulgence a sound investment. But finally we realized that as we submitted ourselves to the media, we allowed our minds — and often our subsequent decisions — to fit into the desires of another person.

There is a nifty proverb that has helped me: "Keep deception and lies far from me, give me neither poverty nor riches; feed me with the food that is my portion, lest I be full and deny Thee and say 'Who is the Lord?' or lest I be in want and steal, and profane the name of my God" (Prov. 30:8).

Every day, as all of us sit in front of television, listen to the radio, or read magazines or newspapers, we receive messages about something new (or improved) that we will enjoy eating, that will invigorate, or will save us time or money.

Many of those advertisements are deception and lies. The products are not enjoyable. They do not invigorate. And while they may save time, they certainly do not cost less than the natural alternative. We are vulnerable to these false advertising for three main reasons.

The first is our frantic desire to save time. A few minutes, a few hours have become our most precious commodity. Strangely enough time is in ample supply in Third World nations, but our work ethic insists that we must work ever harder so we can afford a greater variety of opportunity to relax.

Recently I was visiting a microfarm in Dominica, a small island in the Caribbean between Martinique and Guadeloupe. The coast-to-coast minibus broke down five times in only twenty-five miles. It took many hours longer than normal to make what is, at the best of times, an uncomfortable trip.

As the passengers unloaded and were greeted by family and friends, there was an enormous sense of joy and excitement. A friend explained that a series of breakdowns gave the participants a grand story to tell. This was an event that they would retell dozens of times, always to an audience that had time to listen.

I thought of our fast life. How frustrated I would have been if this had happened in the United States, how critical of the busline. I'd have vowed to fly next time, even though it cost five times as much! And what would I have hurried home to do? For many of us, the answer would be sit in an overstuffed chair and watch television. The latest national figures show that approximately 6.5 hours a day are spent watching tv. That's an average of forty-five hours a week. This is one area where we could start to reallocate our time and have added hours for leisure and creative cooking.

For food is an enormously important area of life-standard change. If one takes time in buying and preparation, the savings can reach $700 a year for a family of four — that is, if you make the switch from multi-convenience foods to a natural source of supply. Good food can also mean a great deal to the quality of life enjoyed by both family and friends. Regardless of how quickly it is eaten, the memory of a good meal not only lingers but actually increases with time.

The second reason we are so vulnerable to advertising is the susceptibility of our senses to certain stimuli. Food technologists know that we have only six primary taste responses: sweet, sour, bitter, salt, piquant (the "hot" sharp taste of chili), and "roundfullness" (the "feel" of eating oil or fat as in ice cream). It follows that if manufacturers can make a product that is sweetened, salted, and has a touch of lemon and a smattering of chili, it's going to have a good chance of success — especially if it's brightly colored, smells typical, and has texture that crunches in the mouth.

Now all the product needs is a package that attracts the eye and feels good in the customer's hands when it is held. Finally this manmade food is given a name and a promotion campaign in order to fix it in the consumer's mind.

Have you ever realized how nonaddictive natural food products are? There seems to be a limit on how many eggs we can consume, or oranges, bananas, lettuce, tomatoes, radishes, spinach, peas. I could go on forever. It is only when we add the salt, the sugar, or honey — when we puff up, crisp, season, and add color that the desire to eat more and more is upon us.

The final reason that we are so susceptible to advertising is our indifference to others, our selfishness. Nowhere else is our self-gratification more easily accomplished, with less judgment from society, than in the supermarket. The enormous choice of food numbs the brain. To choose wisely is to successfully run the gauntlet of one aisle after another.

The supermarket is a highly controlled space. Its designers know that here the largest percentage of the discretionary income of the average home is spent. There are literally billions of dollars at stake and competition is fierce.

Here we can decide to respond to the implanted jingle, to lift the colored crinkle pack, to instantly recall its promise. "Buy me." It almost has a voice of its own.

With a small, half-resigned smile you lower it into your shopping basket. . . . But celebration doesn't depend on how big, or how varied a table you can lay. It's hard to celebrate when we are trying to impress our neighbors — or even ourselves — by trying the latest macrobiotic nut loaf with sesame seed hollandaise! The thoughtful creativity and care is what really counts.

Celebration means using what we have in a way that brings joy and wonderful memories — without heartburn, obesity, or guilt. It means making the very best of what one has, and sharing it with no other feeling than love. And this begins at home.

I don't believe you can celebrate with a credit card. We can eat out, we can perhaps *entertain* others, but the real honest-to-goodness celebration begins and ends in our own houses or apartments. Home is exactly the right place to celebrate because it, too, is worthy of thanksgiving; it, too, is a gift.

Since our homes are of variable size, we need first to discuss the size of a celebration. This obviously depends upon the nature of the occasion. Let's look at some of the options.

*Small dinner party.* This celebration includes only one other couple, people we love dearly — perhaps our closest friends. It may be their anniversary (or ours). Whatever the reason, we want to share it together and look back upon this time with fond memories.

*Table-size party.* Here other friends or close family are included. The number goes up to — but not beyond — eight people. Groups that exceed eight run into a communications problem, and any potential for group celebration is diluted.

*Multiple tables.* This is an expanded version of the table-size party. Card tables or occasional tables can be uniformly covered with red-check tablecloths for a casual plan or with white, starched linen for very special moments such as weddings and certain anniversaries. Twenty is often the limit imposed by the size of our homes.

*The buffet.* This celebration uses the buffet table, from which fork-style food can be served. The number of guests is up to you, but more than twenty often becomes tiresome for both the celebrants and the hosts!

*The barbeque buffet.* Outdoor space is used in the same manner as the buffet, but the style of serving will be more casual.

Variations on these themes can be achieved by the time of day: a breakfast, lunch, brunch, or supper.

## Foods for celebration

To my mind the highest possible goal of any celebration is to be able to give genuine heartfelt thanks to God for the food. The best example of such a celebration is, of course, Thanksgiving. Typically, the foods served are seasonal foods since the harvest is being celebrated.

Whatever food is growing naturally, whatever is "in season," should be your first choice. If it is truly in season, then the food will also be readily available in excellent quality and be reasonably priced (compared with, say, Mexican strawberries served in midwinter). It is often wise to choose foods in the middle of their season in order to avoid the early cropping varieties of certain plants or fruits; they just don't have the flavor of those at the season's peak.

If it happens to be midwinter, and if your climate is harsh, may I add a radical idea. Don't be tempted to cook heavy, rich food because the weather is cold. The days of snow blowing into a log cabin as a fur-clad man comes home from the woods to a hearty bear stew with dumplings are almost completely gone.

We have become cradled in comfort, yet we are still possessed with the notion that our food needs to change with the climate outside. We adopt the hearty stew concept as if it will bless our overweight, underexercised (it's too cold to jog) friends. Winter, of all times, is not for hearty robust fare, but for color, texture, and aroma with small but well-presented main dishes.

Remember you are feeding your family or guests for their sake, not yours!

Now let's look at each of these steps more closely.

## Your guests

Have you ever drawn up a guest list and noted by each name his or her needs? Mary has high blood pressure. Jack had a mild heart attack last spring. Henry needs to lose weight...These are the facts we know, but we can also assume some other probabilities.

When autopsies were performed on young G.I.'s who died in the Vietnam War, doctors discovered that a great many otherwise fit young men were suffering from arteriosclerosis (arteries partially clogged with a fatty substance; it can lead to thrombosis and even death through heart failure).

These young men were in their twenties! Yet they also suffered from digestive malfunctions, ulcers, and all manner of maladies, either directly or indirectly linked to poor food habits.

So, no matter what your guests' ages may be — and no matter how fit they seem — they may be on their way to a serious physical malfunction from either too much to eat or eating unwisely. Since the latest research indicates that 40 percent of the population in the USA is obese (and 28 percent or more are in excess of normal weight), it also stands to reason that they will be watching their weight.

At this point you have two options: you can assist them in over-eating, or, really loving them, you can come up with a creative alternative. What I am about to suggest is no slick panacea, no easy answer. Loving, after all, takes effort.

Learn how to cook!

"Wait a minute," you probably respond. "I've been cooking for years."

Please let me explain what I mean. Cooking involves four steps, one or more of which are often overlooked, resulting in a dull offering that is no more worthy of celebration than a meal at your local fast-food outlet. Cooking is:

*Planning.* This will involve all the decisions about your guests' needs, possible menu, seasonal items that enhance or limit the choices, etc.

*Preparation.* In this step, you will cut, weigh, measure, or otherwise lay out all the ingredients that make up the recipe.

*Assembly.* Here you are following that method of heating or combining the ingredients that is appropriate to the recipe: what we usually think of as cooking.

*Serving.* The presentation of the food to your family or guests.

## Planning

The pace at which we live is ever increasing in speed and complications so the scriptural view of the Kingdom as "righteousness, peace, and joy in the Holy Spirit" (rather than food, drink, or clothing) is of great importance as we make plans.

To Treena and I, righteousness means living in such a fashion that no man has cause to be offended by our behavior. Peace means having an inner smile when chaos surrounds us, and joy means living in continual expectation of God's blessings, either for ourselves or those we love.

To achieve these overall goals of the Kingdom in the practical world of planning a celebration, you need to first of all choose the right time. When you set the date to celebrate, let it be uncrowded, as free as possible from stressful periods. If the date has been set well ahead of time, avoid too many other obligations that would hinder your peaceful anticipation of the coming occasion.

A list is a great planning tool. Now, I know that not everyone likes lists. Treena, for example, hates them; she gets things done by carrying all the facts in her head. Consequently, she has a good memory — and sleepless nights! Only as a last resort will she make a list.

However, using lists from the beginning results in restful nights and less tension (and a poor memory?).

Here is a basic check list for the diligent planner:
1. Reason for celebration
2. Number attending
3. Date _____ Season _____
4. Type of party
5. Guest list (with known physical needs and food preferences or dislikes noted)
6. Seasonal foods locally available
7. Other fresh foods available in good quality and price
8. Flowers in season for decoration (not essential but nice)
9. If guest came before, what did you serve? (You don't have to be different, but it is more creative to break new ground.)

I would suggest a second list to help you decide what you should serve:
1. How many courses? Name them.
2. What will the main food item be (i.e. steak or chicken, etc.)?

3. List vegetables that go well with this main dish.
4. Decide on a first course that does not repeat the foods listed in numbers 2 and 3 (lobster as a main dish when shrimp is the first course, or carrot soup when the orange vegetables are also carrots).
5. List salad items available plus fresh herbs if possible. We like to serve a cleansing salad *after* the main dish.
6. List fruit that is available locally or in season close by. Try to avoid rich sauces or puddings, especially if you have used moderate amounts of fat in the preceding courses. It is far better to gain sweet tastes from natural sources, like fruit. Also be careful not to use too much honey to sweeten the fruit. It is only marginally better than sugar.
7. List one digestive herbal tea together with decaffeinated coffee as creative alternatives to regular tea and coffee. You dont't have to serve them to everyone, but you will be able to offer these substitutes to anyone on your guest list who normally avoids caffeine because of high blood pressure.
8. Review the whole meal. (There are no recipes yet; it's just the basic building blocks at this stage.)

Now look for recipe ideas in your favorite books. *Caution:* do not expect magazine-style, color photographs to resemble your finished dish. All kinds of tricks are used to make the food look more colorful. The result is often discouraging for the home cook who is lured by sight alone!

Keep your meal simple. If you must serve a first course, let it be either soup or a cold plate that is ready to serve. If the main dish needs last-minute cooking, arrange for vegetables, sauce, etc., to be precooked and reheated at the last moment. Too much kitchen activity just prior to serving can produce tensions all around. However some last-minute cooking should be done. Otherwise it all seems unnatural — as if the meal was catered! Desserts, hot or cold, should always be prepared ahead of time, unless your menu plan or personal views require you to make a souffle or souffle omelet, which is more practical.

Now review again all the ingredients used from beginning to end. There should be lots of fresh food, herbs, and spices. There should be potential for plenty of color, aroma, and texture changes (not all soft, not all creamy, not all white or dark).

At this point you need to plan for the beverage. Whatever you choose should not mask or overwhelm the basic combination of tastes produced by the recipes. It must enhance them. I personally do not consume alcohol in any form when I have the choice. My reason is not so much spiritual as practical. A vast amount of the hurt in this world stems from the misuse of alcohol — and so little apparent good flows from it. I have chosen to get at the grape before it ferments. (See page ____ for some ideas.)

Finally, consider a welcome before-dinner drink. This should be very light and attractive. (White grape juice with fresh mint is ideal.) There is no need for salted nuts or other tidbits of conviviality. They only result in excessive salt consumption and a general decrease in the appetite, all negative results. A jug of grape juice and some glasses on a tray should help your guests overcome any initial awkwardness.

In this cookbook, I give you a basic methodology for cooking different meats, vegetables, etc. Now that you have selected the foods you will use, look at the pictures of the basic way to cook that food. Then select one of the recipe ideas following that methodology.

As you do this, make a careful note of the time it takes to cook each item. Decide which items to precook and then make up a schedule that lists each time in order of preparation time, from longest to least. Now you will have the order in which the foods should be cooked. This should avoid the tension that comes from leaving everything to the last moment. It also prevents overcooking, which comes from doing everything too early.

A handwritten menu can add a festive touch. If you have a good handwriting (or one of the family does), write out your menus on small, well-lettered cards with, perhaps, some pressed floral decoration as an ornament.

## Now to the preparation

A good cook always prepares the raw ingredients well ahead of time. The French (who have often made elaborate efforts to complicate cooking) devised one of the most specific and helpful culinary terms, *mis en place:* "to put everything in its right place."

Every single ingredient in a given recipe is washed, peeled, scrubbed, weighed, and cut in the manner called for ahead of time. It is then put in cups or plates and covered, ready for assembly. Failure to do this may mean a search for an ingredient as the sauce is boiling. This can, and usually does, spell disaster!

# Now cook!

In my early days of training, the chef instructor at our hotel school used to pat me on the back, sigh deeply, and come up with such nifty comments as: "O.K., go ahead, do what you usually do; put it in the trash bin" or "ought to give you a fireman's helmet rather than a chef's hat."

My problem, as you may have guessed, was using too high a heat. I was always in a hurry. A high flame or a cherry red element is usually the mark of a careless cook. Except in very rare cases you should lower the heat for better results.

It also helps to clean up as you go. Treena and I have something of a running battle in this area. During the early years of our marriage, I used every pan in the kitchen until one day she declared, "Anymore than two pans remaining after we've eaten, and you do the washing up!" Her logic was hard to refute: The cook shouldn't get all the praise while leaving the kitchen in a total shambles for either husband, wife, or children to clean up!

We still disagree in part. If she is cooking, the whole kitchen is immaculate, every pot in its place. When I cook, my two allowed pans, plus spoons and dishes, are more or less everywhere! After all, my theory is that food is the most important item. The object is to get it to the guests in its best possible condition, regardless of the disorder that may accompany this process. However, I'm prepared to concede that a short wait in the warming oven might not constitute a disaster.

# Presentation

The moment of presentation or service is when the "rubber meets the road!" This takes the least time, is the easiest to execute, and is the moment that seems to matter least in most people's minds.

The French — bless their hearts — came up with another term of even greater significance than *mis-en-place. Ambiance.* It refers to a somewhat mystical aura or general atmosphere in which all things work together to produce a sensation of well-being.

I suppose that in some cases this can be achieved by the finest linen and china with crystal glass and candelabra, but it has not happened that way with us. We used to own Coalport, Wedgewood, Sheffield Silver, Waterford Crystal, and Irish Damask. But frankly, the best memories come from red-check tablecloths and a bottle draped about with candle wax — plus simple muted colors, small wild flowers, and always the right amount of light in the right place.

Again, it's love that matters. There is always a greater danger of straining relationships with luxury than there is with a humble table of earthen pottery. However, please don't let these words allow for carelessness. To my mind, the worst assault on a guest is a scruffily laid table.

Consider the type of entertainment that best represents you, and then plan for a table setting that provides the essential *ambiance.* It may seem to be an unnecessary expense; yet I assure you, it is well worth your while.

# Hints to Enhance Ambiance

An essential part of ambiance is lighting. Treena and I suggest that you light the table from above and control the amount of light with a dimmer switch. Both lights and candles on the table surface seem more romantic than they actually are, so we would advise against candles except for certain occasions. (Candles can smell and almost always throw unattractive shadows.)

To achieve the centerpiece effect that a candle represents, try a small, but very carefully arrayed, grouping of miniature flowers. These should be low and nonaromatic. Tablemats on woodgrained tables also set the atmosphere. Some interesting varieties are representations of fine art backed by masonite and covered with heatproof resin coating. Or a simple quilt with enough packing to provide insulation. When using the quilt idea, it's good to make table napkins that match.

For casual entertaining the flatwear should be stainless steel and comfortable to hold. We particularly like knives with pistol grip ends, which combine comfort and appearance.

China or stoneware is so varied in availability that it presents a special challenge. I personally don't like the scraping sound that a knife makes on some types of stoneware. On the other hand, I see no reason to spend a fortune on fine bone china. The answer seems to be the well-glazed, yet sturdy ironstone with extremely simple decoration. You might want to make sure that it can be easily matched if you should break a piece in years to come.

We tried an amusing idea once that worked quite well. We bought various dishes so that each place setting was different. In this way it isn't such a tragedy when you break a piece that has been discontinued. You need to have a good eye for the "antique pieces" you can pick up from secondhand or antique stores, garage sales, and church bazaars. Finding an especially pleasing place setting is like finding a family treasure.

Glasses can now be purchased quite inexpensively. My favorite is a machine-made wine glass with a heavy stem. Just show a local department store this sketch. The glass holds about eight fluid ounces (1 cup), is sturdy — yet attractive, and can be purchased at a very economical price.

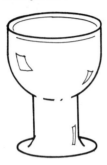

A pitcher or jug for beverages is best replaced by a one-litre carafe, which does not have an easy-to-break handle or hard-to-clean lip. The carafe looks good and fits in the refrigerator well. You can also cover the top to prevent odors, dust, etc., from getting to the beverage before you do.

The actual presentation of the food can be accomplished in a wide variety of ways. I have experimented with dozens of different ideas on how to serve a party, and have finally come to the conclusion that the following equation usually makes the best sense: The host/hostess does all the carving in the kitchen. Then the main dish is placed on a large, one- to one-and-a-half inch deep, oval platter with the vegetables presented as a garnish around the featured food. One additional vegetable dish can then be passed around to each guest, together with a sauceboat (if it is appropriate to the dish). Be sure that you have the serving platter well heated and that your table is properly protected.

Plates should not be stone cold, but neither should they be blistering hot. Experiment to get them just right. Finally, select a suitable serving spoon and fork. The one set will serve each item on the platter.

## Successful Creative Cooking

Trying a new recipe rather than selecting a favorite comes complete with a considerable threat: "What if it doesn't work!"

Many cooks experience failure not because of the recipe (other than in some baked goods), but because both the method and the ingredients are foreign to them. In order to reduce the failure rate — or at least the threat of failure — it is important to use a method of cooking that you thoroughly understand. Then all you need to do is vary the ingredients.

Treena and I have designed this book to give you a good grasp of some basic methods, which will provide a foundation for your cooking skills. We have included additional recipes (creative alternatives) along with hints that can improve your quality of eating. Also, a number of symbols are listed beside the individual recipes to indicate that recipe's particular attributes. These will help you decide quickly which elements build together for a successful celebration.

Here are the symbols with the attributes they represent:

 Cut costs by avoiding waste or replacing commercially prepared products.

 Saves time by eliminating unnecessary steps.

 Enhances good nutrition by reducing salt, fat, sugar, and unnecessary chemical additives.

 Suited to barbeque.

 Radical departure from the normal. For those who are expressing their love through a changed life-style.

## On Your Mark, Get Set — Wait!"

The dining table is the last remaining "tribal meeting place" of our culture. Here we can escape the detached impersonality of our lives outside the home and meet each other as persons. Together we can share our enjoyment of the blessings of God.

The whole secret to a successful celebration is being thoughtful. The more personal care invested, the more loved your guests and family feel. Your meal preparations need not be elaborate in order to reflect your care and concern. In fact, the more simple, handmade, and home-styled it is, the more your love is felt.

Now cook! And put your heart into it!

# breads

# breads

# breads

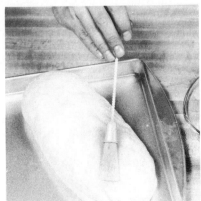

# breads

# Quick Yeast Bread

### INGREDIENTS:

4 cups flour (1 lb.)
¼ cup safflower oil (2 oz.)
¾ tablespoon yeast (¼ oz.)
1 teaspoon sugar
1 cup liquid
2 teaspoons salt

> *To mix bread dough, the conditions must be perfect. All the utensils should be clean and warm. Measure the flour unsifted if using a cup measure, but we recommend a pair of scales and accurately weighed ingredients. There is a difference! But for convenience we do use cups here.*

### PREPARATION

1. Measure flour.
2. Combine liquid and oil, and warm to correct temperature.

**Step 1.** Sprinkle yeast with sugar or honey over warmed liquid and oil. Let it sit for five minutes, then combine well. Pour yeast mixture into a well of flour, add salt, and stir in thoroughly. Knead well for 5 to 10 minutes.

**Step 2.** Place the dough into a greased bowl, then grease the surface of the dough by turning it in the bowl. Cover with a cloth, set in 140° F. oven, and turn off the heat. Prove for 30 minutes or until doubled in size.

**Step 3.** Take dough from oven, punch in the center, and turn out onto a board. Knead again lightly. Cut into 1-ounce pieces and shape into rolls. Place onto a well-greased, "bright" (aluminum) sheet, cover, and allow to rise for 30 minutes.

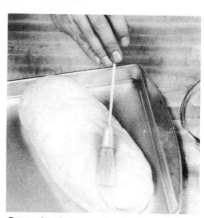

**Step 4.** Brush with egg white or melted butter before baking to give a glaze, then place into a 375° F. preheated oven for 12-15 minutes to bake. Turn out onto a cake rack to cool.

**Flour.** All-purpose flour is fine — you can add various other flours at a 1 to 4 ratio (i.e., 1 cup whole wheat to 3 cups all-purpose). All-purpose flour is needed for proper rising.

**Oil.** ¼ cup (2 oz.) safflower oil for each 4 cups flour. Acts as a keeper by making a batch moist. You can do without, but the bread goes stale very rapidly (after 1 day's time).

**Yeast.** Can be purchased in ¼ oz. (¾ tablespoon) packages. Should support 3-4 cups flour (4 cups means longer prove time).

**Sugar.** Feeds the yeast. Yeast has to grow on some food, and it does well on sugar, honey, or molasses, but sugar is easiest (1 teaspoon to 4 cups flour).

**Liquid.** 50/50 milk and water ratio (1 cup liquid to 4 cups flour) or potato water or rice water can be used, and the salt and sugar eliminated since the starch water satisfies both needs. Milk plus flour greatly increases the protein value of the bread, compared to water alone with flour.

# Egg Braids

### Yields 2 2-lb. Loaves

## INGREDIENTS:

8 cups flour
½ cup butter or oil
2 eggs plus 1 egg white
2 cups reconstituted nonfat dried milk
1 tablespoon salt
4 tablespoons sugar (¼ cup)
2 packages yeast or 2 tablespoons (from jar)

> *A "fancy loaf" is one that employs a complicated recipe or form. This is a simple recipe with an easy form that winds up looking fantastically complicated, a kind of maximum return for a minimum effort!*

## PREPARATION

1. Measure all ingredients. Heat milk and butter to 115-120° F. Place yeast in warmed liquid and stir well. Allow to sit 5 minutes.

2. Mix 6 cups flour, with salt, sugar, and yeast/liquid ingredients.

3. Add 2 eggs and mix well. Stir in enough flour so it doesn't stick (1½-2 cups).

4. Turn out onto a floured board and knead for 8-10 minutes, until smooth and satiny.

5. Place dough in a clean, greased bowl and grease the top of the dough. Cover and allow dough to double in size (1 hour).

6. Punch dough down and divide into 4 equal portions. Roll each piece into a 24-30 inch rope. Then braid each 2 pieces, starting out in an "X" position, with the top piece going to the top left. Bring it down under the top right one, then over and under until it is used up.

7. Place the 2 braided loaves on a greased cookie sheet, cover, and allow to rise for 45 minutes to 1 hour or until double in size. Just before going into the oven, brush loaf with a raw, beaten egg white. Bake at 375° F. for 20 minutes. Cool immediately on a cake rack.

You can get at least 20 large slices per loaf, but we recommend cutting each slice in half (a whole slice is very large). The dough will keep well up to 1 week, and it freezes beautifully. A ½ slice is about 64 calories.

# Lemon Yogurt Bread

### Yields 1 Loaf

### INGREDIENTS:

2 teaspoons lemon peel, grated
⅓ cup sugar (3 oz.)
¼ cup butter (4 tablespoons)
2 eggs
1 teaspoon baking soda
2 cups unbleached flour
1 teaspoon baking powder
¼ teaspoon salt
1 cup yogurt
1 teaspoon vanilla

*" If you make this recipe, you might well argue that it seems more like a cake than a bread. You are quite right! If you want an apology — you have it! But if you want a "bread" you don't feel you have to smother with butter and jam, then you also have it!"*

### PREPARATION

1. Finely grate the peel from 1 lemon and measure out 2 teaspoons.

2. Measure all ingredients. Grease an 8x4x2 inch loaf pan. Preheat oven to 350° F.

3. Cream butter and sugar well. Sift together flour, salt, baking powder, baking soda. Add eggs one at a time to the butter-sugar mixture and blend well after each addition.

4. Add peel and vanilla flavoring. Alternate adding dry ingredients with the yogurt. Mix until just moistened.

5. Pour into a greased loaf pan and bake for 50 minutes. Cool 10 minutes and turn out onto a wire cake rack to cool completely before cutting, otherwise it will crumble badly. Makes 1 loaf of 20 slices.

# Middle Eastern Pocket Bread

### Yields 20-25 Loaves

### INGREDIENTS:

9 cups unbleached flour
1½ tablespoons yeast (2 packages)
1 teaspoon salt
3 cups potato water
¼ cup sugar
(No oil)

*" Some good supermarkets now stock this bread. It makes a great sandwich. All you do is slide the filling into the round bread "pocket" and munch!*

*Some interested cooks with baking skills may want to try this recipe for themselves. It was one of the early Holy Breads for Holy Communion."*

### PREPARATION

1. In a large bowl measure out 3½ cups flour. Mix salt, sugar, and instant yeast with the flour. (If yeast is not instant, dissolve yeast first in ½ cup warm, not hot, potato water and stir into the dry ingredients.)

2. Heat potato water to 115-125° F. Pour water into the center of the flour and mix with a spoon.

3. Gradually add the rest of the flour, ½ cup at a time.

4. Turn dough out onto a floured board and knead 8-10 minutes until smooth and satiny.

5. Place dough in a greased bowl and grease top of dough by turning the dough in the bowl. Cover and let rise again.

6. Divide dough into small lemon-sized pieces. Roll out *very* flat (¼ in. or less). Place on ungreased cookie sheets and bake at 475° F. for 7 minutes. (To brown, put under the broiler 1-2 minutes later on.)
   They puff up when they bake, but go flat as they cool. This is normal.

If you make 20 loaves, each loaf has about 216 calories each. If you make smaller loaves, you can get 28 loaves, with 188 calories each, or 40 loaves at 108 calories each.

# Newfoundland Pizza Teacake

## INGREDIENTS:

¼ cup butter or oil (2 oz.)
6 cups flour (1½ lbs.)
2¼ cups nonfat dried milk,
reconstituted (12 oz.)
1 egg
2 tablespoons sugar
2¼ cups currants and raisins
(6 oz.)
3 tablespoons each lemon
and orange peel (1 oz. each)
2 tablespoons dry yeast
(2 packages)
1 tablespoon salt

## PREPARATION

1. Measure all ingredients. Cut up peels and measure or weigh out. Mix 3 cups flour with the sugar and salt. Heat milk and shortening to 115° F. Add dry yeast, stir well to mix, and let sit for 5 minutes.

2. Pour warm liquid into dry ingredients, add egg, and blend very well. Stir in the fruit and peel. Add the rest of the flour, 1 cup at a time. Stir and then mix well with the hands between additions.

3. When dough becomes stiff, turn out onto a well-floured board and knead for 8-10 minutes until smooth and satiny. Place dough in a greased bowl and grease the top by turning dough over. Cover with a clean tea towel and allow to rise 1 hour or until double in size.

4. Punch dough down and mold it into a greased pizza pan. Brush top with egg white. Allow to double again and bake at 375° F. for 20 minutes or until a deep golden brown. Remove bread from pan immediately and cool on a cake rack. To serve, split bread horizontally, butter each half, and place under the broiler for 5 minutes or less to toast lightly and melt the butter.

*I frankly admit to being the author of this gastronomic pun. You may not receive my humor too well, but the "biggest bun in the business" will receive many compliments.*

*Try it and see, especially when the weather is cold enough to justify the nearly 200-calorie buttered snack!*

# Pumpernickel Bread

### INGREDIENTS:

1½ cup rye flour
2 teaspoons salt
2 packages yeast (2 tablespoons)
¼ cup warm water
1½ cups vegetable stock or
potato water
¼ cup molasses
2 tablespoons oil
1 cup whole-wheat flour
⅓ cup soy grits
2 tablespoons wheat germ
2 tablespoons brewer's yeast
⅓ cup nonfat dried milk
1 egg
2⅔ cups all-purpose
unbleached flour

*This is one of those recipes that should make you jump to your feet, shriek, and leap onto the housetop from which, presumably, you might want to shout out the good news. It is chock-full of **everything anyone** ever asked for from a loaf of bread!*

### PREPARATION

1. Measure all ingredients first. Grease one long pan (13 x 4½ x 2½ in.) or 2 shorter pans (7⅜ x 3⅝ x 2¼ in.).

2. Mix together rye flour, salt, instant yeast (if not instant, disolve in the water first), warm water and stock, molasses and oil. Beat for 3 minutes.

3. Mix in a separate container whole-wheat flour, soy grits, wheat germ, brewer's yeast, nonfat dried milk.

4. Add egg to first (wet) mixture and beat well for 1-2 minutes.

5. Then add the second (dry) mixture to the first and beat very well.

6. Then add 2-3 cups unbleached flour, ½ cup at a time, and mix well after each addition.

7. Turn dough out onto a floured board and knead for 8-10 minutes. Shape into 1 long or 2 small loaves; place in greased pans, cover, and let rise in a warm oven (preheated to 140° F. and turned off) until double in size (1-2 hours).

8. Brush top of dough with egg white. Bake in preheated oven at 400° F. for 10 minutes. Then reset oven to 350° F. and bake for 30 minutes longer (for large loaf) or 10-20 minutes (for small loaves), until golden brown on top and lightly brown on the sides. Loaves should leave the sides of the pans easily when turned upside down. Cool on cake racks. This is a solid loaf of bread with a delicious taste and is very filling. Slice thinly and make open-face sandwiches. Yields 40 slices.

# Bread and Butter Pudding

**Serves 6-8**

## INGREDIENTS:

½ stick butter at room temperature (2 oz.)
3 tablespoons sugar
3 slices white bread
3 slices whole-wheat bread
2½ cups skim milk
½ vanilla pod
2 pieces thin lemon peel
6 tablespoons seedless raisins or currants (2 oz.)
6 tablespoons candied lemon peel (2 oz.)
3 eggs
Nutmeg

> ❝ *We have tried hard to reform this dessert largely because it is so good. We severely reduced the sugar and strove to make this up with dried fruit as a more satisfactory source of sweetness. Note the serving size if you are concerned about calories.* ❞

## PREPARATION

1. Out of the butter, lightly butter the inside of a 2-quart casserole and dust it with ½ tablespoon of the sugar. Preheat oven to 325° F. Spread the bread lightly with the rest of the butter and cut the slices in half diagonally. Measure the remaining ingredients.

2. Place milk, vanilla pod, fresh lemon peel, and 2 tablespoons sugar in a saucepan and scald. Stir to dissolve sugar.

3. Arrange some of the cut bread on the bottom of the casserole.

4. Sprinkle it with some of the raisins and candied peel.

5. Place another layer of bread over the first layer, alternating brown and white layers.

6. Break eggs into a bowl and whisk.

7. Slowly beat in the scalded milk, having first removed the lemon peel and vanilla pod.

8. Pour this mixture over the bread, dust with ½ tablespoon sugar and nutmeg.

9. Bake in preheated 325° F. oven for 35 minutes. Serve warm, with milk, or plain.

Serves 8 at 213 calories or 6 at 283 calories per serving.

# HINTS

## Bread Cases

An interesting — and delicious — use of a loaf of bread is to "stuff" it. For the technique with a sample recipe, see Chicken Treenestar, page 113.

## The Chemical Factor

Our daily bread was once a known commodity, a staple, attractive, homely thing on which we could rely. We can now expect our daily bread to be treated to an incredible barrage of chemical manipulation.

We can assume that the following list has been applied:

Preservatives
Added nutrients
Antisprouting agents
Coloring
Flavoring
Bleaches
Texture enhancers
Emulsifiers
Softeners
Acidifiers
Sweeteners
Anti-foamers
Dough conditioners

The reason for their addition is logical enough: it reduces the effect of human error on the eventual product. Note please that it permits the error to continue, but it fixes up the mistake. We eat chemically remedied mistakes!

What man lacks in genuine honest skill he makes up for with chemical manipulation!

Let's look at a few well-known chemical preservatives so that we can better appreciate the problem.

*BHA (butylated hydroxyamisole).* This is the chief preservative used in our daily food. It causes contractions of the smooth muscle of the intestine in the ileum area (the bundle of intestine just under the duodenum that leads into the ascending colon).

*BHT (butylated hydroxytoluene).* This more toxic relative of BHA can cause metabolic stress, enlarged liver, and weight loss with cholesterol and genetic problems. It is banned in Sweden and Austria. In Britain, the Food Standard Committee took this action: (1958) Recommended an outright ban, but industry protested. (1963) Committee reviewed data and again recommended total ban. (1965) New evidence put to the test. BHT banned in all baby foods and quantity previously considered safe reduced by 50 percent. (1972) New evidence includes brain damage in mice fed large quantities of BHT. Humans thought to suffer chronic asthmatic attacks, extreme weakness, fatigue. Still in use!

*NDGA (Nordihydroguaiaretic acid).* An antioxidant that's banned in Canada; it's no longer GRAS (generally recognized as safe) in U.S., but still in use.

*Polyoxyethylone compounds.* The FDA banned their use but manufacturers went to the Supreme Court and obtained a postponement. Still in use in biscuits, cakes, cake mixes, ice cream, frozen desserts, and pickles.

# HINTS

*Sodium Carboxymethylcellulose.* The U.S. Public Health Service warned, "If used in excess, such modification may have serious nutritional consequences for certain segments of the population." It is an indigestible material supplied as a substitute for normal food in an effort to improve texture and keeping quality, or to lower calories. In other words, it's worth nothing, but it gives the mouth the **feel** of eating real food!

*Sodium Nitrite/Nitrate.* Color fixatives used in almost all cold-preserved fish and meats. Nitrates and nitrites **may** react with secondary amines (an ammonia derivative in which hydrogen atoms have been replaced by a group of two atoms that act as a single atom containing hydrogen and carbon atoms) in the acid digestive tracts to form nitrosamines: one of the most potent cancer-causing agents known to science.

Once again you will note that there is a continual ebb and flow of opinion between industry and those who serve the common good of the consuming public. I understand the problems that industry faces, but I must be realistic about where I am with my family. Since there are so many obvious health hazards, **the least is the best, when it comes to chemical additives.**

If it means, for example, that the entire preserved-meats counter is suspect — then so be it! I am genuinely open to reason, but I will not sacrifice my body for the sake of my senses. I now look for the label that reads "no preservatives," and I consume the product quickly.

# soups

# soups

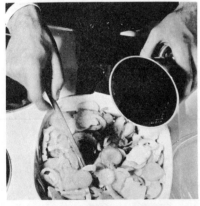

# soups

# soups

# Thin Soups

**Yields 1 Pint**

## INGREDIENTS:

½ lb. shin of beef
1 teaspoon oil
Salt to season
2-in. piece of carrot (½ oz.)
3-in. stalk of celery (½ oz.)
2-in. piece of parsnip (½ oz.)
4 thin slices onion (½ oz.)
2¼ cups cold water
1 bay leaf
1 clove
1 piece garlic (size of pea)
1 stalk parsley
1 white of egg

*I'm not at all sure that the famous consommé isn't on the way out — that is, when it is prepared at home. Yards of bones, a three-gallon pot, and at least twelve hours of pot watching don't make much sense. In this recipe I have tried to produce a seasoned liquid capable of being used as a soup, stock, or sauce base. You could call it a last-ditch stand by the "do-it-yourselfer" to the can.*

## PREPARATION

1. Chop or mince beef finely.
2. Finely slice carrots, celery, and parsnips.
3. Measure water.
4. Crush garlic.

**Step 1.** The meat selected depends upon the end use. If you want a light negative stock, then use veal neck meat. In this case the meat is shin of really old beef. Sprinkle it liberally with salt to draw out the natural juices.

**Step 2.** In oil, fry the vegetables, meat, and garlic together until a golden brown. You can see the pan base where the juices have adhered and become browned.

**Step 3.** Add water and remaining herbs; cover and cook for 30 minutes. Now strain off the seasoned liquid through muslin into a clean saucepan.

**Step 4.** Add 1 white of egg and whip it to a froth in the stock. Bring to the boil, take it off the heat for 2 minutes, then boil again. Now skim the egg white off the top. This clears the liquid, and it can now be used or frozen ready for future use.

# Pressure Beef Stock

**Yields 2 Quarts**

### INGREDIENTS:

1½ lb. beef rib bones
1 lb. hambone (shank end)
2 onions (6 oz.)
Celery (2 oz.)
2 garlic cloves
¼ teaspoon thyme
2 bay leaves
9 black peppercorns
9 cups water (4½ pints)

### PREPARATION

1. Place the beef rib bones and the hambone in the bottom of a 4-qt. pressure cooker. To save as much space as possible, the bones should be quite flat.

2. Add the onions, celery, and spices and cover with the water. *Because of the pressure buildup, the pot should not be more than ⅔ full at most, and ½ full is preferred.*

3. Close the cooker, build pressure to 15 lb. per square inch over moderate heat. Reduce heat and cook for 30 minutes. Turn off heat and let pressure subside gradually, at stoveside.

4. Strain and bottle the stock and put it into the refrigerator to cool. When cook, skim fat and use as needed (for example, Onion Soup, see below).

**❝** *One of the longest, often most tedious, and sometimes the smelliest job in the kitchen is making stock. All these minus points are instantly repealed by the pressure cooker (see page 36 for discussion). The 6-12 hour process is handily reduced to only 30 minutes.* **❞**

# Simple Onion Soup

**Serves 4**

### INGREDIENTS:

1 lb. Bermuda onions
1 tablespoon sesame/safflower oil (page 186)
4 cups beef stock
Salt, to season
Pepper, to season
Parsley, to garnish

### PREPARATION

1. Peel and finely slice onions (should yield 3½ cups), and shallow-fry for 30 minutes in sesame/safflower oil in large, heavy-based saucepan. Just color but do not burn the onions.

2. Add good, rich, brown beef stock (above). Bring to the boil, reduce heat to simmer, and cook 30 minutes longer.

3. Adjust the seasoning, scatter the top with fresh parsley, and serve. I do not add the usual bread and cheese for fairly obvious dietary reasons.

See page 35 for discussion on varieties of onions.

# Chicken Stock

**Yields 4 Cups**

### INGREDIENTS:

1 tablespoon sesame/safflower oil
1 tablespoon fresh ginger root)
(½ oz.)
(or ½ teaspoon dried ginger)
½ lb. chicken feet, bones,
neck, etc.
½ lb. pork bones (optional —
these provide a rounder,
richer flavor)
1 3-inch piece of celery
1 bay leaf
Parsley stalk
Freshly ground salt
Freshly ground pepper
8 cups water

### PREPARATION

1. Place oil in a pan, add ginger, and fry gently.

2. Add chicken and pork bones, celery, bay leaf, parsley, seasonings, and water. Bring to a boil and simmer for 1 hour.

3. Strain. Cool and skim off the fat before using.

# Chicken and Barley Soup $

**Serves 8**

### INGREDIENTS:

8 cups water
2 lbs. chicken backs and necks
¼ cup thinly sliced celery
¼ cup diced onion
1 teaspoon black pepper
1 tablespoon salt
¼ teaspoon thyme
¼ teaspoon sage
⅛ teaspoon marjoram
⅛ teaspoon rosemary
¼ cup barley

### PREPARATION

1. Measure all ingredients. Rinse chicken parts. Chop celery and onion.

2. Combine all ingredients except celery and cook for 1 hour slowly, with the lid on.

3. Cool and skim fat from the surface. Remove meat from the chicken backs and necks. Separate skin from the meat, discard skin, add meat to the broth (we obtained 7 oz. meat from 1.73 lbs. of backs). Reheat and add celery at the end. Serve immediately.

Time to prepare: 1 hour cooking time and 10 minutes preparation.

The number of calories per serving is 62.5.

# Gazpacho

**Serves 7**

## INGREDIENTS:

2 lbs. ripe tomatoes
(2 pints canned)
⅓ cup black olives
½ cup spring onion tops
½ cup green pepper
1-1½ cups cucumber
1 tablespoon fresh parsley
¾ cup radishes (optional)
2 tablespoons lemon juice
¼ cup red grape juice
2 tablespoons rice vinegar
2 tablespoons olive oil
1 tablespoon strong cold tea
1 cup concentrated gelatinous
chicken stock
¼ teaspoon basil
¼ teaspoon tarragon
1 teaspoon paprika
1 teaspoon salt
Pepper to taste
1 garlic clove, crushed

## PREPARATION

1. Skin tomatoes. (page 207). Finely dice olives, onion tops, green pepper, cucumber, fresh parsley, radishes. Squeeze lemon juice, measure grape juice, vinegar, olive oil, tea, chicken stock, and herbs.

2. Rub a large bowl with the crushed garlic clove.

3. Place tomatoes in a blender and blend for 10-15 seconds until well chopped.

4. Pour tomatoes into the bowl, season with basil and tarragon (rubbed between the palms of the hands to bring out the flavor).

5. Add paprika, parsley, chopped vegetables, and all other ingredients.

6. Stir to blend. Chill for at least 2 hours before serving.

There are 96.6 calories per serving.

❝ *No summer soup deserves so widespread a reputation for excellence as this simple recipe. Certainly, the fine dice you have to cut is a tedious business, but oh, the colorful, wonderful result! The standard soup can be 96.6 calories per serving, **but** we have added a list of extras that can increase the protein to remarkable levels and do great things to vary the soup's flavor.* ❞

# Fish Stock

### INGREDIENTS:

14 ounces fish bones
(from 2½ to 3 pounds of
whole fish)
1 medium onion
½ teaspoon thyme
3-inch piece of celery
1 bay leaf
6 parsley stalks
2½ cups water
¼ teaspoon salt
¼ teaspoon black pepper

### PREPARATION

Bring to the boil, reduce to barely moving simmer for 20 minutes, strain, and use.

# HINTS

## Fish Stock

We once had the misfortune to consume a very poor fish soup in the south of France. Since that time I've wondered why such varied results should occur from soup to soup. The answer, I am now convinced, lies in the head and the skin. We have conducted tests with straight "bones," with the head on its own, and again with head and skin.

The result of using only bones is clearly better, less muddy, and more fragrant — so much better in fact that I strongly advise not using the head for fish soups or sauces.

## Hock Stock

Small ham hocks weighing about 10 ounces (variously called "country ham hocks" or "smoked pork hocks") are *not* a good buy — especially if taken from the *hind shank*. They are almost all bone and fat and hardly any meat. Ask for fore shanks and have them cut so that you get sufficient meat to cut for casserole and omelet uses (less expensive and better flavored, and less fatty than bacon). The bones give an excellent flavor especially good for vegetable casseroles (see pages 189-90) — which are great ways to beat the budget!

You simply use the normal vegetable trimmings — celery tops, carrot, and onion peels are all very good — strip back the skin from the hock (which helps speed the cooking time), cut off the meat for casserole use, and add a bay leaf and some thyme, *no* salt. Simmer slowly for 1 to 2 hours. Two knuckles will make 1½ pints (24 fluid ounces) of finished, skimmed, and strained stock of excellent quality.

# HINTS

## Onions

A swift visit to the average supermarket produce section will turn up an interesting array of onions. I'd just like to deal with three kinds:

*Sweet Spanish* cost me 49¢ for 1 pound.* Mild and sweet — the sweetness converts readily to a good color suited to soups like French Onion Soup where a mildness is also required.

*Yellow Dried* —"Downing and Yellow Globe"— cost 49¢ per pound. These are pungent and have considerable holding power in sauces that need long cooking — they're especially good in curries where the onions have to "melt" with the spices to form a base.

*Red Spanish* —"Southport Red Globe"— cost 69¢ per pound and are a *salad* type onion suited to easy slicing. They should perhaps be "blanched" in boiling water 2 to 3 minutes for a salad for people with delicate digestions.

Since the Yellow Globe has the most flavor at the lowest cost, it follows that, for sound economic reasons, you should buy it for all stews and casseroles — in fact for our basic use.

Nutritional advantage. One yellow globe onion (2¼ inches in diameter, raw) contains 38 calories. One-half cup cooked onion is listed at 29 calories.

Onions do also contain some B vitamins, a small amount of Vitamin C, and the yellow-fleshed varieties also have some Vitamin A. However, these amounts would be considered insignificant.

Sense advantage springs from taste and aroma. The onion is vital to successful cooking because *successful* cooking is aromatic and flavorful.

*All prices at the time of printing. Price will vary according to locale.

## Onions without Tears

It is possible to avoid the annoying problem of crying while peeling onions by placing the onion into the freezer 15 minutes before use. This helps to reduce the spray of volatile oils that vaporize upon contact with a knife. You can also *skin* an onion easily: cut it into quarters and peel by slicing into the root end just under the outer skin and pulling back.

Sense advantage. The skins are useful in a good stock for both flavor and color (the brown skins produce an excellent amber color).

## Ice Cube Stock

The soup stock pot is an excellent example of European ingenuity when it comes to preventing waste. Essentially it's the place where all the trim goes. It can become a nondescript "broth." All dishes (except egg custard!!!) benefit from good aromatic stock but the *makings* are not always at hand.

We make up a stock from a chicken carcass — or from some beef bones when we have them as a *natural by-product* from another meal. We clarify the stock and freeze it in ice cube trays — turning the cubes into a bag marked Beef Stock or Chicken Stock, etc. Then all you need is one or two cubes and you are in business.

You will find literally dozens of recipes in your own books and in mine that will help you to use this simple idea. Just keep the stock clearly of one type — chicken, or fish or beef or ham stock. For each pound of bones, add 1 cup (8 oz.) vegetable peelings and always add a bouquet garni (pages 83).

Remember — stock is always better than water!

# HINTS

## Clear Stock

Any stock that is used in a white or tomato sauce should simply be skimmed of fat and surface foam and then strained through a fine sieve.

A stock needed for a brown sauce thickened with arrowroot or one that is destined to become a consommé (clear soup) needs to be *clarified* — cleared of all "specks" of food. To do this you must first remove the fat, foam, and obvious debris by straining. Add 1 beaten egg white for each 2 pints of stock to be cleared. Bring the stock to a slow boil. Take it off the fire and let the egg white settle. Bring to a slow boil again and remove. Skim off the egg with the "collected" particles firmly trapped within.

## Pressure Cookers

My changed attitude to cooking begins with the simple statement that cooking must never be a burden and that, if it is, then something's wrong!

One of the ways in which our daily food gets on top of us is in the cooking of stocks, ox tongues, beans, etc., all needing at least 4 hours to prepare. One piece of equipment gets things moving fast: the pressure cooker, a device that simply *raises* the boiling point of water. At sea-level (14.7 psi [pounds per square inch]), steam won't get any hotter than water's 212° F. (100° C.) boiling point, no matter how much heat is applied; the steam will simply dissipate. That's the situation when you are cooking with water in a pot without a lid or with a loose-fitting lid.

Put a tight lid on the pot, however, and the situation changes. Assuming that heat is continued, the pressure rises, and with it the water temperature. An increase of 5 psi raises the boiling point of water (and thus the temperature of the resulting steam) to 227° F. Add 5 more psi and the boiling point goes to 239° F. At 15 psi above normal atmospheric pressure (the maximum intended for our cookers) steam reaches 250° F., and food gets cooked a lot faster.

There are some old fears that the instruments may blow up. Let me explain that these were warranted at one time, but now the pressure cooker should be considered as safe as many other new appliances. However, be sure you follow directions for cooking time, clean out the release hole (*check it every time),* see that the plunger is loose on the blowout valve, and listen to the "train" in motion. Also, cool first — open later (the Presto top indicates when it's safe to open). Check rubber gasket periodically.

Be very careful not to overfill! The makers recommend to only fill half with liquid and fill two-thirds with solids. This means purchasing a 4-6 quart size for even a small family.

One of the immediate ways in which this unit will bless your daily cooking is in the recipe for stock.

# Farmhouse Vegetable Soup

**Serves 4**

### INGREDIENTS:

2 medium carrots (6 oz.)
1 small parsnip (3 oz.)
1 medium onion (4 oz.)
2 tablespoons safflower oil
1 clove garlic
1 stalk celery (3 in.)
1 tablespoon tomato paste
2½ cups Pressure Beef Stock
(see page 31)
Freshly ground salt to taste
9 black peppercorns
2 bay leaves
4 parsley stalks
3 thyme sprigs or ¼ teaspoon
ground thyme
½ cup yogurt or buttermilk

*This is a rib-sticker that comes out of my "creative" past when Treena and I ran the Royal Ascot Hotel in England.*

*It, like all the "oldies," has gone through some changes, mainly to reduce the fats and calories. It is still delicious; in fact the yogurt really gives it style.*

### PREPARATION

1. Wash and peel vegetables and slice medium thin.
2. Measure stock and yogurt or buttermilk.
3. Tie herbs in a muslin bag.

**Step 1.** Wash and add to your vegetables a collection of vegetable peelings saved from the day or meal before. Keep them in a plastic bag in the refrigerator.

**Step 2.** Heat oil in a small dutch oven, add vegetables, and sauté gently for 4 minutes.

**Step 3.** Add tomato paste and stir well to obtain a medium-brown carmelizing of tomato sugars. Add stock and herbs and simmer 20 minutes or until vegetables are tender. Remove and discard herbs.

**Step 4.** Place liquid and vegetables in a blender and blend until smooth. Add yogurt and blend again. Reheat, but do not boil. Season to taste and serve.

# Swedish Fruit Bloop Soup

**Serves 6**

### INGREDIENTS:

1 cup dried peaches
1 cup dried apricots
½ cup dried apples
½ cup pitted prunes
½ #30 can red tart pitted cherries
¼ cup raisins
1 quart water
1-in. piece of cinnamon
½ teaspoon lemon peel, freshly grated
⅛ teaspoon ground mace
Dash each of cardamom, ground allspice, ground nutmeg
1¼ cups buttermilk
5 tablespoons yogurt
1 teaspoon nutmeg

### PREPARATION

1. In a large saucepan combine all ingredients except buttermilk, yogurt, and nutmeg. Bring to a boil, reduce heat, cover, and simmer gently for 1 hour.

2. Remove cinnamon. Place soup in a blender and purée.

3. Return soup to a double boiler, reheat with the buttermilk.

4. Ladle soup into bowls. Garnish with 1 tablespoon yogurt and a dash of nutmeg and serve hot.

At 248 calories per serving, this soup includes 3.8 mg. iron, 4201 I.U. vitamin A, 11.5 mg. vitamin C, 8 gm. protein.

**❝** *This is great fun, almost a meal in itself, and greatly enjoyed by young and old alike. It's called* bloop *because of its habit of throwing spoonfuls of puree into the air as it boils.* **❞**

# Potato Soup $

**Serves 6**

### INGREDIENTS:

1 onion, chopped
1 garlic clove, mashed
1 cup carrot, chopped (4 oz.)
1 cup celery, chopped (4 oz.)
½ tablespoon butter
1 lb. potato, chopped uniformly
1 stalk and leaves of parsley
1½ cups water
¼ teaspoon thyme
1½ teaspoons salt
¼ teaspoon pepper
2 cups milk
4 tablespoons Parmesan cheese

### PREPARATION

1. Chop onion, garlic, carrot, celery, potato, and parsley. Grate cheese and measure remaining ingredients.

2. In a large saucepan, sauté onion, garlic, carrot, and celery in ½ tablespoon butter for several minutes until tender.

3. Add water, potatoes, parsley, thyme, salt, and pepper and cook for 5 minutes, covered. Add milk and heat until almost boiling. Serve in mugs with 1½ teaspoon cheese on top of each cup. Makes 6 cups.

Each serving has 126 calories.

> *Here is a soup that uses very little the average home doesn't have or couldn't use for many varied dishes. We enjoy it on cold winter nights — especially in the Rocky Mountains!*

# Cream of Lettuce Soup

**Serves 4**

### INGREDIENTS:

1 lb. lettuce
1 large onion (finely sliced)
2 tablespoons butter
¼ cup all-purpose flour
2 cups "cooking milk" (see page 240)
2 cups chicken stock
2 garlic cloves
Freshly ground salt
Freshly ground white pepper
Dill weed garnish

### PREPARATION

1. Thoroughly rinse lettuce and remove cores. Smash garlic and chop to a pulp. Heat a soup tureen.

2. Place lettuce leaves in large, dry saucepan and cook over medium heat for 6 minutes.

3. Place butter in another pan on low heat; stir in finely sliced onion and let cook until soft. Stir in flour, making a roux. Cook 3 minutes, stirring.

4. Stir cooking milk into roux and add ½ of the chicken stock.

5. Remove cooked lettuce from pot, puree in a blender, return to pot, and add soup. Add remaining chicken stock and cook while stirring for 7 minutes or until thickened. Season to taste with salt and pepper.

6. Strain lettuce soup through a sieve into soup tureen and serve at once with a dusting of dill weed.

# Soupe Au Pistou

### Serves 10

## INGREDIENTS:

1 carrot (2 oz.)
1 small leek (2-3 oz.)
1 stick celery (1 oz.)
1 cup fresh green beans (4 oz.)
1 small zucchini (3 oz.)
1 small potato (2 oz.)
2 medium, fresh tomatoes (11 oz.)
1 cup fresh asparagus stalks (4 oz.)
½ green pepper (1-2 oz.)
1 large garlic clove
2 tablespoons fresh parsley
3 ounces sharp cheddar cheese
1 14-ounce can red kidney beans
2 tablespoons olive oil
6 cups cold water
½ teaspoon dried basil (or 1 teaspoon fresh)
½ teaspoon freshly ground black pepper
1 tablespoon freshly ground salt
¼ lb. fine noodles

## PREPARATION

1. Scrape and cube carrot. Wash leek very thoroughly and slice thinly. Slice celery and green beans. Cube zucchini, potato, and tomatoes. Finely slice asparagus stalks and dice green pepper into small pieces. Mash garlic; finely chop parsley. Grate cheese. Open the can of beans and measure out the rest of the ingredients.

2. In a small dutch oven, heat the oil, and fry the carrot in the oil. Add the can of beans. Then add leek, potatoes, green beans, garlic, green pepper, and asparagus. Stir well together.

3. Add zucchini and celery. Cook gently for 5 minutes.

4. Add water and seasonings and noodles. Bring to a boil. Cook until vegetables are tender (8-12 minutes). Add tomato cubes and cheese. Pour into heated bowls. Makes 10½ cups.

1 cup has 131 calories and 6.1 grams of protein.

Complementary protein sources: whole-wheat bread, kidney beans, cheddar cheese.

*Use this soup as a vehicle for extending your own creativity into a protein explosion. Frankly, the writing is on the wall about high-priced meat. As Christians I feel we should begin to understand how to make do when forced out of the luxury market completely!*

# seafood

# seafood

# seafood

# seafood

# Deep Fried Fish

**Serves 4**

## INGREDIENTS:

1½ lb. codfish
Enough cold milk to cover
Flour to coat
Salt to taste
White peppercorns to taste
Yeast Batter (page 216)
Oil for deep frying

> *Before I started my television career, I used to buy my children fish and chips from an excellent local fish shop. This habit ended abruptly one day when a fellow customer pointed at me and yelled with much mirth, "Ah, now we know what you eat at home." All the customers in the crowded shop dissolved in laughter. We now prepare our own and, frankly, I'm delighted.*

## PREPARATION

1. Soak fish in cold milk about 1 hour before cooking.
2. Season the flour.
3. Heat oil in deep fryer to 370° F.

**Step 1.** Dry the fish well with a clean cloth or paper towel. The soaking period in milk both enhances the flavor and obviously whitens the flesh.

**Step 2.** Toss the fillets in the seasoned flour until they are all thoroughly coated.

**Step 3.** Using a pair of tongs, place floured fillets in the batter — allow excess to drip off and then transfer to the hot oil.

**Step 4.** Cook at 370° F. for 4 minutes, turning them after 2 minutes. Place on a dish covered with paper doilies and serve with deep-fried parsley.

# HINTS

## Fish — Whole or Filleted?

I knew the answer before I started. Of course, it was beneficial to buy a whole fish and fillet it myself.

Of course I was wrong — at least in New York City! In every case, in N.Y.C., supermarket frozen, filleted, and packaged fish was clearly less expensive.

You should experiment in your area with cutting up a fish to determine the actual potential savings of buying whole vs. fillets before you add the labor to your life! When you find the fish that do produce savings, keep a note of the edible portion and keep a check on fillet prices.

## Refreshing Oil with a Potato.

Cooking oil or fat can become clogged with flavors and discolored by burned bits of breadcrumb, etc. To "repair" the oil, clean it up and have it ready for further use, just add 2 ounces peeled sliced potato cut ¼ in. thick to each cup of oil. Add potato when oil is cold and gradually bring to the boil. Reduce to a simmer and let it stand until the water has been driven out and the dark color taken up. When the water has left the potato, the surface of the oil becomes still. Remove the potato and strain the oil. It is then ready to use again.

## Deep Frying

Deep frying is a technique that is not exactly high on the list of nutritional techniques, yet it does have extremely high appeal for the taste and we can minimize the adverse aspects.

*Enemy No. 1 is type of fat.* Animal fats, rendered beef suet, and fat trim must be among the worst "saturated" fats, yet when relatively fresh they are among the best for flavor. They are also cheaper and last longer than most commercial solid fats. Use them if you must, but be aware of their adverse effects.

*Enemy No. 2 is the temperature.* It must be about 340° F. to 385° F. Too low and the fat is *absorbed* by the article; too high and the fat will be destroyed and loose its ability to fry quickly. Use a special thermometer, but heat the bulb first in warm water.

*Enemy No. 3 is lack of cleanliness.* Regardless of the use, the oil must be cleaned after each use and kept *skimmed* during cooking with a flat wire skimmer. The greater the proportion of fine particles in the fat, the lower the smoke point, which reduces the frying temperature. The lower the temperature, the higher the fat absorption, and this spells T-R-O-U-B-L-E! — so keep it clean and *hot*.

Frying in beef fat as compared with an oil such as safflower oil would mean greater fat absorption due to the lower temperature of frying necessary for the beef fat and the increased cooking time. There is also an overall increase in saturated fats over using a good polyunsaturated vegetable oil.

RECIPES. I would prefer not to recommend additional recipes to you but would refer you to Squash Chips (page 163) and French Fries (page 162), in which we have tried sincerely to reduce adverse nutritional body impact.

# Shallow Fried Fish

**Serves 2**

### INGREDIENTS:

1 large flounder or turbot (2 lb.)
Flour to coat
Salt to season
White peppercorns to season
¼ cup butter
Parsley to garnish
Lemon wedges to garnish

*Most recipe methods for shallow-fried fish begin with the miller's wife technique. According to the legend, the miller was up to his hocks in the nearby stream fishing, when his wife (hard at work) heard him shout, "j'ai une truite"— literally, "I've got a trout." She sped to his side, clasped the trout to her ample flour-covered bosom, ran for the kitchen, and flopped it into foaming butter — hence the method. Surely a lesson in good feminine behavior?*

### PREPARATION

1. Season flour with freshly ground white peppercorns and salt.
2. Heat frying pan to 350° F.

**Step 1.** Remove fins and detach the head as shown. Carefully peel back the skin from the tail with a sharp knife. Dip fingers in salt and give the skin a sharp even tug. Clean the area from which the head has been taken with a salt-dipped cloth.

**Step 2.** Coat fish with seasoned flour. Add butter to a moderate-heat pan (350° F.).

**Step 3.** Place the fish in the pan skinned side down. Cook for approximately 4 minutes, and then turn and cook 4 minutes more, until the flesh can be lifted from the bone.

**Step 4.** Lay the cooked fish on a dish, dust with freshly chopped parsley, and add some extra butter to the pan. Raise the heat until the butter just begins to go light brown. Pour this over the fish. The parsley will sizzle; the result — delicious. The fish can be neatly divided into two portions by cutting down the middle with chicken scissors or a sharp, heavy knife. Serve with lemon wedges.

# HINTS

## Crimping

I learned this simple idea from the Scottish crofters, folk who live in the north of Scotland. They have perfectly fresh fish but use a technique called "crimping" to *revive* fish that might have been a few hours out of the sea and be less than absolutely fresh (like almost all of *ours!*)

Take the fillet and cut shallow, light incisions diagonally down its skin side. Place the fillet in ice cold salted water (add 1 tablespoon salt to 2½ cups water). Allow no more than 30 minutes in this salt water: otherwise valuable nutrients can be lost. Lift the fillet directly from the water, dry it, and cook immediately while it is still chilled.

Touch advantage is the major plus factor, with many benefits. The fillets are clean, sweet smelling, and fresh to the touch — not that old sticky sensation that puts many people "off" fish.

## Breading

A well-breadcrumbed piece of fish or chicken is a joy to behold. But the old 3-step method of flour, egg, and bread crumbs needs some overhaul for both taste and adherence.

We found that 2 whole eggs, 1 tablespoon safflower oil, 1 tablespoon soy sauce, and ¼ teaspoon white pepper combined with 2 tablespoons flour makes a fabulous coating before pressing into bread crumbs for *all* shallow-fried savory dishes, instead of the seasoned flour that tends to create a doughy skin on the fish. The soy sauce on seafood is really excellent. It was, after all, originally designed for such a use in Southeastern China and in Japan.

## Lemon

Yes, lemons are fabulous, providing two vital things are always remembered.

The first is the shape of the lemon piece provided. If it is sliced into a thin decorative ring, it is a useless waste of money. You can't squeeze it or eat it effectively! A lemon should be cut in wedges that can be squeezed. That is, the pointed ends of the wedge have to be trimmed first to provide a flat surface. I use a fork to jab into the quarter in order to release some of the juice without a struggle.

The other point is that if you are right-handed, you should squeeze the wedge with your left hand. The lemon skin is filled with volatile oils that spray back onto your hand and make it impossible to drink anything without a new "lemon fresh" aroma!

# Grilled Fish $ Ⓨ

### INGREDIENTS:

1 gurnard (filleted) or small
rainbow trout (9 inches maximum)
Flour to coat
Salt to taste
White peppercorns to taste
Clarified butter (p. 77) to brush

> *Apart from certain flat fish such as sole and flounder (or if the fish is not perfectly fresh, see Crimping p. 45), an infallible rule applies to broiled fish: the skin should not be removed before cooking. The reason for this is simple. The skin has a layer of natural fat between it and the flesh. This fat bastes the fish and imparts a wonderful taste and aroma. Removing the skin is like taking all the fat off a leg of lamb before roasting. Silly, isn't it!*

### PREPARATION

1. Season the flour.
2. Melt the butter.
3. Heat broiler (medium hot).
4. Grease the rungs of the broiler.

**Step 1.** Make diagonal incisions into the fleshy part of the fillet, cutting deeper where the flesh is thickest. This helps to speed cookery.

**Step 2.** Season the fillets and brush on the clarified butter.

**Step 3.** Place skin down in the flour and brush the flesh surface with butter. Then flour this side. Shake off any surplus and place onto the broiler.

**Step 4.** Just before broiling, brush over with butter once more. Broil at medium to hot for 5 minutes either side.

# Poached Fish

### INGREDIENTS:

1 young scrod or North Sea cod
(2 lb.)
⅝ cup stock
⅝ cup milk
2 oz. butter
½ cup flour
1¼ cups milk for sauce
¼ cup white grape juice
½ teaspoon rice vinegar
Salt to taste
White peppercorns to taste

*The poaching method of cooking fish is excellent. It is a pity that it is so seldom used. So many varied flavors and garnishes can be added to the sauce, and the whole task, including the sauce, is over in 20 minutes.*

### PREPARATION

1. Brush the poaching dish with butter.
2. Combine stock and milk for poaching liquid.
3. Measure butter, flour, grape juice, and vinegar.

**Step 1.** Place the fillets in a shallow dish and add the milk. Leave to soak for 1 hour.

**Step 2.** Place on a gentle heat (or in an oven set at 250° F.) and add fish stock (made from the bones cooked for 30 minutes). Cover and cook for 8 minutes — do not boil. Test for doneness by easing away the flesh with a knife point.

**Step 3.** While fish is poaching, make up basic White Sauce with milk (page 217) but do not add herbs. Strain off cooking liquid from fish into the sauce. Add the white grape juice and rice vinegar and beat well.

**Step 4.** Add whatever seasoning or garnishes you wish to the sauce and pour it over the fillets (see, for example, Dill Weed Fish Sauce-page 218).

# Walleyed Pike Pie

**(Serves 4)**

### INGREDIENTS:

1 lb. walleyed pike fillets (or halibut, haddock, flounder, snapper)
1 lb. spinach
6 cooked asparagus spears
2 lbs. potatoes
2 tablespoons butter
1 egg
Freshly ground salt to taste
Freshly ground white pepper to taste
2 tablespoons sesame/safflower oil (page 186)
1¼ cups milk
Parsley and paprika for garnish
½ lemon

**❝** *Walleyed pike is a classic local specialty of Minnesota. If not available, other solid white-fleshed fish can be used. Strip away the skin and prepare as follows:* **❞**

### PREPARATION

1. Crimp fish in mixture of salt and water for 30 minutes (see page 45).* Wash spinach thoroughly. Trim stems and slice into 1-inch strips. Puree asparagus well in a blender. Any strings will clog the pastry tube. Peel and boil potatoes. Mash, adding butter, egg, and pureed asparagus; season with pepper and salt. Roughly chop parsley. Oil an oven proof dish.

2. Place spinach in a large saucepan with 2 tablespoons oil. Season with salt and pepper. Put lid on pan and set over low heat for 5 minutes, giving spinach a good shake after 2 minutes to distribute the oil.

3. Cover the pike fillets with cold milk in another pan, season with white pepper, cover, and allow to poach gently for 8 minutes. (Count 8 minutes after you see bubbles around the edge of the pan.)

4. Drain spinach and place half of it in the oven proof dish. Add drained fish, and sprinkle with juice of ½ lemon. Cover with rest of spinach.

5. Cover spinach with half of the potato, smoothing it with a spatula; then place the rest of the potato in a pastry bag with a star-shaped nozzle and pipe potato decoratively around dish.

6. Bake in a hot oven for 6 minutes until browned. Sprinkle with parsley and paprika before serving.

   *The colder the salt and water mixture the better. It should almost have ice flakes on top.

# "A. J. Rockfish"

**Serves 4**

### INGREDIENTS:

4 7- oz. fillets of fish (rockfish,
striped bass, or whiting)
2½ cups fish stock (page 34)
1 tablespoon safflower oil
2 cups mushrooms (4 oz.)
1 lemon for juice
Cayenne pepper to season
1 tablespoon arrowroot
¼ cup milk
¼ cup cream
1 tablespoon soy sauce
Dill weed to season

> *You will need four fillets of fish weighing about 7 ounces each. I like rockfish, striped bass, or whiting — each poaches well and can look, as well as taste, excellent.*

### PREPARATION

1. Lay the fillets in iced salt water (see page 45 for crimping).

2. Prepare fish stock.

3. Oil a skillet with 1 tablespoon oil, strain fish stock into it, and bring to the boil, then reduce to simmer.

4. Take fillets straight from the iced water to the poaching liquid, cover and cook gently for 8 minutes.

5. During this time take the firm white mushrooms and slice them finely across the cap. Sprinkle with fresh lemon juice and cayenne pepper.

6. Remove fish from the skillet when cooked with a long, flat, perforated "fish lifter" and keep them warm on their serving platter over a saucepan of boiling water.

7. Bring the cooking liquid to the boil and reduce it by rapid evaporation for 2 minutes. Dissolve arrowroot in the milk and stir arrowroot into the hot (not boiling) cooking liquid. Return to heat and stir until it thickens.

8. Add enough table cream (about ¼ cup) to lighten the color and add 1 teaspoon of soy sauce (to replace the fat taken out by not using the roux-based sauce). Taste and adjust the seasoning.

9. Place mushroom pieces like large scales down the back of each fish fillet and coat with the hot sauce. Sprinkle with dill weed and a little cayenne pepper and serve.

# Simple Court Bouillon

### INGREDIENTS:

1 large onion (⅝ cup, coarsely
chopped)
2 medium carrots (⅝ cup, coarsely
chopped)
1 teaspoon oil
7 quarts water
1 cup rice vinegar
⅔ cup coarse salt
2 tablespoons black peppercorns
1 tablespoon chopped parsley
2 bay leaves
½ teaspoon thyme

### PREPARATION

1. Shallow-fry vegetables in oil, turn into the fish kettle, and add remaining ingredients.

2. Cook over moderate heat for 20 minutes. Strain before using in recipes.

# HINTS

## Skinning Fish

If you wish to skin your fish or your fish fillets, here are the directions for doing it easily. But first, why skin the fish?

If it has been deep frozen for more than 6 months there is a fighting chance that the "oil underlay" beneath the skin has become rancid, which can seriously affect the taste. I suggest you take off the skin if you are in any doubt. Simply grasp the tail end of the fillet and place the knife blade carefully between the skin and the flesh (the skin is placed down against the board). Dipping one's fingers into some salt (for a firm grip), hold the blade at about a 25° angle and pull the tail, bringing the flesh over the knife and the skin under in a seesawing side-to-side motion.

## Fish Kettle

If you should happen to be a fisherman who habitually catches six- to eight-pound fish or if you know someone who does, then you'll need a fish kettle.

The most inexpensive kettle is made of tinned steel, is oblong with rounded ends, and has a lid and perforated lifter tray insert. It is so long that it must be placed over two heat elements. Fish are poached in the kettle in a well-seasoned liquid called a "Court Bouillon" (page 49) — a technique first mastered by the French.

Thoroughly clean the gutted fish by wiping with a damp salt-encrusted piece of cheesecloth. Lay the fish gently in the precooked liquid, cover tightly, and turn on the heat to bring to the boil *gradually* (takes about 30 minutes). When it boils, time it accurately at 3 minutes per pound (18 minutes for a 6-pounder). Immediately remove from the stove and allow fish to cool in the liquid for an hour. Remove and serve hot or cold with Light Mayonnaise (see page 214).

*Nutritive information.* Note the relative calories for some of the different fish that can be cooked in this manner. These approximate calorie counts are for a 3½-ounce serving:*

| | | | |
|---|---|---|---|
| Bass | 287 calories | Lake Trout | |
| Bluefish | 192 calories | under 6½ lbs. | 241 calories |
| Catfish | 103 calories | over 6½ lbs. | 524 calories |
| Cod | 150 calories | Brook Trout | 101 calories |
| Salmon | 217 calories | Rainbow Trout | 195 calories |

Appearance, texture, flavor, and aroma advantages are extremely high; small pieces of fish when poached just don't measure up (except for fillets of sole).

*Charles F. and Helen N. Church, *Bowes and Church's Food Values of Portions Commonly Used*, 11th edition (Philadelphia: Lippincott, 1970).

# Baked Fish

## INGREDIENTS:

2½-3 lb. butterfish, trout, or small salmon
Salt to taste
½ teaspoon white pepper
2 tablespoons sesame/safflower oil
1 tablespoon fennel seed

> *A whole baked fish can be delicious. If you can't lay your hands on a trout, then there are many commercially available fish that make a good substitute. If you can get a trout, then toss away the wet newspaper and try this method — it works.*

## PREPARATION

1. Prepare a muslin pad dipped in salt for cleaning fish.
2. Wash fish thoroughly and dry inside and out.
3. Preheat oven to 350° F.

**Step 1.** Wipe inside fish with a muslin pad dipped in salt. All whole fish should be cleaned in this way. Remove head & tail if you like.

**Step 2.** Cut through thickest part of body with diagonal strokes to a depth of ½ to 1 inch. Combine seasonings with oil.

**Step 3.** Rub seasoned oil into slashes on both sides, and scatter fennel seed on bottom of dish. You will note that the fish is placed on grill bars in a roasting dish. This provides all-around heat and helps to turn the fish onto the serving dish.

**Step 4.** Bake the fish at 350° F. for 8 minutes each side or until the flesh comes easily from the bone. Turn the fish onto an oval dish and strip off the skin.

# Shrimp

**Step 1.** Shrimp must be perfectly fresh. When shrimp has been "sitting about," the head shell goes a very dark color. Beware of these. Grasp the head firmly and break it downward from the tail.

**Step 2.** Strip off the outer shell by loosening it first from the underside.

**Step 3.** Cut into the back of the tail with a sharp knife. Do not cut deeply — only the slightest pressure is needed.

**Step 4.** Peel back the flesh to uncover the waste tract. In this photograph you have, on the right, a clear view of the tract — remove this completely. On the left you can see the tract covered with coral. Remove the tract but retain the coral for use as a garnish or for incorporation in a cocktail sauce.

# Steamed Shrimp

### (Serves 4)

#### INGREDIENTS:

1 lb. medium-size raw shrimp
¼ cup rice vinegar
¼ cup water
4 spring onions
2 garlic cloves, crushed
2 stalks parsley
2 bay leaves
Peel from ¼ orange and ¼ lemon
1 tablespoon fennel seed

> **❝** *I must insist that precooked shrimp are tasteless; in fact, they just look the part. Better by far to buy them raw and frozen ("green") and steam them yourself.*
>
> *Here is a simple recipe. Remember, shrimp are a good source of protein with very little fat.* **❞**

#### PREPARATION

1. Keep shrimp frozen until ready to use. Prepare or otherwise measure out all ingredients.

2. Put vinegar and water in the bottom of a large saucepan. Place all other ingredients except the shrimp in the liquid after it has been brought to a boil.

3. Place a metal vegetable steamer over the hot liquid and put the shrimp in the steamer. Cover tightly and steam for 10 minutes.

4. Serve hot or cold, but remove shrimp from steamer after cooking or they become too strongly seasoned.

Another great use for shrimp is in salads. See page 203.

# Shrimp Cocktail

### (Serves 4)

#### INGREDIENTS:

½ lb. shrimp
½ cup mayonnaise (page 212)
1 stiffly beaten egg white
2 teaspoons horseradish sauce
2 teaspoons ketchup
¼ teaspoon dill weed

In this section I really want to show *two* ways to avoid spoiling this splendid appetizer. Restaurants use a very powerful prepared tomato "dressing" as a sauce dip and they also *couch* the shrimp in a large uncut lettuce leaf as garnish.

I prefer a milder sauce that doesn't overwhelm the delicacy of the shrimp, and I like the lettuce to be in an edible state. Therefore this dressing is mayonnaise-based and seasoned with tomato.

Appearance advantage: you only need 2 ounces of shrimp per person, and served this way it looks like more, in fact, it looks *great!*

Taste advantage comes from the balance in flavor between the shrimp and the sauce, together with the *cleansing agent* of the lemon-dressed lettuce.

Nutritional advantage is pretty good. By using whipped egg white, you reduce the normal mayonnaise calories by almost half, and the shrimp provides about 26 calories per ounce.

#### PREPARATION

1. Make up mayonnaise, fold into this 1 stiffly beaten egg white, the horseradish sauce, ketchup, and dill weed. This provides 1 cup sauce. Chill well.

2. *Finely* slice some lettuce, mix with salt, pepper, and lemon juice and place in a fancy glass. Top with shrimp and cover with cooled sauce. Dust with a *little* fresh chopped parsley and paprika. Serve with *thin* slices of buttered whole wheat bread.

# Rock Lobster

*There are at least eight different ways to kill a crayfish. I'm a coward when it comes to dealing with a live crayfish, and the one on this page was not only active but quite large. The method chosen here shows the boiling process. You can, however, stop at Step 3 if you want to broil or shallow fry the flesh. Another simple way to deal with a live crayfish is to place it into a deep freeze. It keeps very well and the method appeals to my nature.*

**Step 1.** When buying live shellfish, make sure its tail moves vigorously when the shellfish is held in the air. Never cook a dead crayfish.

**Step 2.** All edible crustacea die at 98.6⁰ F. Place the crayfish in the sink and allow warm water to run in slowly. I have found that in this way the crayfish does not struggle and appears to pass away peacefully.

**Step 3.** For the most flavorsome results, prepare a lightly salted water mixture containing the following ingredients for each 3 pints of water; 8 ounces carrot, 2 shallots or 1 medium onion, 1 bay leaf, 1 sprig thyme, 1 ounce salt, ¼ pint white vinegar, 6 stalks parsley, 6 black peppercorns. Boil this for 30 minutes before you add the crayfish.

**Step 4.** Boil for 7 minutes for a 1½-pound crayfish if you wish to reheat the flesh for a made-up dish. If you prefer to eat it cold, then cook for 10 minutes. In both cases transfer the cooked crayfish straight into a bowl of very cold water. This prevents the crayfish from continuing to cook.

# Oysters

*Oysters should, by right, only be eaten raw — straight from the shell. This is how to open them.*

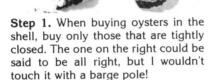

**Step 1.** When buying oysters in the shell, buy only those that are tightly closed. The one on the right could be said to be all right, but I wouldn't touch it with a barge pole!

**Step 2.** Scrub the outer shells thoroughly in cold water.

**Step 3.** Use a cloth and a sharp knife exactly as shown here. You can cut yourself to ribbons if you don't take adequate precautions. Cut into the hinge end and feel along the flat shell until the muscle is detached.

**Step 4.** With the top shell removed, you can release the oyster from the bottom and turn it over. The underneath side looks better, but gourmets prefer to cut them from the shell at the table. Please keep the natural juice surrounding the oyster in the shell. Serve with wedges of lemon.

# Squid

❝ *Squid is mostly used for bait. This seems to be a gross waste of a delicious seafood.*

*In some countries it is a luxury. I admit that it looks utterly repulsive at first, but as you will see from Steps 3 and 4, when it is properly prepared it looks highly edible — and it is!* ❞

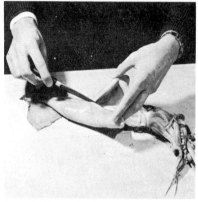

**Step 1.** Open the hood down the back with a sharp knife. Lay the hood open flat.

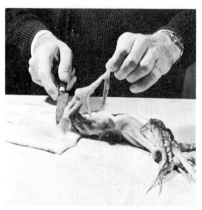

**Step 2.** Starting at the top, gently detach the gut and ink sac and cut through at the base of the hood. Cut off the tentacles just below the beak and throw the center portion away (or freeze it ready for the next fishing trip!).

**Step 3.** Rub the outer skin with a coarse salt-dipped cloth to remove the skin. Peel out the backbone (seen at the bottom of the picture) and then slice into ½-inch-wide strips.

**Step 4.** Place hood and tentacles together in a steamer and steam gently for 45-60 minutes. Remove when completely tender and use in casserole or fried dishes. It tastes like a combination of oyster and chicken.

# Scallops

*Scallops are one of our finest seafoods. Some like to buy them in the shell, and if you should want to join them, this is the method of opening and basic preparation.*

**Step 1.** Scrub the shells well in cold water. The shells don't close as tightly as oysters, but it is obvious when they are dead.

**Step 2.** One way of opening scallops is to put them into an oven set at 200° F. for 5 minutes and then cut them open by detaching the muscle from the flat shell. I'm not completely sold on this technique as they are really quite easy to open with a knife without heating. The acceptable ones are those on the top shelf — the ones below are very dead.

**Step 3.** Open the scallops over a bowl containing ½ cup white grape juice, 1 tsp. rice vinegar, 1 ounce sliced onion, 1 sprig thyme, 6 black peppercorns, and 1 crumbled bay leaf. Any juices will mix with this poaching liquid and help the finished flavor.

**Step 4.** Cut the scallop from the curved shell and strip off the beard, leaving only the trimmed center core and the bright orange flap. Put the trimmed scallops into the grape juice mixture and poach gently for 4 minutes; remove and use as the recipe requires.

# Clams

> *Mussels are easy and fun and delicious and inexpensive (if you live by the sea!).*

Here are a few pointers that help to make the first experience a happy one:
* Select large shells that are tightly closed.
* Scrub them free from all surface mud, etc.
* Shake each one; if it rattles, discard it — it has a stone inside!
* Grab hold of its "beard" and pull hard; this is much better than leaving them attached, only to be dealt with while eating.
* When you have boiled them for the 2 minutes and the extra 1 minute (see following recipe for Standard "Soup"), look to see if any *haven't* opened. Toss out those that haven't.
* Please respect the advice to strain the "soup" through a cheese-cloth. This removes all the grit and sand that can, so often, ruin a good mussel.

*Nutritional advantage.* The food value of mussels is splendid. Here is the profile for 3½ ounces (100 grams) of the mussels, *meat only* — the weight of one dozen good-sized mussels: 95 calories (good); 14 g. protein (good); 2 g. fat (good); excellent iron and iodine.

*Effort advantage.* Look closely at the following recipe and you will see that while it may *look* complex it only actually takes about 8 minutes of work to make.

# Standard "Soup"

This soup will steam open 80 mussels — 4 portions

### INGREDIENTS:

2 medium onions (1½ cups chopped)
1 tablespoon garlic oil (see page 78)
1 teaspoon thyme
2 tablespoons parsley
2 bay leaves
1 tablespoon whole peppercorns
1 garlic clove
1½ cups white grape juice and 2 tablespoons rice vinegar
¼ cup cream
1 tablespoon chopped parsley
1 tablespoon arrowroot

**Step 1.** Bring to boil all ingredients except cream, parsley, and arrowroot; cover and cool. Strain and press out through cheesecloth.

**Step 2.** Pour seasoned juice into large pan or split into 2 large pans with tight covers. Bring to a boil and add mussels, then cover and time 2 minutes. *Shake pan well* (hold lid on firmly) then boil 1 minute.

**Step 3.** Place cheesecloth in colander and pour soup and mussels into colander. Dish mussels into a large *heated* bowl.

**Step 4.** Pour strained sauce into a pan and bring to a boil. Combine cream with parsley and arrowroot *(don't add salt)*. Stir this cream mixture into the soup, remove from fire, and dish into 4 soup plates. Serve mussels on flat plates with finger bowls. Use mussel shells as tongs to remove other mussels and drop them into the soup — just fabulous!

# meat & poultry

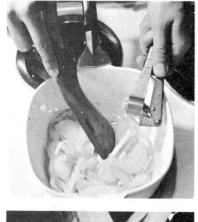

# meat & poultry

# meat & poultry

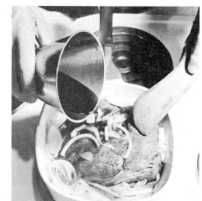

# meat & poultry

# Roast Meat $ ⍟

Serves 6-8

### INGREDIENTS:

5-6 lb. leg of lamb
2 garlic cloves
Salt to taste
Black peppercorns to taste
Enough flour to dust

> ❝ *In accordance with ancient tradition, many gourmet authors and leading chefs prefer to cook their roasts at a high initial temperature and then reduce heat to roughly 400° F. I am not a traditionalist. It has been proven time and time again that a stable temperature of 300° — 325° F. throughout cookery produces a tender, succulent, and above all economic result. We can no longer afford to let such expensive meat cuts evaporate.* ❞

### PREPARATION

1. Peel cloves of garlic and cut into thin slices as shown in Step 1.
2. Dry meat with a clean cloth.
3. Preheat oven to 325° F.

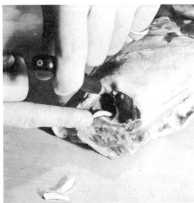

**Step 1.** Place slivers of garlic in the joint at points nearest to the main bones. This carries the flavor through the joint, and the result is "gently aromatic."

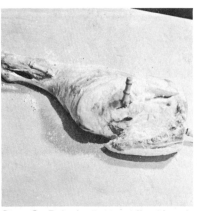

**Step 2.** Rub the joint well with salt and freshly ground black peppercorns. Then dust it all over with sifted flour. The bamboo spikes indicate the position of garlic in this leg of lamb.

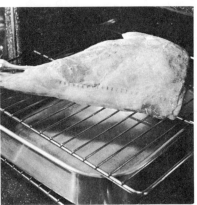

**Step 3.** Place the joint directly on the rungs of your oven shelf with a roasting dish underneath. In this way you get all-round circulation of hot air, and it definitely improves the quality. Always put fat side up. Roast for approximately 30 minutes per pound — internal temperature 168° F.

**Step 4.** Unless the joint is very lean do not baste during cookery and NEVER add the dripping from one animal to a roast of another, i.e. pork dripping for lamb roast.

You can see the advantage of the oven shelf position here. You can stack in vegetables if you want, whereas space is limited with the joint in the same roast tray.

# Roast Leg of Lamb Nelson

**(Serves 6 to 8)**

### INGREDIENTS:

1 4-lb. leg of lamb (wipe dry with a clean cloth)

1 tablespoon flour, sifted and seasoned with salt and white pepper

6 sprays parsley, very fresh and well washed

1 10-oz. can apple and orange juice, opened and placed in a small saucepan

(If you cannot find apple/orange mixed simply combine ⅝ cup each of orange juice and clear apple juice.)

### PREPARATION

1. Rub the lamb with the seasoned flour and shake off surplus.

2. Make several even and decorative shallow incisions in the heavy outer fat layers and pack into these some well-washed pieces of parsley. (If you have some marjoram, it also gives a delightful flavor to lamb, but it must be used very sparingly.)

3. Preheat your oven to 325⁰ F. Place the leg, fat side up, on the cleaned rungs of your top oven shelf; place the drip pan two shelves below the roast. This is used to collect the drippings and to roast root vegetables if you wish to add them.

4. After 10 minutes of cookery, draw out the top oven shelves so that the joint is exposed and place another drip pan immediately underneath the joint. Now baste the leg with the apple and orange juice. The pan immediately below the leg will collect the surplus fruit juice and will save the vegetables from becoming saturated. Allow 30 minutes per pound of meat and baste with the juice at least four times during cooking.

5. When the joint is cooked, remove the vegetables, boil down the juice in the other pan to ¼-⅓ cup, and spoon the syrupy mixture over the joint, having raised the temperature of the oven to 500⁰ F. This high heat will form a crisp golden orange and apple glaze on your lamb in 5 to 10 minutes, which is as delicious as it is attractive. The balance of the fruit juice can be added to the meat drippings in the vegetable pan, to form a fruit gravy.

# Baste for Pork Crackling  $

### INGREDIENTS:

½ cup safflower oil
½ teaspoon caraway seed
2 garlic cloves (crushed)
¼ teaspoon salt

### PREPARATION

1. Place the ingredients in a small saucepan. Cover and simmer slowly for about 10 minutes.

2. Cool and strain the liquid; discard the solids. Use the remaining oil as a baste on roast pork to get the crackling crisp.

# Pork Shish Kebab  $

### Serves 4

### INGREDIENTS:

2 tablespoons soy sauce
1 tablespoon rice vinegar
¼ teaspoon fresh ginger root
1 garlic clove, crushed
2-3 tablespoons water
1½ lbs. loin cut pork, bone out
(or pork butt)
4 cups cooked long-grain rice
Aluminum foil
9 inch round or square cake pan
4 skewers
Vegetables (optional)
1 tablespoon oil

### PREPARATION

1. Measure and combine marinade ingredients: soy sauce, vinegar, ginger root, garlic, and water. Use marinade only with pork butt; not needed with loin cut. Cut meat into 1½ inch chunks. Soak meat in marinade mixture several hours or overnight. Be sure there is enough marinade to cover the meat.

2. Prepare the rice.

3. Line the cake pan with foil. Put 5-6 ounces of meat on each skewer. Place pan with skewers laid rim-to-rim on top, under the broiler. The fat will drip down. Turn every 5 minutes (10-15 minutes total cooking time).

4. Cut vegetables to be eaten with meat into 1-1½ inch squares. Pan-fry them in 1 tablespoon oil to the crisp-tender stage.

Serve bowls of hot vegetables to be dipped in different mustard, chili, or soy sauces or mixed with the meat, which has been pushed off the skewers onto a bed of rice. This is a very versatile meat, at 620 calories per serving.

*❝ Quite apart from the conven-ience of handling a quantity of cubed meat, the skewer has the added advantage of allowing a maximum area to be coated in a glaze as a result of the radiant heat playing directly upon a marinated surface. Try this simple idea that uses only ordinary kitchen equipment. ❞*

# HINTS

## Meat Thermometers

Described by all modern authorities as an *essential*. This simple instrument can save a great deal of money when used in association with an in-oven thermometer and a set of scales. You need to know exactly how much the meat weighs and that your oven is accurate at 325° F., which is the temperature most suited to most dishes.

A good thermometer will cost about $3 to $6, with the professional one about 3-4 times as much. Consider two things about the unit. First, you should select a unit with a large head; that is, the dial needs to be about 2 inches in diameter. The head must be large so that there is enough air to expand without destroying the dial when left in the oven for the full cooking time. (The professional model reads almost instantly, but this is *not* for home use. The professional uses it to jab in *large* cuts to confirm his opinion. To keep on jabbing at a domestic cut will drain out the juices, and if you leave the professional one *in,* its small dial will be destroyed due to there being insufficient room for the air in it to expand.) Second, you must place a thermometer in the meat correctly, with the dial facing you from the oven. The point must be in the middle of the muscle and not touching a bone. The dial must not be closer than 3 inches to an overhead oven element. Lastly, they don't work in microwave ovens.

*Nutritional advantage.* Studies done on rare and well-done roast beef indicated a higher retention of B vitamins when cooked to the rare stage. Thiamin is particularly sensitive to heat and is reduced the most when beef is cooked to the well-done stage.

## Pork Crackling

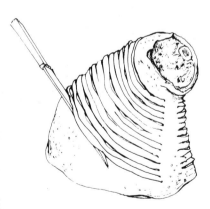

When anything is as good as this, there simply has to be a drawback! In this case it's the fat content of the skin and its double effect of saturated fat intake and calorie burden. But, we have some escapes for you!

First, we must advise on the cut. You should *order* ahead of time from your meat supplier a *5-pound fresh ham shank, with the rind (heavy outer skin) left intact.* You will now have fresh pork from the lower hind leg with the skin on.

In order to get the crackling crisp you make ¼-inch deep incisions with a sharp knife every ¼ inch in hoops right about the leg (see illustration). Rub salt into these "scores" and baste well with the mixture given. Roast at 375° F. for 25 minutes per pound until the internal temperature is 175° F. (see Meat Thermometers, above).

Sense advantage is clearly a visual one at first, but when the pieces are eaten they are delicate, crisp, and full of flavor, an ideal foil for the smooth meat they cover.

*Nutrition Comment.* A word of caution here. There is a danger of consuming too much fat by leaving the rind in place. To avoid this you *must* cut away the crackling from the underfat and then carve all the underfat away and remove it from the table. It should not be eaten. By doing this, the small piece of crisp skin will not be out of balance with the normal fat-to-meat ratio.

# HINTS

## Cooking a Standing Rib Roast

Some cuts of beef have become real public enemies in our lives. The standing rib of beef is a perfect example. Yet I believe it warrants a closer look.

The cut is large and it looks big. It weighs about 4 lbs. when cut to include 2 ribs (the minimum size to purchase). Choice grade at time of writing was $2.89 lb. Thus 4 lb. cost $11.56. We get 1 lb. 5 oz. trimmed meat, or 11 good slices serving 5 people with excellent portions of 6 oz. each at a cost of $2.31 per portion with all fat trimmed off (14 oz. fat) and the bones (10½ oz.) to be used for stock.

Certainly it's a treat, and because of this it is essential to treat it with great care. Roast not a degree over 325° F. I roasted an identical cut at 385° F. and look at the difference:

| CUT | WEIGHT | TEMPERA-TURE | COOKING TIME | INTERNAL TEMPERA-TURE |
|---|---|---|---|---|
| A) 2 ribs | 4 lb. 2 oz. | 325°F. | 120 minutes | 140°F. |
| B) 2 ribs | 4 lb. 2 oz. | 385°F. | 110 minutes | 140°F. |

| | PAN GREASE | WEIGHT OUT | BONE WEIGHT | FAT TRIM* |
|---|---|---|---|---|
| A) | ½ c. | 3 lb. 13 oz. | 10½ oz. | 14 oz. |
| B) | ⅔ c. | 3 lb. 3 oz. | 11½ oz. | 16 oz. |

| | PURE MEAT | NO. SLICES | COST PER OZ. |
|---|---|---|---|
| A) | 1 lb. 15 oz. | 11 | 37.3¢ |
| B) | 1 lb. 7 oz. | 8 | 50.2¢ |

*Contains some meat layers that were not removed in either case.

Rub a little salt and freshly ground black pepper into the meat, cut a little pocket between the ribs and push a garlic clove up into the incision. Then rest the roast (standing fat uppermost) on the bones in an oven proof roasting pan. Place roast in an oven set at 325° F. and roast to an internal temperature of 140° F., tested with a good meat thermometer. Don't add any fat; it has plenty of its own. Turn the oven off. Let the cut stand in oven with door open for 20 minutes before carving. This way you will get outside end slices well done, inside medium, and middle slices rare.

# HINTS

## Heat Prongs

Since the increasing cost of living for both fuel and food has hit us, we are being besieged by the heat prong as an economy-oriented proposal.

Heat prongs work by carrying heat into a large muscle or dense object, like a potato, and by conduction hastening the cooking from the inside out as well as the normal outside in. The question is, does this save time and money?

Potato nails resulted in 5 minutes less baking time, when used from both ends. The Hang and Bake strips (in which the prong is twisted to hold the potato as it hangs from the oven rungs) didn't work. The test on the cooking pin* was, however, interesting. We took 2 similar rolled loins of pork, one with a pin in, one with no pin. Side by side roasting at 325° F. for 90 minutes resulted in our usual satisfying perfectly cooked roast without the pin. But with the pin, the roast was overcooked badly. Later tests revealed a 15-minute saving of time from use of the cooking pin with a resultant weight saving of 1 ounce. All you have to do is ensure that the tip of the pin is higher than the black knob and that no part of the pin touches anything other than the meat or clear air (avoiding the bone, for example).

*Budget advantage.* One ounce on 1 pound 12 ounces (the weight of the above roast) equals a 1/28 saving. Based on the consumption of 1 roast per week for a year, the saving was less than the cost of the pin! I used this whole examination to prove a point. We may well be attracted to what appears to be a logical little gadget, but it is my experience that, armed with a meat thermometer (see above), a portable timer, and an oven with an accurate thermostat — all you need as gadgets are two hands and a brain!

*Sense advantage.* One disadvantage here is that the pin cooks the meat well done or close to it. In this way it isn't possible to get meat cooked rare, unless you can put up with a roast with rare rings!

*This is a heat conductor fluid-filled prong about 9 inches long that is used to insert into meats being cooked.

## Beef Seasoning from the Inside

Mix ¼ teaspoon each of cinnamon, cardamom, nutmeg, and black pepper with 1 teaspoon of ground ginger and 3 crushed cloves of garlic. Spread this "paste" evenly upon the cut surface of a 3- or 4-pound rolled beef roast, then roll tightly and retie. You can modify the seasoning for lamb or veal breast — all manner of super flavorings are yours to invent and use.

## Carving a Rib Roast of Beef

Carving a small roast prime rib has more to it than meets the eye.

There are four things to look out for: setting, fat and bone removal, heat, and slice size.

*Setting.* Each roast should be internally measured to 140° F. and then allowed to set in an open oven turned *off* for 20 minutes before carving. It will be easier to handle this way.

*Fat.* We get between 14 and 16 ounces of solid fat off a 4-lb. rib roast. This must come off. It represents close to 3,000 calories or 200 calories per ounce of saturated fat. The bones are also removed for ease of carving, and they make excellent stock.

*Heat.* Slices should be carved onto a heated dish.

*Slice size.* We highly recommend thin slices for better flavor. Smaller pieces also look better on the plate and are easier to cut, chew, and swallow.

## Roast Only What You Need!

The use of cold roasted meats in leftover dishes is, in my opinion, the most wasteful practice in the North American kitchen. A family of 4, for example, will purchase a 4-pound roast of beef for a family dinner. It will cost about $2.89 per pound or a total of $11.56. After roasting it will weigh about 3 pounds — at $3.85 per pound. Each person likes to see about 5 ounces (cooked weight) of sliced beef; for our family of 4, we like 20 ounces. This leaves 28 ounces *surplus to requirement* at $3.85 per pound — or $6.74 for 1 pound 12 ounces of cold roasted meat! Either it is eaten up at the meal *in excess of even our emotional needs* or it is used as "leftovers" within another recipe that could easily have used, say, hamburger at $1.70 per pound with a subsequent saving of $2.15 per pound!!!*

*Nutritional advantage.* Dietary surveys indicate that Americans are not lacking for protein in the diet. In fact, even in underdeveloped countries, the problem of malnutrition seems to be associated with total calories available and not only with protein. We are "hung up" on protein, and specifically on meat. Protein is an important nutrient, but most of us greatly exceed our needs. Protein eaten in excess of bodily needs is either used for energy — that is, burned as calories — or stored as *fat!!!* if the energy is not expended. In this context, excessively high meat consumption, as with any food, is *fattening.*

*Budget advantage.* Depending upon how often you eat roast meat, you could save considerable amounts of money. I once was able, by instituting this theory in a large-scale catering responsibility, to save about $153,600 in an overall budget of $5,700,000 — or nearly 3 percent of the total. You might manage the same with your total budget.

To roast what you need, order your roast next time by multiplying the number you will feed by 8 ounces — i.e., for 4 people, 4 x 8 ounces = 2 pounds of *boneless* meat. Roast it at 325° F. and carve in thin slices. If this works *then* reduce the quantity until you sense an adverse reaction — and may God bless your efforts!

*All prices at time of writing.

# Pot Roast $

### INGREDIENTS:

3 lb. blade roast
Flour to coat
Black peppercorns
Salt
6 tablespoons clarified butter
2 medium onions
1 medium parsnip
1 large carrot
2 garlic cloves
1 bay leaf
Red grape juice
1 teaspoon cold, unsweetened tea
2 teaspoons rice vinegar
3 tablespoons arrowroot
NOTE: ½ cup stock can be used in lieu of grape juice, tea, and vinegar.

*Forgive me if I get immodest over the recipe given here. Although it is a basic method, it is really very pleasant. No, delicious! The meat is a roast blade of beef (well matured), and it melts in your mouth. Pot roasting should really be reserved for tougher meat cuts — those with a good deal of connective tissue — but I find that now and again a tender cut can be given added flavor when cooked in this fashion.*

*You can add fresh vegetables half an hour before the roast is cooked, removing the old ones. The new vegetables are then served with the roast.*

### PREPARATION

1. Peel and cut vegetables into ¼-inch thick slices.
2. Peel cloves of garlic.
3. Measure grape juice, tea, and vinegar.
4. Make an arrowroot paste with 3 tablespoons each of arrowroot and water.

**Step 1.** Because of its long slow moist heat this method is good for cuts containing a good deal of sinew. The selected roast should be wiped with a clean damp cloth and then dried thoroughly. Now lightly flour the roast.

**Step 2.** First shallow fry the vegetables with crushed garlic in the saucepan or casserole dish — remove the vegetables when browned slightly. The size of utensil is important; it should be just large enough for the roast.

**Step 3.** Add the roast and brown well on both sides over a high heat. This builds up a delicious crust that both flavors and colors the sauce. Replace the fried vegetables and set the roast on top.

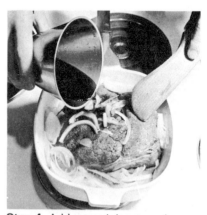

**Step 4.** Add grape juice, tea, vinegar, and bay leaf. Place a lid on top and cook either on the ring or in an oven set at 350° F. to simmer for 40 minutes per pound. When cooked, throw out vegetables (they will be "pappy" and tasteless) and clear the fat from the sauce. Thicken this with arrowroot paste, correct the seasoning, and serve.

# Pot Roast Brisket  $

### (Serves 4)

## INGREDIENTS:

1 large carrot
1 medium onion
1 garlic clove
1 pint beef stock
1 lb. long straight carrots
¼ cup polyunsaturated vegetable oil
2 lbs. brisket
Salt to taste
A dash of black pepper
2 heaped tablespoons tomato paste
1 bay leaf
¼ teaspoon thyme

## PREPARATION

1. Preheat oven to 350° F. Peel and roughly chop the carrot and onion. Peel and squash the garlic. Measure beef stock. Peel the long carrots and leave whole.
2. Trim excess fat from the brisket (if any).
3. Heat a moderate-size Dutch oven — it should *just* provide enough room for the brisket. Add the oil and shallow-fry the vegetables and garlic.
4. Remove the vegetables and add the brisket; brown all over and season with salt and pepper.
5. Add the beef stock mixed into the tomato paste and the herbs. Cover and allow to cook in the oven for 1½ hours (in some cases, 2 hours may be necessary — if the meat is "older" or has been working harder); at the end of this time turn the oven off and allow the meat to cool in the oven for 30 minutes.
6. Drain off the cooking juices and sieve the vegetables so that the pulp thickens the juices. Adjust the seasoning, reserve (heated) to use as a sauce, and replace the brisket to heat through on a very low heat in the same Dutch oven on top of the stove.
7. Cut the carrots in quarters lengthwise, place in cold salted water, cover, and bring to a boil. Boil for about 8 minutes or until *just* done.
8. Carve the brisket in the kitchen and lay overlapping slices on an oval dish. Cover with bubbling hot sauce and garnish with the long carrot sticks.

## HINTS

# Be Your Own Butcher

This is a tip for getting more out of a large cut by being your own butcher. Here we get some great value by cutting 18 portions from a 6½ pound boneless beef chuck roast. This is enough for 4 different meals for an average cost of 55¢ per serving.*

*Beef chuck cost $1.59 per pound and weighed 6 pounds 3.2 ounces for a total of $9.86 — price at time of writing.

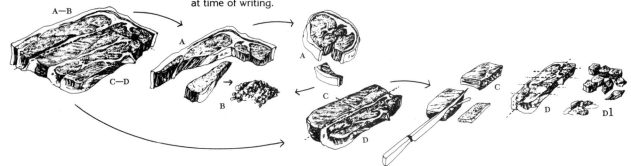

# Braised Meat  $

## INGREDIENTS:

1½ lb. blade steak
1 medium onion
1 large carrot
1 bay leaf
1 spray parsley stalks
2 sprigs thyme
1 oz. clarified butter
Salt to season
Black peppercorns to season
2 garlic cloves
½ cup meat stock (page 31 for quick method)
You can also add tomato sauce for additional color
Flour to dust

> *It has been said that there is no difference between braising and pot roasting. They are similar, but a braise should be covered with liquid at the beginning of cookery, not just ¼ to ½ way up as is the case with a pot roast.*
>
> *Ox tongue is another meat that is delicious when finished by braising.*

## PREPARATION

1. Tie up bay leaf, parsley, and thyme with a piece of string.
2. Dry steaks thoroughly.
3. Heat frying pan to 400°F.
4. Peel and cut vegetables into ¼-inch-thick slices.
5. Measure stock and tomato sauce.
6. Season the flour well with salt and ground peppercorns.

**Step 1.** Cut the steaks into relatively even-size pieces. Dry them well and then press into the seasoned flour.

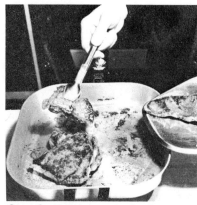

**Step 2.** Melt butter in the frying pan and sear the steaks until beautifully browned. Remove. Add a little more butter and fry the vegetables until they too are browned.

**Step 3.** Replace the steaks, add the herbs, and pour in sufficient stock to cover. With a wooden spoon, scrape all residue from pan base into the liquid. Cover and cook at the simmer for 1½ hours.

**Step 4.** When meat has cooked, remove the herbs, skim off the fat, and thicken with an arrowroot paste if necessary. I sometimes add ½ cup of tomato sauce. This improves the color and helps to thicken the cooking liquid. Dust with parsley and serve.

# Quick Sauerbraten

**(Serves 4)**

### INGREDIENTS:

2½ lb. beef chuck
½ cup rice vinegar
2 tablespoons lemon juice
½ cup water
½ cup red grape juice
1 tablespoon safflower oil
1 garlic clove, crushed
2 tablespoons tomato paste
Salt and pepper to taste
1 teaspoon fresh or
¼ teaspoon ground ginger
2 bay leaves
2 onions cut into quarters
1 tablespoon cold tea
2 tablespoons arrowroot mixed
with 2 tablespoons water

### PREPARATION

Marinate meat in vinegar, lemon juice, water, and grape juice for 2 hours. Do not use an aluminum pot for either marinating or cooking the meat. Measure or otherwise prepare other ingredients before cooking.

1. Dry off meat, brown in a Dutch oven in the oil, then add the garlic, tomato paste, and further brown until paste is caramelized. Add salt, pepper, ginger, bay leaves, onions, cold tea, and the marinade to the pot. Cover and cook gently for 1½-2 hours.

2. Remove the meat from the pot and place on a warmed platter. Slice the meat and keep warm while thickening the sauce.

3. Strain the marinade stock and return to the heat. When it boils, remove from the heat, stir in the arrowroot cream and return to the heat. Stir constantly until it boils again and thickens. Remove from the heat immediately. Spoon a little over the meat and place the rest in a gravy bowl to serve at the side.

Using lean beef, the dish has 554 calories per serving.

*❝ Sauerbraten is a marinated block of beef that is then braised and served fork tender and juicy. The cost in calories per serving is a shade over 550, which makes it the villain of this volume, but on the other hand it is a good rib-sticking repast for the hungry man — especially after a day in the snow.* ❞

# Slow-Cooked Beef Casserole

### (Serves 4)

#### INGREDIENTS:

2 lbs. beef chuck
2 medium carrots in 1″ chunks
2 medium onions cut in quarters
1 tablespoon naturally brewed soy sauce (8% sodium)
1 tablespoon tomato paste
1 tablespoon arrowroot mixed with 2 tablespoons cold water
1 tablespoon parsley, freshly chopped
Freshly ground black pepper
1 cup water
2 bay leaves
½ teaspoon thyme
6 black peppercorns

#### PREPARATION

1. Cut off all fat from the meat and divide meat into 8 4-ounce pieces.

2. Put water in the bottom of a Dutch oven. Add bay leaves, thyme, and peppercorns. Bring to a boil and reduce heat to the *lowest* setting on the stove; add bundt pan (as suggested below).

3. Place dry meat and vegetables with soy sauce in bundt pan. Season with pepper and cook for 4 to 6 hours. Be sure the Dutch oven is covered during this time.

4. When meat is cooked, remove onion, and place it in a small saucepan with the tomato paste over a medium heat. Stir and brown paste. Add the liquid from the meat, stir, and thicken with arrowroot cream.

5. Pour sauce back over the meat and serve in a casserole. Dust with freshly chopped parsley.

# Your Own Slow Cooker

Slow cookers are all the rage, but they do have two disconcerting problems. One is that you probably don't need another large pot, the other is that in some makes the center meat doesn't reach the needed 148° F. until *at least* 4 hours have passed. This means that some slow cookers are perfect incubators for bacteria. I'll try to take care of both problems by showing you how to use two pieces of equipment for one job and provide you with a very inexpensive slow cooker that takes up very little space.

Just buy an aluminum, preferably Teflon coated bundt pan and slip it into your largest Dutch oven. (Be certain to measure the opening before you make a guess purchase!) Pour about 1 cup water into the Dutch oven and add 2 bay leaves, ½ teaspoon thyme, 6 black peppercorns. Bring to the boil and reduce to a simmer (lowest heat). Add meat and vegetables to bundt pan according to the recipe and cook with lid on for up to 6 hours. The meat is cooked at 5 hours but will be in excellent condition at 6 or even 8 hours. Check the water level after 4 hours or place glass marbles in the bottom. They will rattle if the water level drops too far.

# Cold Ox Tongue

### INGREDIENTS:

1 fresh ox tongue
1 onion
1 teaspoon salt
2 bay leaves
6 peppercorns
6 cloves of garlic

*One of the really excellent low-cost cuts you can buy is fresh ox tongue. Low in fat yet high in succulence, it is unique for its texture. It is recommended as a good food for babies since it is easy to digest.*

### PREPARATION

1. Soak tongue in cold water for 1 hour and then rinse well.

2. Cut away surplus fat and discolored areas.

3. Then place tongue in a Dutch oven to boil with the onion (cut in quarters), the seasoning, spices, and garlic (not crushed) for 4 hours; or pressure cook for 40 minutes and let pressure fall gradually (keep the natural juices for later addition to the finishing sauce).

4. Skin the tongue and finish off by braising in a 300° F. oven for 1 hour (see next recipe).

# Braised Ox Tongue

### INGREDIENTS:

6 oz. mixed vegetables (celery, carrots, onions)
1 garlic clove
1 tablespoon oil
1 tablespoon tomato paste
1 tablespoon ham hock stock (page 34)
1 bay leaf
1 boiled tongue (previous recipe)
Tongue cooking liquid
Arrowroot
Parsley

### PREPARATION

1. Blend or chop vegetables and garlic until fine. Fry these fine vegetables in oil and add tomato paste. Cook until the mixture caramelizes.

2. Add the ham hock stock and the bay leaf. Stir.

3. Add tongue, cover, and braise for 1 hour.

4. Test tongue by prodding it with a drinking straw — it should be that tender!

5. Strain the sauce, bring to a boil, add the first cooking liquid from the boiled tongue to make 2 cups, and thicken with arrowroot (1 tablespoon arrowroot to 2 tablespoons cold water).

6. Slice the tongue finely and place it in layers on a shallow dish. Coat with the sauce, dust with parsley, and serve.

# Boiled Meat (Ham)

### INGREDIENTS:

1 country-cured ham

### PREPARATION

1. Put in a large kettle and cover completely with boiling water.

2. Reduce the heat so that the water barely simmers. Cover. Cook 20-30 minutes per pound.

*Traditionally thousands upon thousands of people buy a ham for Christmas. It has become as normal a piece of festive fare as the English Christmas pudding. It is boiled in clothes kettles, kerosene cans, or in the baby's bath. Apart from this annual "boil up" there are a few roasts cooked in this manner. Because of this I have selected the ham as a "basic" in order to suggest a rather unusual way of approaching the problem.*

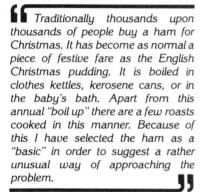

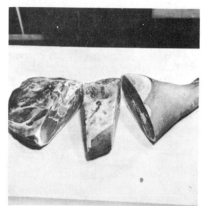

**Step 1.** Ask your supplier to cut a country-cured ham into 3 pieces as shown above. The hock, or shank, end (on the right) is a good boiling piece, as is the gammon or butt, end. The middle gammon is excellent for frying or boiling, and by keeping it for this purpose you avoid that frightful business of eating cold ham until you look like one.

**Step 2.** The first task is to soak the ham for approximately 12 hours. This is necessary unless you have a ham specifically labeled as mildly salted. This hock end weighed 5 pounds 2 ounces before soaking and 5 pounds 6 ounces after. From this you will gather that it also makes the joint beautifully moist. After soaking, give it a good scrub.

**Step 3.** Place the scrubbed ham in cold water with *no added seasoning* and bring to a gentle boil (this means simmer, but I happen to like the description gentle boil). Leave at this heat for 20 minutes per pound.

**Step 4.** Allow to half cool in the liquid and then strip off the skin. Place the naked joint in the refrigerator to finish cooling.

# Shallow-Fried Meat

### Serves 1

## INGREDIENTS:

½ lb. Porterhouse steak
Salt to season
Ground black peppercorns to
season
1 garlic clove
Clarified butter to cover pan

*Have you ever stopped to con-sider how interesting is the choice of titles for food. Take for example, the word* broiled *when applied to steak. It is so much more appetizing than the word* fried, *and yet I'm certain that in seven out of ten cases where broiled steak is served, it is in fact fried. I believe that unless you have a really excellent broiler, it is better to shallow-fry a steak. If you are careful with the fat, it need not be fattening, and the method allows for numerous variations.*

## PREPARATION

1. Heat frying pan to 400° F.
2. Melt butter.
3. Peel garlic.

**Step 1.** Porterhouse is my favorite steak. One way in which it is spoiled is by failing to remove the sinew that lies beneath the fat at the backbone end. Always cut this out, as this stops the steak from "bunching" (see page 77).

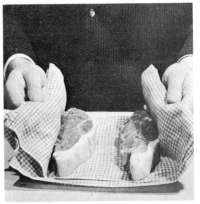

**Step 2.** It is good to wipe steak with a clean damp cloth and to dry the surface thoroughly.

**Step 3.** Before you add the seasoning, place the clarified butter in the pan to heat. Now season the steak with salt and roughly ground black pepper-corns. Garlic can be added by using a cheese knife (with the barbed end); jam the garlic onto the points and cut the clove. This is an easy, nonmessy way of adding a "sigh of garlic." Then fry immediately. Never keep a steak hanging around when seasoned.

**Step 4.** Always handle the steak with a blunt pair of tongs. Sear the meat first on both sides, and then cook to the stage you prefer.

# Steak Au Poivre

### INGREDIENTS:

24 oz. sirloin or porterhouse steak
1 garlic clove, crushed
2 tablespoons whole black peppercorns
1 tablespoon safflower or corn oil
Salt to taste

> *In an effort to reduce the incidence of huge steaks (12 oz. or more per head!) we suggest one large steak, highly seasoned, that can be carved into four pieces at the table.*

### PREPARATION

1. Wrap garlic in small piece of aluminum foil. Crush garlic with flat edge of French chef's knife. Place peppercorns in an envelope and crush roughly.

2. Rub crushed garlic on both sides of the steak and then remove and discard garlic. Pour pepper out onto a plate and press both sides of the steak into the crushed peppercorns.

3. Pour oil into a frying pan and heat. Lightly salt the steak and fry.

Serves 4 at 660 calories per serving, 40 gm. protein and 54 gm. saturated fat.

# Pan-Fried Steak

### INGREDIENTS:

4 New York strip steaks (6-7 oz. each)
1 garlic clove
Salt to taste
Black peppercorns, ground

### PREPARATION

1. Remove sinew from the steaks (page 77).

2. Crush the garlic and spread it over the steaks, then scrape it right off so that no shred of garlic fiber can be seen.

3. Season with a *little* salt and ground black peppercorns.

4. Heat sesame/safflower oil (page 186) in a skillet and pan fry until browned on each side.

5. Serve with mushrooms (page 194) and watercress dipped in our new French Dressing (page 214).

# Steak: When to Salt?

More concern has been expressed on when to season than on almost any other facet of meat cookery.

We conducted experiments to test the validity of the claims that juices are drawn out by the salt, that the finished color is impaired, and that the meat is toughened — serious allegations, to be sure. We cut identical slices of beef and seasoned each piece with salt only: the first was salted 5 minutes before cooking; the second was salted in the pan. The juice loss was not significant, the color was unchanged, and the taste was better with the advanced seasoning. Tenderness appeared also to be unchanged.

As a result, we recommend that steak be properly seasoned before cooking by massaging a *small* quantity of salt into the flesh.

# HINTS

## Steak

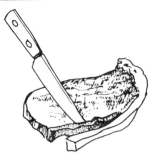

We look upon meat costs as one of the great burdens of our era, especially when such costs part us from our supersteaks. So you will find this technique especially important and well worth the little extra effort so you get the maximum enjoyment from those occasional steaks. I'm talking about removing the small sinew found in almost all the back steaks that, if left in, contracts, hardens, and can bend a thin steak out of all proportion. This causes parts of the steak to overcook and others to undercook. It's a lousy spectacle whichever way you look at it! So here is the way to "cut it out"!

*Sense advantage* is almost entirely visual, but there are certain textural plus factors: removing the hard gristle and retaining greater juiciness.

## Clarified Butter

Butter burns at about 200° F. unless it is *clarified.* The easiest method is to place 1 pound of butter in a small saucepan on a low heat; leave for 10 minutes, until a foam has risen to the top. Skim this off and place in a bowl. Pour remainder into a glass jar — this is clarified butter. Add the sediment dregs to the "foam" and use for buttered vegetables. The clarified butter will fry foods in a temperature as high as 475° F., at least the equal of oil.

Place both containers, covered, in the refrigerator. The clarified butter will keep for about 5 weeks.

*Sense advantage* comes almost entirely from aroma; there is some flavor, but it is discernible only when used in large quantity — and then it has some obvious nutritional problems.

*Nutrition comment:* I'm concerned enough to give you a word of caution here. I'm no longer convinced that saturated animal fats are harmless; neither, for that matter, am I yet convinced that hydrogenated margarines are harmless. I believe that correctly processed polyunsaturated vegetable oils can provide the *least* harmful means of culinary frying. There are, however, some foods — such as mushrooms — that cannot be prepared with oils or margarines as well as they can with butter. There is, therefore, a place for a *frying-temperature butter,* but please be *very* sparing in its use.

## Olive Oil

We always looked upon olive oil as one of those saturated fats to be avoided at all costs. Yet it always held a fascination for its unique flavor.

In Europe they use freshly pressed crude oil, very pungent to the average American cook. By law, we insist that it be pasteurized when it reaches us. There are various grades:

*Virgin.* The first oil to be pressed from the crop.

*Pure.* Both blended and refined, which Italian experts claim destroys, removes, or alters the vitamins, lecithin, and unsaturated fatty acids.

*Genuine Imported Virgin Olive Oil* (how can you resist a title like that!). This product undergoes less modification than most domestic refined oils, it oxidizes less readily than most other oils, and has one great plus factor:

Olive oil is only 11% saturated fatty acids and 83% unsaturated fatty acids (oleic and linoleic). By comparison, safflower is 10%, sesame is 14%, and coconut is 80%.

So Olive Oil is *In!*

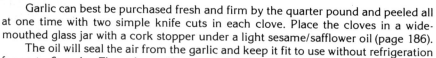

## Garlic

Garlic can best be purchased fresh and firm by the quarter pound and peeled all at one time with two simple knife cuts in each clove. Place the cloves in a wide-mouthed glass jar with a cork stopper under a light sesame/safflower oil (page 186).

The oil will seal the air from the garlic and keep it fit to use without refrigeration for up to 6 weeks. Flavor loss will occur if the cloves turn pale brown.

The external peeled leaves can be used to flavor the cooking liquid for rice and pasta. Just bring the peel to the boil, then strain and use the clear, flavored water to cook the pasta!

P.S. You can use the garlic-flavored oil in many of our dishes — you only need to keep refilling the jar with oil.

## Minute Steaks

The objective here was to select a beef steak that would give at least a 4-ounce serving and cover as large an area of the plate as possible.

Our selection was the *real* "London broil," a cut from the flank (an extension of the tail end of the T-bone). It is very lean and can be cooked and sliced diagonally or pre-sliced and fried individually. We feel it is best cooked whole. Having first "seasoned" it with an instant meat tenderizer (per the instructions on the bottle), cook in a heavy skillet over moderate heat for about 2 minutes on either side; then carve it through diagonally. A *full* 1-pound piece will serve 4 people for an everyday meal (4 ounces of a complete protein food at night is enough). The lack of fat and bone makes it the same price as a beef chuck arm or shoulder steak, which can also be broiled — but these cuts are more fatty and don't "present" as well.

*Nutrition comment:* the flank steak is an excellent cut as seen by this profile (for 120 g. or 4 oz.): 252 calories (good); 41.1 g. protein (good); no carbohydrate (good); 8.32 g. fat (very good); B Vitamins (good). *Caution:* Some popular tenderizers have salt and dextrose added to the papain (tenderizer). This *could* be a problem to people on sodium-restricted diets.

*Budget advantage:* flank at $3.99* per pound costs $1.00 per 4-ounce serving. Hamburger at $1.79 per pound costs only 45¢ per 4-ounce serving, but regular hamburger contains approximately 22 percent fat. Flank has very little fat and looks much better, covering a larger area of the plate and thus providing great visual satisfaction.

So essentially it must be regarded as a "better buy" or more "value for your money" and that is what makes up the word *budget.* Cheap food is a poor substitute for satisfaction. I view the available money as finance for good health and enjoyment, not for bulky, dull fodder!

*Prices at time of writing. Price may vary with locale.

# Broiled Meat

**Serves 4**

### INGREDIENTS:

8 lamb cutlets
Clarified butter to brush
Black peppercorns to season
Garlic to season
Salt to season

### PREPARATION

1. Peel garlic.
2. Prepare seasoning.
3. Brush broiler rack with clarified butter.
4. Heat broiler medium hot.

*I hope you will forgive the obvious plug for New Zealand Lamb in the Step 1 photograph below. I have no reservations in this direction because I am confident, having tasted lamb from many countries, that New Zealand leads the world in over-all quality. My favorite lamb comes from the coastline stations where up to one ton of sea salt falls to the acre per year. This adds a tang to the meat, which places it beyond international competition. Here endeth the commercial — now on with the method!*

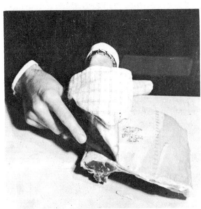

**Step 1.** In the case of lamb (and this is why I have chosen it for the basic method) you must first remove the "fell" or outer skin. If this is not done, then the skin contracts, pulling the cutlet out of shape and making it go brittle. At least ask your butcher to see that it is done!

**Step 2.** Cutlets look so much more attractive when the bones are trimmed as shown above. The trimmings make an excellent addition to an Irish stew. A further refinement in trimming can be made by getting the butcher to remove the backbone completely, leaving only the rib.

**Step 3.** Dry the cutlets and then season immediately before placing under the broiler. Brush with clarified butter and cook for 5 minutes either side. Turn only once.

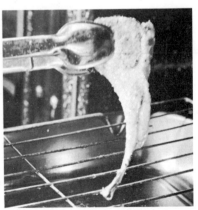

**Step 4.** When turning the meat use a blunt pair of tongs. If you use a fork or knife, you release the natural juices and spoil the supreme succulence.

# Sausage 'N' Cardamom

**Serves 4**

### INGREDIENTS:

1 lb. link sausage
in the casing, 16 per lb.
2 tomatoes
Ground cardamom

*Cardamom is a spice native to India, but we get some quantity from Guatemala and Sri Lanka as well. We know that it grew in the garden of the king of Babylon in 721 B.C., and it is used in some cosmetics today. The plant is a member of the ginger family, and the spice comes in the pod, or decorticated (pod off), or ground. It is good as a breath freshener. Used as a principal spice in Danish pastries, it is also good in pickles, grape jelly, fruit punch, fruit pies, and important in curry powder. We use it to bring sausage to life in this great breakfast recipe.*

### PREPARATION

1. Fry sausages in a pan until lightly brown and cooked through.

2. Remove sausages and drain well. Make a lengthwise slit down each sausage. Sprinkle the tops gently with cardamom.

3. Skin (page 207) and core 2 tomatoes, chop finely, and spread over the top of the sausages, which have been placed in an ovenproof shallow dish.

4. Place the pan under the broiler for 5 minutes and serve immediately.

*Nutrition profile:* from ½ pound of sausage links (16 per pound), ¼ cup grease was drained off. This left 4⅛ ounces of sausage meat. Therefore, 1 pound will yield 8¼ ounces of meat, and each person gets 2¹/₁₆ ounces at the rate of 65 calories/link (4 links per serving is 260 calories per serving). One serving is 9.6 grams protein and 22 grams fat.

# Light Stews

### Serves 4

### INGREDIENTS:

1½ lb. white veal boned neck
2 medium carrots
1 medium parsnip
1 large onion
2¼ cups chicken stock
2 stalks parsley
2 sprigs thyme
White peppercorns and salt
to season
1 clove of garlic
1 bay leaf
2 egg yolks
4 tablespoons cream

*The French have a method of preparing light pigment meats in a stewed form called **blanquette**. This is one of my favorite dishes. The meat used in this basic recipe is milk-fed white veal. The quality and quantity of the milk produces an excellent product, and modern farming techniques avoid the unpleasant methods used in Europe. If you cannot get local supplies, then try young lamb or pork.*

## PREPARATION

1. Cut meat into 1-inch cubes.
2. Peel and slice vegetables into 1-inch-thick pieces.
3. Peel garlic.
4. Prepare chicken stock.
5. Ready the herbs.
6. Separate yolks from whites of egg.
7. Measure cream.

**Step 1.** It is essential to use cuts of meat from the neck and shoulder for a white stew. The connective tissue melts during cookery and adds flavor and texture. As much fat as possible should be trimmed from the meat before cutting.

**Step 2.** Season the meat well and then place all the ingredients in a saucepan. Add the cold stock and squeeze in the garlic clove; stir and bring to a simmer. Skim the surface from time to time during cookery.

**Step 3.** After 50-60 minutes, strain off the liquid. You should then have 1¼ cups. Combine the cream and egg yolks in a small bowl and add the stock by degrees — it will start to thicken.

**Step 4.** Pour the egg- and cream-enriched stock back over the meat and stir over a very gentle heat until thick and glossy. Do not allow to boil; otherwise the eggs will curdle.

# Kare Poaka No. 1

**Serves 4**

### INGREDIENTS:

1¾ cups coconut milk (14 fl. oz.)
2 lbs. pork (blade steak)
Salt, preferably freshly ground
Freshly ground black pepper
1 medium onion
1 medium green pepper
1 garlic clove
Juice of ½ lemon
¼ cup ketchup
2 tablespoons sesame/
safflower oil (p. 186)
1 tablespoon curry powder (mild)
1 teaspoon mustard seeds
1 bay leaf
1 tablespoon red currant jelly
1 heaped teaspoon chili powder

### PREPARATION

1. Make coconut milk. Remove the fat from the pork and cut into 2-inch cubes. Season with salt and pepper. Slice the onion into 1-inch-wide rings. Cut the pepper into 1-inch squares. Smash the garlic and squeeze the lemon. Now combine coconut milk with ketchup.
2. Heat the oil in a large saucepan, add the meat, and fry gently. Add the onion and curry powder, then add mustard seeds, green pepper, bay leaf, and garlic, and continue to fry, stirring gently.
3. Pour in lemon juice, red currant jelly, ketchup, and coconut milk. Simmer in the open pot for 1½ hours. This recipe is better if it's made the day before.
4. Skim off all fat and pour off ¼ cup of the sauce. Blend this sauce with chili powder and pour into small sauce boat. This extra-hot sauce can be added by those who prefer "undemocratic curry."

❝ *This is a dish that I had the honor of creating for Her Majesty the Queen Mother's visit to New Zealand in 1965.* ❞

# New White Cooking Wine

### INGREDIENTS:

½ cup white grape juice (4 fl. oz.)
1 teaspoon rice vinegar

### PREPARATION

Combine and use immediately.

❝ *This can be used in place of dry white wine called for in recipe books.* ❞

## HINTS

## Bouquet Garni $

Aromatic herbs give up their natural volatile oils to the sauces or liquids in which meats, poultry, and sometimes seafood are cooked.

There is a "classical" bundle that includes — *almost without thought* — bay leaf, thyme, parsley, and a piece of celery. Exactly why the culinary profession has bowed down to this singular lack of imagination is hard to understand unless it be their convenience in the sprig form (they are usually available fresh or dried, in the leaf, or on the sprig). Tied in a bundle, they can be removed before service; if only dried is available, then they can be crumbled up and placed in a piece of muslin, securely tied and dropped in. It can be used in a variety of soups, stews, and casseroles (see, for example, Navarin on page 85). Whatever or whichever — the truth is that, by it addition, the average casserole or stew ceases to be average!

Variations can be made by adding marjoram or rosemary or dill weed for beef, lamb, and pork respectively; the choice and opportunity are really yours, and it's *wide* open for initiative — so try today, won't you?

*Sense advantage* is primarily aromatic with perhaps a small taste fringe benefit. Try to see it as an *infusion* of herbs — it works better that way.

*Budget benefit* comes from its use with low-cost foods that need some sparkle.

# Dark Stews $

### Serves 4

## INGREDIENTS:

1½ lb. blade steak
Flour to coat steaks
¼ cup clarified butter
Black peppercorns and salt
to season
2 medium carrots
1 large onion
1 medium parsnip
2¼ cups beef stock (page 31
for quick method)
1 bay leaf
2 sprigs thyme
2 stalks parsley
1 clove of garlic
Parsley, chopped, to garnish
2 tablespoons arrowroot

> *You could just as easily call this a casserole, and most people do because it sounds better. The method is identical. This is a great favorite of mine, because there is virtually no limit to your attempts at improvisation; and they will be basically successful if you apply this simple method.*

## PREPARATION

1. Slice vegetables into ¼-inch-thick slices.
2. Tie herbs in bundle.
3. Peel clove of garlic.
4. Cut steak into 1- by 2-inch pieces.
5. Measure stock.
6. Mix arrowroot with 3 tablespoons water to a smooth paste.

**Step 1.** Meat cooks better by this method when cut into large pieces. The meat is first dried thoroughly, coated with seasoned flour, and then fried really brown in the butter. Remove the meat and add the vegetables. Fry these until well colored.

**Step 2.** Place cooked meat back in the casserole and add the stock and herbs. Scrape the meat residues from the casserole pan up into the liquid. Cover and simmer for 1½-2 hours or place in an oven set at 325° F. for the same length of time.

**Step 3.** If you can plan far enough ahead, place the casserole in the refrigerator to cool overnight. The next day the fats will have set on the surface, and they can be easily removed. If you are in a rush, then skim off the fats and remove the herbs.

**Step 4.** Bring the casserole to the boil and pour in the paste of arrowroot, stirring until it thickens and clears. Taste for seasoning and dust with parsley before serving. Fresh vegetables be included if added 30 minutes before cookery is completed.

# Navarin of Lamb

**Serves 6**

## INGREDIENTS:

1 tablespoon sesame/
safflower oil
2 lbs. mutton shoulder meat, as
lean as possible, cut into
2-inch pieces
Salt
Freshly ground black peppercorns
4 garlic cloves, well crushed
1 tablespoon sugar
½ cup red grape juice
1 teaspoon cold tea
2 teaspoons rice vinegar
½ pint lamb or veal stock
4 black peppercorns, 4 parsley
stalks, ½ teaspoon each rosemary
and thyme, 2 bay leaves,
all placed in a muslin bag
12 whole small onions
(pickling size)
1 teaspoon sugar
12 small potatoes (all the same
size), peeled
1 tablespoon chopped parsley

## PREPARATION

1. Pour oil into a heavy-based saucepan and add the shoulder meat; season in the pan with salt and ground black peppercorns, and brown.
2. Add garlic and sugar when the meat has become a little brown. Continue to cook until the sugar darkens.
3. Add the grape juice, tea, and sufficient stock to just cover the meat and pop in the Bouquet Garni (bunch of herbs in muslin bag). Cover the pan and simmer for one hour.
4. Shallow fry the onions in a little oil and add a teaspoonful of sugar to give them a deep golden brown color.
5. When the first hour of cookery is up, remove the herbs and add the onions and the small potatoes; add some more stock to cover all these ingredients, replace the lid, and simmer for another 30 minutes until the potatoes are cooked.
6. Skim the surface of any surplus fat, add 2 teaspoons rice vinegar, pour off the liquid, and thicken with arrowroot (see page 220 for the technique). Dust with chopped parsley and serve.

# Freezer Casserole

**Serves 8 dinners for 4 people**

## INGREDIENTS:

1 20-lb. picnic ham
2 lbs. onions, chopped
2 lbs. carrots, chopped
1 lb. celery, chopped
¼ cup safflower oil
8 bay leaves
1 tablespoon thyme
8 garlic cloves
2 tablespoons salt
2 tablespoons ground black
pepper
6 quarts water

> *The bulk precooking of a single, delicious casserole so that in one afternoon one makes the base for eight fully flexible dinners for four people isn't a bad project — especially if the family can be pressed into service!*

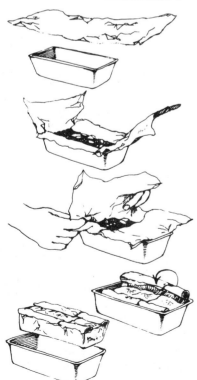

## PREPARATION

*The pot.* Absolutely essential to this idea is a large cooking pot. We suggest the inexpensive enameled clam cookers that hold truly vast quantities. But use one that will fit into your oven and will hold at least 10 quarts (2½ gallons). It can be used for other work such as boiling large chickens, cooking a ham, steaming clams, boiling a lobster, or even as a water bath for preserving.

*The meat.* Select a cut that has good connective tissue content (i.e., it works hard — like the neck and shoulder muscles of lamb, pork, and veal). It should be a "young meat" like veal or pork or lamb because it can be "finished" in a greater variety of ways than beef or mutton. I selected as a test an unsmoked picnic ham weighing about 20 pounds. *True,* they have to be boned and skinned, but this way you control the fat content and the size of the pieces (12 2-inch cubes — 3 each for 4 persons), and you get the bones for the broth. After discounting the trim and bones the cost per pound will almost double, *but* you get good lard — at least 1 pound. You also have 5 pounds of bones that can replace some of the flavor material gained otherwise from stock cubes or powders.

*The juice.* This is the vital difference in *our* technique. We believe that vegetables cooked, frozen, and then reheated are *awful.* Thus we make our stock with the bones from which you've trimmed the meat. 1. Roast the bones in the big pan in the oven at 375° F. until nicely browned. Drain off the fat. 2. Fry the roughly chopped vegetables in the oil in the big pan until limp, then add the rest of the ingredients. 3. Cover and place in 350° F. oven for 1 hour. Strain. Throw out vegetables and herbs (they are without value at this stage) and retain bones in broth which should now measure about 10 pints. You can make this stock while you are cutting and trimming meat.

*The meat.* The meat must be fried in a little garlic oil in a hot skillet, piece by piece, until well colored. Then turn directly into the big pot containing the hot strained stock plus bones. When filled, cover the pot and cook 1 hour at 350° F. The meat will then be completely cooked, an essential for pork. The fat must be carefully skimmed off, which will leave approximately 8 pints.

*Wrapping and freezing.* The meat must be laid on a shallow tray to lose heat *quickly.* Select a dish approximately 8 by 5 by 2 inches. Line it with foil 3 times its length (i.e., 24 inches long). Press foil into the "mold," fill each dish with ⅛ of the cooled mixture (12 pieces of meat, plus juice), fold the ends over, and roll edges together (see illustration). *Label and date* 3 months hence; this is the date by which it must be eaten. Remove foil packet from dish, lift onto backing sheet, and slide into deep freeze. Have free space around each one to hasten freezing (you can stack them later). Meat must be kept at 0° to −10° F. to be safe, and then for no more than 6 months. It's very important to freeze promptly and to use sanitary handling practices — e.g., don't handle cooked meat with utensils used to handle raw meat.

*Resuscitation.* Divide your recipe ideas into 3 groups.

- *Spice Fry Off:* Curries, chili.
  1. Fry onions first with spices for 10 minutes.
  2. Add frozen meat, cover pan, and cook slowly to heat through (10 minutes).
  3. Thicken with arrowroot (page 220) and serve.
- *Root Vegetable Precook:*
  1. Cook fresh root vegetables such as potatoes, turnips, carrots, etc., in a little oil with tomato paste for color; add a little water. Cook 10 minutes, then add frozen meat.
  2. Cook over low heat to heat through (10 minutes). Thicken and serve.
- *Pre-made Sauce:*
  1. Defrost over low heat for 10 minutes. Drain, reserving all liquid. Add small vegetables (peas, etc.).
  2. Cook the vegetables in the broth. Thicken with cream or milk and arrowroot, then add the meat and heat through.

# New Red Cooking Wine

### INGREDIENTS:

½ cup red (or purple)
grape juice (4 fl. oz.)
1 tablespoon strong cold tea
1 tablespoon rice vinegar

### PREPARATION

Combine and use immediately.
You will find that I separate the grape juice and tea from the vinegar in some recipes for specific effects.

> **"** *Use in lieu of red wines called for in recipe books.* **"**

## Superchunk

For stews and casseroles it is better to cut meat rich in connective tissue (such as beef chuck, lamb shoulder and neck, pork shoulder, veal shin) into large pieces, rather than the usually suggested 1-inch cube.

It is easier to do the initial browning because there are fewer pieces to turn, they cover less area on a restricted pan base, and there are fewer exposed cut surfaces (i.e., a 6-ounce portion raw weight, cut into 2 large 3-ounce cubes, has 12 sides. Six 1-ounce cubes would have 36 sides). In addition, the connective tissue has a greater chance to dissolve through low moist heat transfer than does that in the smaller cubes which tighten by initial "shock" browning.

## Tomato Paste

I do not know quite how I could function as a cook without a good, thick tomato paste. Much of my cooking is vivid in flavor, with deep, rich colors, and this is precisely what tomato paste provides.

I use it as a deep coloring by adding it after the meat has been browned. The paste is stirred into the *frying* dish and cooked until it goes through a deep red into almost a dark brown color. The cooking liquid (stock, etc.) can then be added and the whole dish looks fabulous. What happens is that the heat hastens the non-enzymatic browning, which occurs in tomato products, and with its color change comes a decided flavor change that imparts a strong and highly acceptable finish.

Sense advantage is visual, aromatic, taste, and even textural — a "grand slam" of the senses.

# Lamb Roll

*I have devoted two pages to the lamb roll because it should become a specialty meat cut. It is quite simply a double lamb chop without the bone, and it is the absence of bone that makes it a fitting dish for such excellent meat. A chop or cutlet is an easy, quick, pleasant dish, but the remaining bones give the finished plate a messy appearance. Lamb roll makes the ultimate best of the cutlet.*

**Step 1.** As with all loin of lamb dishes, the outer membrane must be removed first. Cut lightly in 4-inch-wide strips, loosen the skin at the neck end — grip and tear off.

**Step 2.** Cut the meat away from the bone, starting at the backbone. Keep the knife close to the bone all the way.

**Step 3.** Trim the fillet from the leg end and place this on the boned loin so that it makes it appear even. Season the open loin with salt and freshly ground black peppercorns. You can also add a filling at this stage. Roll up and cut off excess breast.

**Step 4.** Tie the joint every 1½ inches — long end toward you.

# Lamb Roll *continued*

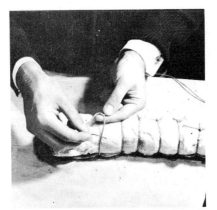

**Step 5.** Short end under long end, then over itself.

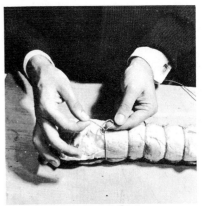

**Step 6.** Pull short end through loop and pull tight.

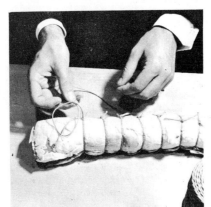

**Step 7.** With long end make a lasso and throw it over the short end. Pull tight again and cut off excess string. See page 90 for diagram of knot.

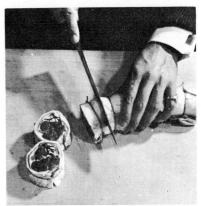

**Step 8.** Cut between the strings just before they are cooked.

# Lamb Roll Arneb

**Serves 6**

**INGREDIENTS:**

1 whole loin of lamb
Garlic salt
Black peppercorns
½ cup clarified butter
Small bunch fresh mint
1 lb. potatoes
8 teaspoons mint jelly

**PREPARATION**

1. Prepare loin as shown in basic method. Season inside with garlic salt.
2. Heat pan.
3. Finely chop mint.
4. Peel, boil, and mash potatoes.
5. Preheat oven to 325° F.
6. Season lamb rolls again with a little garlic salt and freshly ground black peppercorns.
7. Place in hot pan with a little butter and sear both sides quickly.
8. Transfer to small roasting pan, brush with butter, and sprinkle with mint. Place in oven for 10 minutes. Turn. Give another 10-15 minutes. Brush again with mint and butter.
9. When cooked, cut strings and place in rows on serving dish. Decorate around their base with creamed potatoes. On top of each, place a spoonful of mint jelly. Parsley and quartered tomatoes may also be used as garnishes.

## HINTS

# Butcher's Knot

This is one of the truly basic skills that can mean so much in your kitchen. It helps you to do your own cutting up, which saves you a good deal of money. It also lets you untie what the butcher did and season or stuff the rolled piece to make it taste better or go further. This is how it's done:

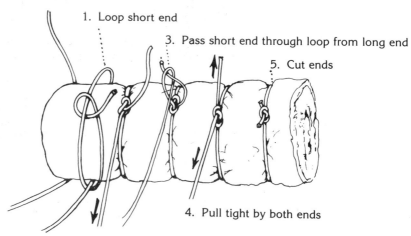

1. Loop short end
2. Pull tight by long end
3. Pass short end through loop from long end
4. Pull tight by both ends
5. Cut ends

Sense advantage comes largely in the fields of appearance and flavor. A well-boned and -tied roast just looks terrific, and it's much easier to carve without ugly and difficult-to-negotiate bones. The flavor is improved by seasoning from the inside out — a technique that simply must be better than "surface crop dusting"!

# Sweetbreads and Brains

*Sweetbreads are glands. They come from either the pancreas (stomach sweetbread) or the thymus (neck or breast sweetbread). We eat sweetbreads from either lambs or calves. The lamb sweetbreads are small, and as you can see from these photographs, those from the calf are large. It doesn't matter how you prepare them later on, the basic preparation remains the same. You can also apply the same method to brains, leaving out Step 4.*

**Step 1.** Soak sweetbreads for at least 1 hour in plenty of cold water. Rinse well and place in a saucepan of cold unsalted water.

**Step 2.** Slowly bring the water to a boil. When the water boils, remove the sweetbreads and place immediately into cold water.

**Step 3.** When cooled, strip off the surrounding skin and pieces of fat.

**Step 4.** Place the stripped sweetbreads between two plates; wrap in a cloth and place them under one leg of your dining table. (This is the best improvised press I know). Leave it for 30 minutes; then dry the flattened sweetbreads. They can now be used for a wide variety of dishes.

## Brains — Camouflage

Calves' brains are a good buy at about $2.19* a pound — that is, if you don't mind the idea. From the cook's viewpoint, the repugnance can often be overcome; it's when the brains hit the plate that things start to go wrong! We have an idea you might like that avoids the limelight or at least manages to change the color!

Brains must first be soaked in cold water for at least 4 hours to dilute residual blood. Rinse and trim off any discolored areas.

Place in cold water, bring slowly to the boil, drain and place in cold tap water to prevent overcooking. Dip into beaten egg, and then in breadcrumbs and shallow-fry for 2 minutes on either side in sesame/safflower oil (p. 186). Serve with lemon.

And when they ask — just smile!

*Price at time of writing.

# Liver

**Serves 4**

**INGREDIENTS:**

1 lb. liver
½ cup flour
Salt to season
Ground black peppercorns
to season
Clarified butter (page 77)

*A well-known television personality admitted to me that he was a keen consumer of lamb's fry. A little later on he described lamb's liver as one of his pet hates. Digging deeper into this curious contradiction, I (and he) discovered that his mother had used the title "lamb's fry" to overcome his aversion to liver. This proves, to me at least, that you should never reject a food before giving it a reasonable chance.*

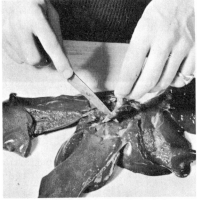

**Step 1.** This liver is obviously too large for a lamb. It is in fact pork liver, and I consider it to be second only to calves' liver in quality. Remove the heavy sinews with a sharp knife, and then wipe the liver with a clean damp cloth.

**Step 2.** Cut into slices about ¼ to ½ inch thick. Allow 4 ounces per portion.

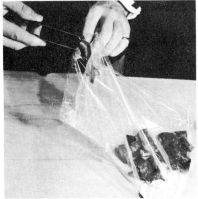

**Step 3.** Place ½ cup of well-seasoned (pepper and salt) flour into a plastic or paper bag and add the liver. Shake vigorously in order to coat the slices.

**Step 4.** Melt some clarified butter in pan set at 300° F. and cook until small drops of meat juices percolate through the flour (see above); turn and cook for 2 minutes. Maximum time for ½-inch-thick slices — 5 minutes. NEVER (please) overcook.

# Chicken Livers in "New Wine"

**Serves 4**

### INGREDIENTS:

1½ cups sliced onion
Juice of 1 lemon
2 cups fresh mushrooms (¼ lb.)
2 tablespoons chopped parsley
4 slices whole-wheat bread, toasted
1 lb. chicken livers
1 tablespoon butter plus
2 tablepoons sesame/safflower oil
(page 186)
Freshly ground salt and
white pepper
½ cup red grape juice
1 teaspoon cold, concentrated tea
2 teaspoons rice vinegar

### PREPARATION

1. Slice the onion finely, juice the lemon, and reserve. Slice mushrooms after washing and drying them. Chop parsley. Toast bread and lightly butter it (optional). Pour lemon juice on mushrooms.

2. Now fry the onions and liver in butter and oil for 5 minutes only, no longer.

3. Add the mushrooms, lemon juice, salt, and pepper. Stir in grape juice and boil rapidly for 1-2 minutes.

4. Add the tea and rice vinegar, stirring to keep boiling. Remove from heat, spoon over toast, sprinkle with parsley, and serve immediately.

One serving is about 372 calories.

*These small livers provide an excellent meal that cannot take more than 10 minutes to prepare! The secret is to keep the tender livers only just cooked. I would prefer to purchase grain-fed "yard" chicken livers so that I might avoid the chemical seasoning that the battery-bird liver receives. Ask a good health food store about purchasing these.*

# Kidneys

**Step 1.** Grasp your kidney in the left hand and run a knife lightly over the skin — peel back the skin and detach. *Note:* On looking back over this instruction it looks odd. By "your kidney," of course I mean the lamb's.

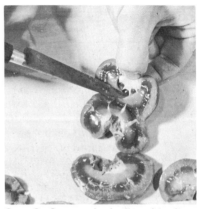

**Step 2.** Cut out the heavy white ligament by cutting through the kidney from the dimpled side — do not cut right through.

**Step 3.** When you broil kidneys (a perfect technique), you should push wooden spikes through each "wing" to keep them flat.

**Step 4.** Season the kidneys with salt and freshly ground black peppercorns, then spread with melted clarified butter. Place pieces of lightly browned toast under the kidneys. The meat juices and butter drip down and are soaked up — fabulous! I recommend you slightly undercook the kidneys — 3 minutes on each side under a medium hot broiler, 3 inches from the heat.

# HINTS

## Kidney Casserole

As a quick, general example of how to create your own dishes using kidneys, cook some small pork sausages and make up a combined dish with chopped bacon, mushrooms, baby onions and the kidneys (but remember — don't ever overcook the kidneys). You can tie these ingredients together with a simple brown sauce (page 222), ¼ cup red grape juice, 1 teaspoon rice vinegar, and ½ teaspoon cold unsweetened tea.

## Lamb's Kidneys

A somewhat stale lamb's kidney can be one of those experiences that turns one away from almost all variety meats for the rest of one's life! But all is not lost. There is a way to bring them back to a state where the senses can applaud their return!

Prepare the kidney by following steps 1, 2, and 3 of the basic method.

Heat 2 tablespoons sesame/safflower oil (page 186) in a frying pan. Place kidneys in the pan so that the cut surface is uppermost and fry briskly for 2 minutes. Turn them over for a few seconds, and then turn out onto a paper towel to cool.

Blot dry and then reheat gently in the frying pan (so as not to overcook). All those "off flavors" will be gone.

*Sense advantage* is largely an aromatic one — the ammonia smell is clearly destroyed. There is a slight reduction in juiciness.

*Nutritional content:* kidneys are an excellent food — just look at this for a 3½-ounce (100-gram) lamb's kidney: 105 calories (good); 16.8 g. protein (good); 3.3 g. fat (good); and high in Vitamin A and in B Vitamins.

# Ground Meat

## INGREDIENTS:

12 oz. lean ground beef
8 tablespoons TVP
1 tablespoon soy sauce
2 tablespoons tomato ketchup
2 tablespoons water

❝ *The natural aversion to the use of soy extenders with hamburger is understandable; if the soy, or textured vegetable protein (TVP), is added in the usual manner, the hamburger tastes like the bottom of a horse's feedbag on a wet day. Here is a recipe that goes a long way toward restoring the flavor to hamburgers with TVP.* ❞

## PREPARATION

1. Cut meat into 1 or 2-inch chunks.
2. Measure the TVP and get the rest of the ingredients handy.

**Step 1.** Grind the meat. A simple hand-operated meat grinder readily found in most good hardware stores works well.

**Step 2.** Combine the TVP, soy sauce, ketchup, and water. Allow the TVP mix to sit for 10 minutes to rehydrate and combine flavors.

**Step 3.** Add the TVP to the meat and combine well. Shape as usual.

**Step 4.** Cook immediately! As each minute goes by, the flavor deteriorates rapidly.

# Barley Meat Loaf

**Serves 4-6**

### INGREDIENTS:

¼ cup pearl barley
1¼ cups beef stock
1 tablespoon soy sauce
½ lb. ground beef shin
1 lb. ground heel of round
1 medium onion, diced
1 garlic clove, crushed
1 teaspoon chopped parsley
¼ teaspoon ground pepper
¼ teaspoon ground oregano
¼ teaspoon ground thyme
2 tablespoons catsup
1 bay leaf
Tomato Sauce (see below)

### PREPARATION

1. Simmer barley in beef stock and soy sauce for 1 hour or until tender, and all excess liquid has been absorbed.

2. Measure the rest of the ingredients and mix them together (except the bay leaf and barley). This blends best by hand. Add the barley and stir to blend well.

3. Press mixture into a 4-cup, oven-proof container. Place bay leaf on top. Bake at 375° F. for one hour.

4. Drain off into a small saucepan the moisture that forms. Make the Tomato Sauce (below).

5. Turn out Barley Meat Loaf onto a plate, cover with the Tomato Sauce, and serve.

> **"** *We have attempted to produce an attractive meat loaf that uses less meat, has higher nutritional value at a lower cost, and isn't difficult to make. We think we've done it after 10 different tests using a wide range of ingredients. We used barley to replace part of the meat and a combination of ground beef shin and heel of round that provides meat that is both lean and tasty. The completing sauce is most unusual, yet guaranteed to please even conservative tastes.* **"**

# Tomato Sauce

### INGREDIENTS:

¼ cup juice from meat loaf
¼ cup tomato juice
1 teaspoon lemon juice
1 teaspoon soy sauce
1 teaspoon arrowroot
1 teaspoon fresh parsley

### PREPARATION

1. Place meat juice in a small saucepan and add tomato juice, lemon juice, and soy sauce. Heat to almost boiling.

2. Dissolve arrowroot in a little water and stir into the hot mixture.

3. Stir constantly, remove from the heat, and add parsley.

4. Pour over turned-out Barley Meat Loaf.

Serves 4 at 395 calories per serving or 6 at 263 calories per serving.

# Children's Meat Loaf

### INGREDIENTS:

½ lb. calf or pork liver
⅓ - 1½ cups cooked carrots or
String beans (optional)
1 teaspoon onion (optional)
½ lb. lean ground beef (shin)
⅓ cup tomato puree
⅓ cup milk
1 egg yolk
⅓ cup rolled oats
¼ - ½ teaspoon salt

### PREPARATION

1. Put the raw liver, vegetables, and onion in the blender and blend on the lowest speed. Add the ground beef, tomato puree, milk, and egg and blend on a low speed. Turn out into a bowl. Add the oats and salt, and stir to mix.

2. Two options are available:
   Lightly grease an oven-proof dish that holds 1½ pints, fill with mixture, and bake at 325° F. for 25-30 minutes; or
   Put into ice cube trays, freeze, and turn out into a freezer baggie. Then seal and store in the freezer.

3. When you need it, remove one or more meat-loaf cubes and bake in aluminum foil in a 325° F. oven for 15 to 20 minutes. Be sure it is completely cooked. Do not under- or over-cook. Cubes can be mixed with milk, or vegetable, or meat stock to thin.

   Makes 2 cups of uncooked mixture. Each ice cube divider tray holds 2 tablespoons of food at 55.3 calories per cube. 2 cups of mixture fills 16 divisions.

*Young children are just as entitled to some consideration as adults. Here's a small meat-loaf recipe for them. I would encourage you to let the older daughter or son prepare it for the youngster — it's great fun and fulfills a frequent desire to do something loving and practical for a toddler in the family.*

# Stuffed Sourdough Meat Loaf

### Serves 6

#### INGREDIENTS:

1 loaf sourdough or French
bread, about 4"x 14"
2 tablespoons butter
2 garlic cloves
FILLING:
1 medium onion
1 garlic clove
¼ cup tomato paste
¼ cup soy sauce
¾ cup water
1 tablespoon safflower oil
1 lb. finely chopped beef
1 tablespoon chili powder
1 teaspoon oregano

#### PREPARATION

1. Peel and chop onion. Crush garlic (keeping cloves for bread and for filling separate). Measure tomato paste, soy sauce, and water.

2. Saute' 1 garlic clove and onion in oil. Add beef and cook until meat changes color. Drain all the excess fat from the pan.

3. Add the tomato paste and cook until it begins to brown. Then add the chili powder, soy sauce, and water.

4. Cover, reduce heat to low, and simmer for 30 minutes. Add the oregano.

5. While the meat is simmering, remove the center from the bread loaf by hinging back the top and spooning out the bread. Leave about ½-inch wall all around.

6. Melt butter, add 2 cloves of garlic, and brush on the inside of the loaf.

7. Spoon in the chili mixture and cover with Hot Bean Dressing (recipe follows).

8. Replace the top of the loaf and heat in a 350° F. oven for 20 minutes or until loaf is brown and crusty.

9. Cut diagonally to serve.

# Hot Bean Dressing

#### INGREDIENTS:

1 cup dried red kidney beans
1 smoked ham hock (12-oz.)
bone in
4 slices bacon
1 medium onion
1 tablespoon chili powder
½ cup sour cream
1 fresh red "hot" chili pepper
2 tablespoons chopped bread-
and-butter pickles

#### PREPARATION

1. Soak the beans in cold water for 24 hours. Then place in clean fresh water with the ham hock and bring *very slowly* to the boil (should take about 30 minutes). Now reduce heat to simmer and cook for another 1½ hours until beans are tender. Allow to cool in the stock, ready for use. Chop the bacon finely; peel and finely dice the onion. Measure the chili powder and the sour cream.

2. Fry the chopped bacon with chopped onion — no need to add any oil.

3. Add the chili powder and continue to fry for one minute. Add the drained cooked red beans; stir gently. Pour on the sour cream and cook gently over a low heat for 30 minutes more, until the beans have partially absorbed the "sauce." Serve hot or cold with the chopped pickles and chili peppers stirred in at the end — or the pickles and peppers can be served in separate small dishes to be added according to preference by the individual at the table.

*Note:* This is a general recipe that can be used to spice up other dishes, especially Mexican or Spanish ones.

# Idaho Chili Pie

**Serves 4**

### INGREDIENTS:

4 large potatoes
Salt
1 lb. 2 ounces ground beef
1 garlic clove
1 medium onion (2 oz.)
¼ cup soy sauce with ¾ cup water
1 tablespoon safflower oil
¼ cup tomato paste (2 oz.)
3 teaspoons ground chili powder
1 teaspoon oregano
2 tablespoons butter
White pepper
1 tablespoon chopped parsley

### PREPARATION

1. Scrub potatoes and roll in salt. Weigh ground beef. Peel and crush garlic. Peel and finely chop onion. Mix the soy sauce and water. Measure remaining ingredients.
2. Place salted potatoes in an oven set at 350° F. for 1 hour 15 minutes until *just* starting to soften — don't overcook!
3. Cut a long, thin, even (¼-inch) slice off the top of each potato to form an "open boat" shape. Scrape out most of the flesh but leave about ¼ inch secured to the sides and bottom. Set aside and cover.
4. Fry the crushed garlic and the chopped onion in the safflower oil. Add the ground beef and fry until the meat separates, *drain excess fat from the pan,* then add the tomato paste and cook until it browns.
5. When a good, even dark brown color is achieved, sprinkle in 2 teaspoons chili powder (adding more if your tongue is abestos!). Add the soy sauce/water mixture and stir well. Cover, reduce the heat to low, and simmer for 30 minutes. When the meat is cooked, add the oregano.
6. During the 30 minutes' simmering, take the potato flesh removed from the "boats" and whip this with a teaspoon chili powder, the butter, some salt, and white pepper. Place it into a piping bag with a half-inch fancy star nozzle, if available.
7. Place the boats onto a white oval serving platter. Spoon the cooked chili mixture into them and pipe a good layer of potato decoratively on top (or spoon it on and mark the top with a fork).
8. Return the dish to the oven for 10 minutes to heat through, then brown the top under the broiler. Serve super-hot, dusted with chopped parsley.

## HINTS

# Hamburger with Ice

Here is a quick, easy, and definitely unusual way to build some excitement and originality into the backyard burger! Simply dilute some soy sauce with an equal quantity of water and freeze it solid in a small ice cube tray. It's better if you can find a ball-shaped ice tray but not vital. Use unseasoned, freshly ground hamburger (better if you grind it yourself in an old-fashioned meat grinder. Weigh up 6 ounces, roll into a ball, and spread out flat. Place the soy cube in the center, fold the meat about it, shape, and broil as normal.

The ice cube will keep the fats from melting out and that keeps the flavor in — it will be juicier and more flavorsome than the usual hamburger. You can adjust the soy content until, to your taste, it is only just there.

*Sense advantage* is in better texture, flavor, appearance, and aroma.

*Nutrition comment:* there is an advantage *if* you grind your own beef and aim for a low fat content. You will find the soy sauce replaces the flavor lost by using less fat.

## HINTS

## Chicken Versus Hamburger

When we look for the best buy, I think we have to consider what the word *best* really means. Do we mean literally the cheapest, or does it mean the best-liked at the lowest price. I go along with the latter because I believe that variety and enjoyment generate peace at the table and greater reward for all. We found the following in our tests:

We bought hamburger at $1.79* per pound and a fryer chicken at $2.55* for 3 pounds 11 ounces.

We cooked the chicken *gently* by slow boiling, then stripped off all the flesh (discarding skin and using bones for stock). We got 17 ounces of edible *cooked* meat (15¢ per ounce).

To compare this with hamburger, we fried the hamburger and poured off the fat. The cooked meat (less the fat) weighed 13 ounces (13.7¢ per ounce).

We were able to feed 4 people with the hamburger and 6 people with the chicken; there was more apparent size for weight with the chicken. This meant that, for the meat content, the hamburger meal cost 45¢ and the chicken cost 42.5¢ per head. The chicken was the hands-down winner on appeal and price (at this writing) and was, in our case, worth the little extra effort.

*Prices at time of writing.

## Home-Ground Hamburger

As a simple test we purchased "freshly ground" hamburger straight from the counter, took it home, and prepared it within 24 hours. It was greasy, fatty, had "off" tastes, and cost $1.79 a pound — it wasn't worth it! So we decided to try several different cuts and grind them ourselves. We tried:

- Two parts beef chuck blade steak (at $1.69 per pound) to one part beef shank (at $1.69) = 42¢ per person (1 pound serves 4).
- Beef flank steak (at $3.99) = $1.00¢ per person.
- Two parts beef heel of round (at $2.49) to one part beef shank (at $1.69) = $2.22 per pound = 55.5¢ per person.*

Of the above, the flank gave an excellent product, but the heel of round plus beef shank had more texture and flavor. This is, therefore, the top selection at $2.22 per pound or 55.5¢ per person against 45¢ for regular store-ground meat.

However, the big issue must be *taste,* and whether or not you do your own grinding at home. We believe you can make an infinitely superior product that is worth the effort — especially considering the reduction in fat and calories.

*Nutritional advantage:* calorie value is reduced by using lean ground beef, and note that the protein goes UP. Some hamburgers contain 30 percent fat (the maximum permitted under law); thus my figures can get even "better." Note also that the higher the fat percentage the greater the shrinkage.

The following figures are for ¼ pound (4 ounces) of raw meat, when broiled:

|  | COOKED WEIGHT | CALORIES | PROTEIN | FAT |
|---|---|---|---|---|
| Regular (21.3% fat) | 85 g. | 224 | 21.8 g. | 14.5 g. |
| Our mix (10% fat) | 86 g. | 140 | 25.9 g. | 3.4 g. |

(You *save* 84 calories per ¼-pound hamburger!)

# HINTS

Sense advantage can become a problem due to fat reduction. Fat equals flavor, therefore less fat equals less flavor. In order to remedy this, add, at the last moment, 1 teaspoonful of naturally brewed soy sauce per patty. The fat flavor is returned without fat! (See "Soy Sauce Versus Animal Fats" following.)

We do get sense advantages in visual and aromatic areas. Ground beef is subject to rapid bacterial growth — the longer it is exposed to the air the more discolored (oxidized) it gets and the more it is potentially subject to off flavors.

Equipment needed is a very small, hand-operated meat grinder available at most good hardware stores.

*Prices at time of writing.

## Soy Sauce

Cooking is, to say the least, an inexact science. If it were more exact, a great deal of the emotion would be lost and the need to cook might be removed.

But we do know that an excess of certain foods can be bad. Too much animal fat, too much sugar, and too much salt are well-known examples. Therefore, when a chance comes to reduce fat and salt in one move, it looks like a winner. We have experimented and are now convinced that fat can be reduced in traditionally high-fat dishes without adversely affecting the flavor — by adding a dash of naturally brewed soy sauce.

*Nutritional advantage:* reduction of both animal fat and salt is first-rate "reforming" of our excessive misuse of food. In one pound of regular hamburger there is usually about 3 ounces of fat (600 calories) that can be removed. This is all saturated fat, and while we need about 33 percent of our calories to be fat calories, the fact is that we get an average of 40 percent and in many cases as much as 50 percent from fats. This national average might include us, so it's reasonable to look for ways to reduce the impact.

The salt consumption is also a grave problem. We only need about ¼ teaspoon of sodium per day. Just imagine how much we get in processed foods that rely upon large salt doses to perk up their otherwise bland products! And when all the salted potato chips, olives, and crackers are done with, we pick up that salt at the table and lay it right on without tasting it first. This form of addiction can kill. In northern Japan, where huge quantities of salt (in excess of 30 pounds per year per person) are consumed, the stroke rate is reported as the highest anywhere in the world. Salt is also said to harden the arteries.

If our average need is only ¼ teaspoon sodium per day, let's try to reduce our intake.

On this point there is a special soy sauce made by Kikkoman with an 8 percent salt content. You may wish to taste it. Most other commonly found natural soy sauces have a 16 percent salt content.

*Sense advantage* comes from taste, aroma, and color (in dark dishes). Soy sauce has been used by Zen Buddhists for generations to replace the animal fat forbidden by their religion and it does work. To test this theory, fry 1 pound of regular store-bought hamburger in 1 teaspoonful of sesame/safflower oil (page 186) over a medium heat; keep stirring to release the fat. Pour off the fat (should be about 3 ounces) and add 2 tablespoons naturally brewed soy sauce. Stir in and cook lightly. Combine with 1 cup of cooked rice (page 164) and ¼ cup of *just* cooked green peas. Simple and delicious. You cut out the fat, but retain the flavor.

# Preparation of Poultry for Cooking

*The most fascinating experience in hotel kitchens is the first time you are permitted to sew up a chicken. When I went through this part of my early training, I was as excited as a young surgeon after completing a neat appendectomy. With great pride I presented it to the chef for his approval. His comment was "Very good — now do it in under thirty minutes." I have had a complex ever since about using needle and thread. I have now overcome this problem by devising a method that requires no needle. It's quicker and just as neat.*

**Step 1.** Having first thoroughly dried the bird, cut a piece of string about 2 feet long. Loop the center piece of the string over the drumsticks and pull tight.

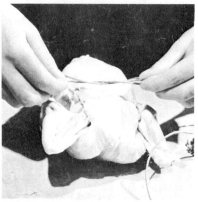

**Step 2.** Turn the bird over and tie the string in the center of the backbone.

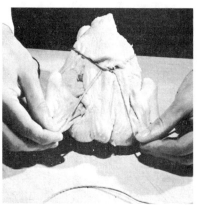

**Step 3.** Pass the ends around the wing pieces next to the breast.

**Step 4.** Bring the string up and tie it in the middle. Tuck the neck flap under the knot. The chicken is now perfectly tied for roasting or boiling.

# HINTS

## Pin Lace-Up for Poultry $

A chicken, when stuffed, has a far juicier texture than a "hollow bird." But how can we fill it and secure the dressing, preventing it from oozing everywhere?

I adopted the "ski-boot" technique of sliding pins through the flesh on either side of the opening and then using one piece of string interlaced tightly (see illustration).

The neck end is securely tied by string.

The best part of this is the ease of removing the string before serving. You extract the pins and lift the string right off.

## Chicken: Cut Up or Whole? $

When we look at the meat counter for good, inexpensive protein, the lure of the chicken is pretty strong. It comes either in pieces or whole. In some cases it can make sense, for a special dish, to buy only legs or thighs, but, from the purely economical aspect, you must face up to the fact that you are paying for the extra weighing and packaging. How much is this, in reality?

We discovered that you will pay a premium of at least 10¢ per pound for the "cut up" procedure. There are other, even higher, costs for specialty cuts such as fully deboned chicken breasts.

We feel that cutting up your own chicken will save roughly $15.00 per year if only one chicken is purchased each week.

The following diagrams show how a 3-pound, raw chicken gets jointed in five minutes, saving at least 18¢ ($2.16 an hour labor, tax-free!).

*Budget advantage* springs from the direct savings of doing your own cutting plus the indirect benefit to the quality of your overall cooking by using the carcass and trimmings to make a good chicken stock (page 32). The stock can be frozen in ice cube trays for use as required.

*Prices at the time of writing.

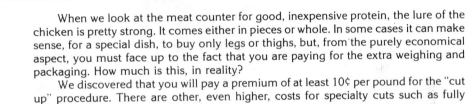

1

2

3

4

# Roast Poultry

**Serves 4**

### INGREDIENTS:

3½ lb. chicken
1 medium onion
4 cloves
Enough flour to coat
Fresh ginger
Salt
White peppercorns
Clarified butter

*Roasting is an extremely expensive method of cookery. It gets ridiculous when you try to economize by buying an old bird and part boil, part roast it. The older the bird the more fat it carries, and I have proved the point time and time again that it is as cheap to buy a bird under 12 weeks old as it is to pick up a so-called pot roaster, and the texture is far superior.*

## PREPARATION

1. Peel onion, stud with cloves.
2. Dry chicken thoroughly.
3. Prepare seasoning and flour.
4. Preheat oven to 375° F.
5. Melt butter.

**Step 1.** Detach end sections of the wings (as seen on right of picture). Place prepared onion in the cavity. Rub the flesh well with a piece of cut root ginger or sprinkle with ½ teaspoon ground ginger and rub in well. Tie chicken as on page 104.

**Step 2.** Always weigh the bird before you roast, and then calculate the time with great accuracy. At 375° F. a chicken of this size will be perfectly cooked if given 25 minutes per pound.

**Step 3.** If you are at all doubtful as to the age of your "roaster," cut up 1 small onion, 1 medium carrot, and 2 slices of bacon into thick pieces; add a little butter and simmer for 2 minutes. Add the trussed chicken, fix a lid on top, and steam for 10 minutes. Remove the now plump bird and dry thoroughly.

**Step 4.** Season the bird with salt and pepper and dust with flour. Brush well with clarified butter (page 77) and place on a wire rack or on the oven rungs with a tray underneath. Brush during cookery. When cooked, remove, cut strings, and serve.

# Ginger-Flavored Chicken

**Serves 4-6**

### INGREDIENTS:

3½ lb. roasting chicken
and giblets
2 tablespoons sesame/safflower oil
(page 186)
2 cups water
Freshly ground salt
1 teaspoon freshly grated ginger
2 teaspoons arrowroot
1 teaspoon soy sauce

*This recipe sets out to prove only one thing. Ginger is an excellent yet seldom-used spice for chicken, especially when it is roasted.*

### PREPARATION

1. Chop giblets and brown well in 1 tablespoon hot oil. Cover with the water; allow to simmer until giblet stock is reduced to 1 cup.

2. Season the inside of the chicken with salt and ½ teaspoon grated ginger, and tie it up (page 104).

3. Mix ½ teaspoon ginger with 1 tablespoon oil and ½ teaspoon salt, and brush this mixture over the chicken on both sides.

4. Place giblet stock in the roasting pan and place chicken on its side in the stock. Roast for 25 minutes at 375° F.; turn to other side for another 25 minutes, and, finally, turn breast up for 10-15 minutes.

5. Skim fat off the stock and thicken with a little arrowroot and 1 teaspoon soy sauce.

Serves 4 at 546.5 calories/serving or 6 at 364 calories/serving.

# Potato and Apple Stuffing

### INGREDIENTS:

1½ cups cooked mashed
potatoes (¾ lb.)
1 raw apple, finely diced
and mixed with 1 tablespoon
lemon juice
¼ teaspoon sage
¼ teaspoon thyme
½ teaspoon parsley
½ teaspoon salt
½ teaspoon white pepper

*We wanted to see if the potato could be developed into a stuffing and serve the double purpose of a seasoned dressing (which is moisture retaining for the bird) and a starch accompaniment. We based the quantity upon a 3½-lb. roast chicken, which should serve four portions. The stuffing makes 3 cups, which is adequate for this roast.*

### PREPARATION

1. Boil the potatoes. Pour off water and return to a low heat, covering with a towel, and steam dry for 10 minutes.

2. Mash potatoes. Finely chop the apple and mix with the lemon juice.

3. Mix all ingredients together and stuff a 3-4 lb. whole chicken. (See page 105 for pin method of closing).

4. Rub a little safflower oil over the chicken; salt and pepper to taste. Bake at 350° F. for 1½ hours.

88 calories per serving. (Bought stuffing mix = 180 calories per serving +9 gm. fat [butter or margarine] per serving.)

# Carving Poultry

Chicken

*Ladies — protect your males from obscurity and let them carve. The joint **must** be carved by the man of the house, and it is better to do this at the table — except with duck.*

**Step 1.** Remove string from bird. Place carving fork into thickest part of thigh. Cut through between breast and inside leg until joint is reached. Lever leg away with the fork, and detach the whole piece at the ball-and-socket joint.

**Step 2.** Take a thin slice off the breast — holding the bird firmly with a fork pressed into the wing.

**Step 3.** Continue to slice the breast, laying the pieces onto the carving dish. It follows that the dish must be very hot — in this way the thin slices stay hot, and, as you will see, they sit in the natural juices of the bird.

**Step 4.** After the meal is over, put the carcass in a plastic bag, and, if you have space, deep-freeze it. Later you can prepare a delicious thin soup.

# Carving Poultry | *continued*

**Duck**

**Step 1.** Remove string and pins. Cut thin slices from the breast on both sides, laying the slices onto the hot serving dish.

**Step 2.** Cut down from the top of the wishbone right through to the joints of the wings. This provides easier access to the slices nearer the breastbone.

**Step 3.** Cut the leg away, pulling it down with the fork. Detach at the ball-and-socket joint seen just in front of the knife blade.

**Step 4.** Lay carved pieces on a hot serving dish with stuffing down center. Pour juices over meats and serve. Duck is one joint that should be "attacked" in the kitchen until you are thoroughly proficient. Keep the carcass for use later on as a soup base.

# HINTS

## Carving Roast Chicken

The usual idea is to give the legs to the men and the sliced breast to the ladies. Well, since our society is now so preoccupied with equality — let's do better!

1. Carve off the whole leg with thighs first.

2. Then detach the thigh from the drumstick — 4 portions of dark meat.

3. Carve off the top breasts. Cut down either side of the breastbone and remove the breast meat intact; serve these with the oyster cuts from under the backbone.

4. Carve off the bottom breasts. Cut in at a 45° angle (with the base of the angle behind the wing) across the breast and turn the knife in to cut down and through the wishbone. This gives you two breasts with wings.

You now have 8 pieces to play with: Equality!

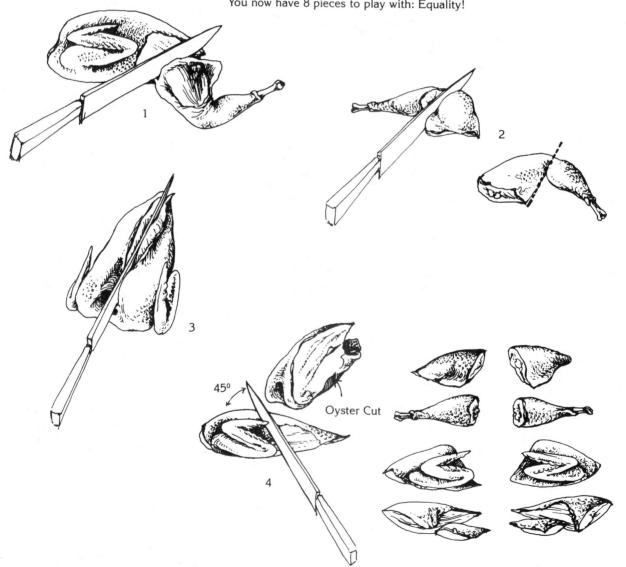

Oyster Cut

45°

# HINTS

## Cutting Instructions For Turkey $ R

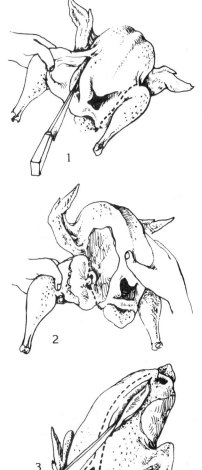

1. Position turkey on its back, as shown. Cut along dotted line to detach drumstick and thigh. Pull away and down, making cut between the seam that joins the thigh and drumstick to the carcass.

2. After the initial cut, pull the drumstick and thigh down and away from the carcass while holding with the other hand. This will expose the joint where the thigh is joined to the carcass. Insert knife blade at the center of joint and cut (as illustrated) until leg and thigh are detached. Repeat procedure for the other leg and thigh.

3. Now remove the turkey breasts by cutting along the dotted lines shown. Cut closely to the breastbone on both sides all the way down to the bottom of the rib cage where the wing joins the base of the breast.

4. Where the wing joins the breast, we have another joint. Cut through at the center point of the joint until the breast portion and wing are detached. Repeat procedure for the other breast.

5. Now detach the wings from the breast portions. This is done by first extending the wing, as shown. Cut through at angle shown to detach wing, cutting away as little of the breast meat as possible.

6. Here the left hand is holding the tender fillet portion of the turkey breast called the "supreme." The drawing immediately to the right shows the shaded area of the breast from where it was removed. It lies in the *inner* part of the breast and is easily lifted out without cutting.

7. Here we have all the portions assembled. First, we have the carcass A, which can produce four pints of jellied turkey stock. This is done by gently simmering the carcass in eight pints of water for four hours. Do not add any seasoning until you actually use it. You can strain it, pour into ice cube trays, freeze, and then place in a plastic bag for later use. It will also make a delicious soup for four by thickening with rice or potatoes or mixed vegetables. B is 4 ounces of turkey liver, which is just like chicken liver. It has an excellent flavor and can be chopped up and stirred into rice for chicken liver risotto.

The next pieces C are giblets and the neck, which can be added to the carcass for some good stock. We then come to the two wings D for BBQ Turkey Wings (page 122). The drumstick and thigh E are great in Turkey Lima, which serves at least four people. Next are the two breasts F for Braised Turkey Breast (page 117), which are cooked by moist heat to retain the breasts' moisture and tenderness. Last, the two supremes (also at F) are poached gently in Supreme of Turkey Cornell.

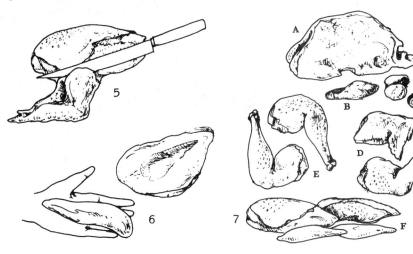

# Boiled Poultry

**Serves 8**

### INGREDIENTS:

4 lb. boiling fowl
5½ cups chicken stock
1 bay leaf
1 sprig thyme
Lemon slices to cover breast
1 medium onion
1 large carrot
1 slice bacon

*Chicken can be made to go a very long way if you boil it. Cool the carcass, and then strip off every vestige of flesh. It can then be made into many delicious dishes by using the stock as a base for a quick, creamy, soft white sauce. You can also carve up the chicken like a roasted bird if you wish, but I consider this a gross failure in home economics.*

### PREPARATION

1. Peel and slice vegetables.
2. Dry chicken well and tie up.
3. Prepare stock.

**Step 1.** If a really old bird has been selected, then place the sliced vegetables with a slice of bacon in the bottom of a saucepan. Place the fowl on this vegetable base, cover the pan tightly, and cook over a moderate heat for 10 minutes.

**Step 2.** After this initial "tenderizing" process (you can see how the bird has swollen), add the stock (or water if you must), and then the herbs.

**Step 3.** The fowl is then simmered with a lid on for approximately 23-25 minutes per pound. Keep a check on the liquid level and add more from time to time. In most family-size saucepans, the breast will not be covered. If this should happen to you, just keep it covered with thinly sliced lemons.

**Step 4.** Skim off the chicken fat and foam during cookery. When the chicken is cooked, strip off all the flesh, strain, and clarify (page 36) the cooking liquid and proceed with making a good White Sauce (page 217), using the clear chicken broth as the liquid.

# Bread Pastry Case with Chicken Treenestar

### Serves 4

#### INGREDIENTS:

1 3-3½ lb. chicken
1 onion
1 medium whole carrot
1 bay leaf
3 parsley stalks
3-in. piece of celery
1 quart water
1 large carrot, thinly sliced
½ lb. asparagus tips
1 cup skim (1%) milk
2 tablespoons arrowroot
1 4½ oz. can of shrimp
1½ teaspoons freshly ground salt
¼ teaspoon freshly ground pepper
1 1-lb. loaf unsliced Italian bread

#### PREPARATION

1. Place chicken, onion, whole carrot, bay leaf, parsley stalks, and celery in a large dutch oven.

2. Cover with 1 quart water and simmer gently for 1 hour with the lid on.

3. *Bread case:* Using a standard loaf, slice off the top, leaving a hinge to raise and lower the lid. Raise and support the lid (so it doesn't break off) then scoop out the interior, leaving about ½ inch soft white bread next to the crust. Lightly butter the interior of the loaf, using butter at room temperature.

4. At the end of 1 hour, remove chicken, separating pieces on a platter to cool quickly. Strain the stock. Allow it to cool and skim off the surface fat.

5. Cut the meat into fork-sized portions, removing skin, bones, and cartilage.

6. Toast loaf, lid open, for 4 minutes at 350⁰ F.

7. Measure 1 cup of the chicken stock into a medium-sized saucepan, add sliced carrot, cook 5 minutes, add asparagus, and cook to the crisp-tender stage (3-4 minutes).

8. Add milk, mix arrowroot with 2 tablespoons (from the ½ cup) milk and stir in. Bring to a gentle boil, stirring all the time.

9. Add the shrimp and chicken, and reheat just to the boiling stage.

10. Turn immediately into the toasted and buttered bread case and heat at 250⁰ F. for 10 minutes. Serve immediately.

   If this serves 6, each serving is 448 calories. If this serves 4, each serving is 672 calories.

# Supreme of Turkey Cornell

### Serves 2

#### INGREDIENTS:

3 cups turkey or chicken stock
¼ cup whipping cream
¼ cup small white mushrooms
1 tablespoon arrowroot
1 tablespoon naturally brewed
soy sauce
1 teaspoon fresh lemon juice
1 tablespoon chopped fresh
parsley leaves
2 6-oz. turkey supremes
(inner fillets of breast)
1 teaspoon paprika

#### PREPARATION

1. Measure stock and cream. Weigh, wash, and dry mushrooms and cut them into quarters; measure the arrowroot and combine with soy sauce; squeeze the lemon; chop the parsley into fine pieces.

2. Lay the supremes in a shallow skillet; add the stock and cover tightly. Poach over a low heat for 8 minutes until just cooked without undue shrinkage of the meat.

3. Remove the supremes and keep them warm. Boil the poaching liquid vigorously to concentrate its flavor until only 1 cup is left.

4. Add the mushrooms to the reduced stock and boil for 60 seconds only. Add the lemon juice and pour in the soy-arrowroot mixture; let it thicken, just coming to a boil. Remove it from heat. Now add the cream very slowly, stirring all the time. Add parsley and return the supremes to the sauce — heat through, but do not boil. Serve, dusted with paprika, on a shallow dish.

# Chicken or Turkey Lima

### Serves 4

#### INGREDIENTS:

1 10-oz. pkg. frozen lima beans
1½ cups chicken or turkey stock
½ cup chopped celery
½ cup chopped onion
2 tablespoons sesame/safflower oil
(page 186).
1 tablespoon curry powder
1 tablespoon arrowroot
2 tablespoons water
1 lb. cooked chicken or
turkey meat
1 large apple, sliced

#### PREPARATION

1. Boil the lima beans in chicken or turkey stock for 5 minutes; drain, reserving the stock.

2. Sauté the celery and onion in oil, then add the curry powder, and strained stock.

3. Bring the mixture to a boil and thicken it with arrowroot mixed with water.

4. Stir in the cooked chicken meat and heat through.

5. Add the apple and lima beans.

## Quick Sauce

## HINTS

For your next casserole (or stew), try adding *no* flour or thickening *at any stage*. Just before you serve it, skim off all the fat and strain off all the thin juices. Bring these to the boil in a small saucepan and pour in the arrowroot, which has been mixed with a little water (about 1 tablespoon of arrowroot per cup of liquid to be thickened). Stir rapidly and return to the stew; fold in gently and serve. It will look brilliant and glossy, just like a *McCall's* food page!

# Braised Poultry  $

### Serves 4

#### INGREDIENTS:

3½ lb. duckling, preferably
Long Island or Brome Lake
Salt to season
Black peppercorns, freshly ground
to season
1 large carrot
1 medium onion
2 garlic cloves
Clarified butter
½ cup apricot juice from the can*
1 bay leaf
2 sprigs thyme
1 sprig parsley
2 tablespoons arrowroot
3½ cups water
1 20-oz. can apricots

*Two pounds of fresh apricots can be gently poached in a light syrup when in season.

> My main "grouse" with duck is that when it is roasted, there appears to be very little meat left. My favorite method is to braise duckling, and, if this is done carefully, the results are fabulous, filling, and tender.
>
> Tenderness is quite a point with me, because I once planned a dinner for New Zealand's Governor-General. The roast Aylesbury duckling was so tough that even a fiercely wielded viceregal fork could not penetrate its golden crust!

#### PREPARATION

1. Peel and slice vegetables and cloves of garlic.
2. Measure apricot juice and water.
3. Preheat oven to 375° F.
4. Prepare arrowroot paste for thickening sauce.
5. Tie up herbs.
6. Dry duck inside and out, and tie up.

**Step 1.** Season the duck well inside and out. Place a little butter in the casserole dish, brown the sliced vegetables, and add crushed garlic. In a frying pan, brown the duck well in some more very hot clarified butter.

**Step 2.** Place the duck on the browned vegetables and add the apricot juice and water. Add the herbs, and place in an oven set at 375° F. to cook, with lid on, for 1½ hours.

**Step 3.** Skim off the fats from the surface and then remove the duck. Strain the juice and bring it to the boil; add the arrowroot thickening and stir until it clears. If not dark enough, add some vegetable or meat flavor concentrate.

**Step 4.** Take the string off the duck, and, holding it with a wooden spoon, give it a little extra golden crispness by placing it under a very hot broiler for a couple of minutes. Serve on a carving dish surrounded with the apricot halves.

# Mild Chicken Curry  $

**Serves 4**

### INGREDIENTS:

1 medium onion
¼ cup sesame/safflower oil
(page 186)
3 teaspoons curry powder
½ teaspoon ground chili
3 mashed garlic cloves
1 3½-lb. chicken cut into
8 pieces
¾ cup chicken stock
¾ cup plain yogurt
Freshly ground salt to taste
¼ teaspoon ground ginger
Pinch of ground cloves
¼ teaspoon black pepper
Pinch ground cumin

### PREPARATION

1. Finely slice the onion and measure the other ingredients.

2. Brown the onion in oil in a skillet, then remove to a small dish. Put the curry powder, chili, garlic, and stock in the oil in the pan. Stir to mix.

3. Add the chicken and boil for 20 minutes with the lid on.

4. Mix onion and yogurt in the blender; add salt, ginger, cloves, pepper, and cumin, and add to the chicken. Stir to mix well.

5. Simmer with the lid off for another 15-20 minutes. The chicken is in a lovely sauce and ready to serve.

Has 333 calories per serving.

> *I haven't got an asbestos tongue, but I do enjoy a good curry.*

# Karewai Chicken Barbecue

**Serves 4**

### INGREDIENTS:

1 roasting chicken
1 cup chicken stock
6 tablespoons tomato paste
¼ cup naturally brewed soy sauce
¼ teaspoon ground allspice
Ground black pepper to taste
1 teaspoon basil
1 teaspoon chopped parsley

### PREPARATION

1. Tie chicken as on page 104 and spit-roast over coals.

2. Reduce chicken stock to ¼ cup by boiling.

3. Add the seasonings and parsley to the stock and baste over chicken when it is almost done.

# Braised Turkey Breast

**Serves 4**

**INGREDIENTS:**

2 bacon slices
1 large carrot (5 oz.)
1 large onion
¼ cup tomato paste
1 cup turkey or chicken stock
1 tablespoon rice vinegar
½ cup white grape juice
2 teaspoons arrowroot
1 tablespoon chopped parsley
1 turkey breast (2 lbs.)
(minus the inner fillets)
1 tablespoon naturally brewed
soy sauce
1 bay leaf

**PREPARATION**

1. Cut bacon in 1-inch squares. Peel and slice carrot and onion. Measure tomato paste, turkey stock, grape juice, and rice vinegar. Measure arrowroot and combine with the soy sauce. Chop parsley. Preheat oven to 300° F.

2. Heat bacon in dutch oven to release fat. Remove the bacon pieces and color the turkey breast in the bacon fat (5 minutes at medium-high heat on each side). Cover the pan for best results.

3. Remove the meat, replace the bacon, and add the carrot and onion. Fry 2 minutes. Add tomato paste, stir well, and cook until the tomato browns.

4. Add turkey stock, grape juice, and bay leaf. Return meat to the pan, cover, and place in oven for 50 minutes. Test for tenderness — it should be just underdone. Strain the "sauce" through a sieve, pressing out the moisture, but *not* pushing through the softened vegetable fiber.

5. Skim off *all* fat. Bring sauce to the boil and thicken by beating in the arrowroot/soy-sauce mixture. Adjust the seasoning. Add rice vinegar. Carve the breast into 12 thin slices (it should be slightly pink), reassemble into the breast shape in a shallow serving dish (with lid), and coat with the finished sauce. Garnish with boiled small onions and carrots and sprinkle with parsley.

# Your Own Light Curry Powder

**INGREDIENTS:**

1 tablespoon ground turmeric
1 tablespoon ground cumin
2 tablespoons coriander seed
1 tablespoon ground ginger
1 tablespoon ground white
peppercorns
2 teaspoons hot chili powder or
hot dried chillies
2 teaspoons ground cardamom
2 teaspoons mace
1 teaspoon mustard seed
½ teaspoon ground cloves
1 teaspoon poppy seeds
1 bay leaf
1 teaspoon fenugreek

Some folks like to be different. I suppose I'm one of them, because I just love the idea of making up my very own curry powder. Try the blend and add or subtract until you have it right for you!

# Deep-Fried Poultry

**Serves 4**

### INGREDIENTS:

2 lb. chicken
Flour to coat
Salt to season
Pepper to season
1 egg
2 tablespoons oil
Bread crumbs to coat

*❝ As this method of preparation needs more illustrations, I shall not list the recipe. A 2-pound chicken will satisfy 4 people, and the beaten egg is made up with 1 whole egg and 2 tablespoons oil. ❞*

### PREPARATION

1. Prepare seasoned flour in a plastic bag.
2. Beat eggs and oil together thoroughly.
3. Break bread into fine crumbs.

**Step 1.** Detach the wing pieces as shown on the right of this picture. Cut off the legs at the thigh joint, shown just under my left thumb, and then remove the skin.

**Step 2.** Cut the whole of the breast away from the bony backbone and remove the outer skin.

**Step 3.** Cut the breast in two down the center. Chicken scissors are best for this job, but it can be done with a sharp heavy knife.

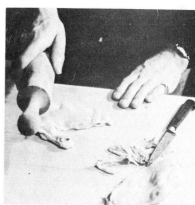

**Step 4.** Beat the breast gently with a rolling pin — this will loosen the bones. Cut out the bones carefully.

# Deep-Fried Poultry *continued*

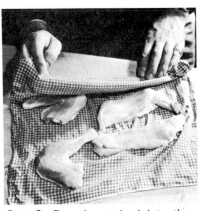

**Step 5.** You will now have the joints shown above. From a 2-pound bird, you get 2 legs (each 4 ounces), 2 breasts (each 3 ounces), 2 wings (each 2 ounces), and 15 ounces of jolly good trimmings for an excellent soup base (see page 32).

**Step 6.** Dry the main joints thoroughly in a clean cloth.

**Step 7.** Toss the pieces in well-seasoned flour in a plastic bag. See extreme left of picture. Now coat the pieces in the egg-and-oil mixture and finally coat with fine bread crumbs. Shake to remove surplus.

**Step 8.** Place chicken into a deep fryer set at 300° F. for 12 minutes. Allow to drain and then serve very hot.

# Breading by the Two-Step Method

A well-breadcrumbed piece of fish or chicken is a joy to behold. But the old 3-Step method of flour, egg, and bread crumbs needs some overhaul for both taste and adherence.

We found that 2 whole eggs, 1 tablespoon safflower oil, 1 tablespoon soy sauce, and ¼ teaspoon white pepper combined with 2 tablespoons flour makes a fabulous coating before pressing into bread crumbs for *all* shallow-fried savory dishes. This lets us avoid, for example, the seasoned flour that tends to create a doughy skin on the fish.

The soy sauce on seafood is really excellent. It was, after all, originally designed for such a use in southeastern China and in Japan.

# Broiled Poultry

Serves 2

### INGREDIENTS:

1½ lb. chicken
Flour to season
Salt to season
White peppercorns, freshly ground
to season
¼ cup clarified butter (page 77)

> *Broiling poultry, especially young, tender chicken, is a very attractive method of cookery. A small bird should be chosen — about 1½ pounds.*

## PREPARATION

1. Preheat broiler (medium hot).
2. Melt butter.
3. Prepare seasoned flour.

**Step 1.** Cut the chicken in half, starting by cutting through the backbone. Remove the wing ends and the neck.

**Step 2.** Beat the chicken lightly with a rolling pin to loosen the major bones. Remove only the heaviest bones (found below the thigh nearest to the board in the photograph).

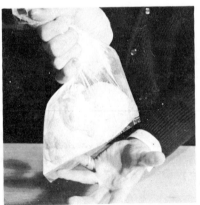

**Step 3.** Toss the halves well in seasoned flour.

**Step 4.** Brush the rack well with butter, then place the chicken halves on top. Now brush the surface thoroughly and broil outer side for 10 minutes until golden brown; turn over and broil for a further 8-10 minutes. Serve immediately.

# Chicken Polese

**Serves 2**

### INGREDIENTS:

2 chicken breasts
1 garlic clove
2 tomatoes
2 ounces green pepper
2 ounces low-fat Mozzarella cheese
½ ounce (4 slices) anchovy fillets
1 tablespoon sesame/safflower oil
(page 186)
2 teaspoons Worcestershire sauce
1 teaspoon capers
Parsley

**❝** *In its original form, this dish came from a small Italian restaurant called Beppie's in Sydney, Australia. The technique it so clearly illustrates is the use of mozzarella cheese in lieu of sauce. Step 7 shows how the "sauce" is made in only 3 minutes. It saves time and reduces the calorie and fat level compared with Béchamel (rich white sauce).* **❞**

### PREPARATION

1. Remove skin and bones from chicken breasts.

2. Peel and mash garlic; seed, skin, and chop tomatoes; cut pepper into thin strips; cut cheese into 2 thin slices; soak anchovies in a little milk, drain, and cut lengthwise.

3. Heat oil in a skillet, add chicken, and brown on both sides.

4. Add garlic, onion, tomatoes, and pepper. Season to taste.

5. Cover skillet and simmer on lowest heat for 30 minutes.

6. At the end of this time, place a slice of cheese and 2 strips of anchovy on top of each chicken breast.

7. Stir Worcestershire sauce in, cover, and simmer until cheese melts (3-5 minutes). Place on a heated dish and keep warm.

8. Reduce vegetable pulp and juices until thick (about 5 minutes on medium-high heat). Pour over or around chicken. Sprinkle with capers and parsley, then serve.

Number of calories per serving is 204.

# BBQ Turkey Wings

**Serves 2**

### INGREDIENTS:

2 turkey wings (detached from the breast at the wishbone)
¼ cup tomato ketchup
1 tablespoon naturally brewed soy sauce
3 cups turkey stock (made from carcass)
1 large garlic clove
1 tablespoon chopped parsley stalks
1 tablespoon safflower oil
1 tablespoon rice vinegar

### PREPARATION

1. Cut wings into three pieces each at the natural joints. Measure ketchup, soy sauce, and turkey stock. Peel and crush clove of garlic. Chop parsley stalks.

2. Combine turkey stock and turkey pieces. *Simmer* the wings for 40 minutes in the turkey stock in a covered pan until *just* tender. Remove meat and pat dry with paper towels. Reserve ¼ cup stock.

3. Heat safflower oil in small skillet; add cooked turkey pieces and brown.

4. Add garlic and ketchup. Cook stirring, until the ketchup is deep brown, then add ¼ cup stock, the soy sauce, and vinegar. Cool in the sauce.

5. Using tongs, place coated turkey pieces under (or over) broiler to heat through and become glazed. Dust with finely chopped parsley stalks and serve with finger bowls to help clean up your hands. There's no other way to eat them!

# pies

# pies

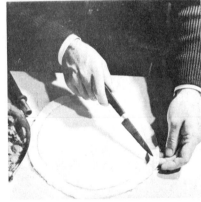

# pies

# pies

# Suet Pudding

**Serves 6**

## INGREDIENTS:

PASTRY:
1 lb. flour
1 heaping teaspoon baking powder
Pinch of salt
1⅛ cups suet
1⅛ cups water

FILLING:
1½ lb. blade steak of beef
½ lb. ox kidney
1½ teaspoons fresh thyme leaves
1 tablespoon parsley stalks
Salt and pepper to season
Flour, to dust
Water (approximately 1¼ cups)
to fill basin ¾ full.

> *"My mother makes a wonderful steak and kidney pudding." This is the kind of statement that usually leads to music-hall comments being made about mothers-in-law. As I am the cook in our home, I face a curiously psychological problem when my wife says, "Yes, it's good. But not as good as your mother's!" What would you do?*

## PREPARATION

1. Measure flour, baking powder, salt, suet, and water for pastry.
2. Grease pudding bowl with butter.
3. Chop parsley stalks.
4. Cut meat and kidney into 1-inch cubes.
5. Measure thyme leaves, parsley stalks, and water.

**Step 1.** Sift flour with salt and baking powder. Rub in suet or mix together in beater. Add the water and mix to a smooth dough. Take ⅔ of paste and roll out ½-inch thick. Line the pudding basin (7 inches diameter).

**Step 2.** Combine the meat and kidney with seasonings, herbs, and a little flour. Pack the mixture into the basin until it comes level with the rim. Add sufficient water to fill the basin ¾ full.

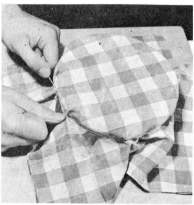

**Step 3.** Roll out the remaining paste, dampen the top of the crust in the basin, and lay on the top. Press the top on well and tie on a well-floured cloth, knotting the ends in the center.

**Step 4.** Place in a large saucepan. Add cold water until it comes halfway up the basin. Fix a lid on top and boil gently for 3 hours. It is a good plan to put 2 marbles in the saucepan. When the water level get very low, they make a fearful din! When cooked, strip off cloth and serve from the basin.

# Pastry Pies

**Serves 4**

## INGREDIENTS:

FIVE-MINUTE PIE PASTRY:
¾ cup butter
2 cups flour
Salt to season
½ cup water

FILLING:
1 medium onion
1 medium carrot
1½ teaspoons clarified butter
1½ lb. neck of lamb
Flour to dust
Salt to season
Black peppercorns, freshly ground
to season
¾ cup water
Meat stock, half fill pan

❝ *I have found from experience that an old, heavy-based frying pan makes the best pie dish — that is, for a top-crust pie like this one. The handle has to be taken off, but this doesn't prove too difficult once you make the decision; and the end results are worth the trouble.* ❞

## PREPARATION

1. Measure flour; cut butter into 1-inch squares, each ¼ inch thick.
2. Peel and cut vegetables into ¼-inch-thick slices.
3. Cube meat from neck of lamb.
4. Preheat oven to 375° F.

**Step 1.** Sieve flour and salt together and add the butter pieces. Pinch these pieces flat with thumb and forefinger. Add the water gradually, mixing with a wooden spoon.

**Step 2.** Fry the vegetables in the pan with a little clarified butter. Dust the meat with flour and season with salt and pepper. Add this to the vegetables. Brown the meat well. Take the pan off the heat and allow to cool.

**Step 3.** Roll out the pastry, using plenty of dusting flour — fold several times — roll ⅛-inch thick and allow to stand for 10 minutes to relax (see page 130). Cut a round piece the size of the rim of the pan and another about 1 inch oversize. Place the outer ring onto the cooled pan rim. Now brush the top with water.

**Step 4.** Add the stock to half fill the pan, and then roll the pastry top onto a pin and lay it over the meat. The pie filling should always rise slightly higher in the center than the outer rim. (I added some extra filling after this shot was taken.) Brush the pastry top with beaten egg, and bake for 1 hour 20 minutes. Cover with damp brown paper if top browns too quickly.

# Five-Minute Flaky Pastry Pie Top

### INGREDIENTS:

1 lb. all-purpose flour
(4 cups sifted)
½ cup safflower oil
½ cup ice water
Pinch of salt

### PREPARATION

1. Measure all ingredients first.

2. Mix salt and sifted flour, then add the oil and *shake the bowl* to combine flour and oil.

3. Stir in water and turn out on a floured board to knead lightly and quickly.

4. Roll out *twice*, wrap in waxed paper, and cool before use. Roll out thin and cover your already prepared pie.

**"** *A really good, full-of-flavor, crusty pie top is almost the perfect topping for a meaty stew. Too often the crust is sodden, pallid, chewy, and, worst of all perhaps, riddled with calories from the saturated fats.*

*We made up a pastry that needs speed, always works, and uses only ½ cup of polyunsaturated safflower oil to a 1½ lb. mix. This is usually enough for a top crust for 12 people.*

*If you look at any good French-style cookbook, you'll see that a puff pastry uses 3¾ cups flour (1659 calories), 1 lb. butter (3240 calories), 2 egg yolks (120 calories), and 8 fluid ounces water — a total of (5019 calories) for 2 lbs. 9 ozs. pastry. Comparing it ounce for ounce, this gives us: Safflower oil pastry = 110.5 calories per oz., puff pastry = 122.8 calories per oz. — and the latter is all saturated fats.*

*So, if, in addition to its nutritional value, you also want to make a top crust in 5 minutes instead of taking at least 1 hour, join us with this easy idea.* **"**

# Treacle Tart $

**Serves 10**

## INGREDIENTS:

PASTRY TO LINE TART:
1½ cups self-rising flour
6 tablespoons butter (¾ stick)
¼ cup milk
½ egg
Pinch of freshly ground salt
TOP PASTRY:
8 tablespoons butter (1 stick)
¼ cup sugar
1½ eggs
1½ cups self-rising flour
2 teaspoons sugar
FILLING:
1 pint Tate & Lyle's golden syrup
(16 fl. oz.)
or use a thick, light corn syrup
1¼ cups fresh white bread
crumbs (5 oz.)

**"** *This is a treacle tart that Her Majesty, Queen Elizabeth, the Queen of England, likes very much (so I was told second hand!)* **"**

## PREPARATION

1. Make bottom pastry by mixing butter lightly into sifted flour, and then stirring into a dough with milk, half an egg, and salt. (To divide egg in half, beat lightly first). Knead lightly, refrigerate 30 minutes.

2. Make top pastry by creaming butter with sugar, adding half a beaten egg, and, when thoroughly mixed, folding in the sifted flour. Refrigerate. Lightly beat remaining egg.

3. Measure golden syrup. Make bread into 1¼ cups. Preheat oven to 375° F.

4. Roll out bottom pastry on a floured surface to an 11-inch circle; leave for 10 minutes to "relax." Line a 9-inch flan ring standing on a greased tray. Trim off pastry and prick base with a fork.

5. Combine bread crumbs with golden syrup and fill pastry case.

6. Roll out top pastry or press out with hands to a 9-inch round on a well-floured board. Roll lightly with rolling pin, turn it over, and again allow to relax.

7. Brush rim of tart with beaten egg, and then place pastry top onto tart. Press edges together and trim off any excess pastry. Crimp edges and brush surface with beaten egg. Prick surface with a fork. Sprinkle with sugar and bake in oven for 20 minutes. Remove and allow to cool for an hour.

8. It can then be reheated at 250° F. for 5 minutes. Whipped cream goes well on the side — but then, so does yogurt. (Please note that this is a dish highly suited to one who needs to *increase* weight!)

# Parmesan Rice Crust

### Serves 6

### INGREDIENTS:

⅔ cup long-grain rice
½ teaspoon salt
1 beaten egg white
1 teaspoon soy sauce
¼ cup grated Parmesan cheese
Pepper to taste

**"** *Would you be interested in a piecrust that used, instead of the regular flour, fat, and water, a combination of rice, egg, soy sauce, and Parmesan cheese?*

*The idea fascinated us. After some trial and much error, this technique evolved. It is actually quite easy, delicious, and slightly less fattening than piecrust — but more expensive. The spinach filling can be used with your regular piecrust.* **"**

### PREPARATION

1. Cook rice 20 minutes in 1½ cups of water.

2. After the rice is cooked, mix the egg white, soy sauce, cheese, and pepper; add to the rice. Stir well to mix, and press into a 9-inch Pie pan. Bake at 375° F. for 25-30 minutes until it begins to get crusty and dries out.

# Spinach Souffle′ Filling

### Serves 2-6

### INGREDIENTS:

1 lb. trimmed spinach
1 tablespoon sesame/safflower oil (page 186)
1 tablespoon arrowroot
¼ cup whole milk
Nutmeg, grated
Black pepper
Trace of salt
3 egg yolks
4 egg whites
4 ounces Swiss cheese

### PREPARATION

1. Weigh 1 lb. trimmed spinach (or defrost 2 8-ounce frozen packages). Cut off heavy stalks before weighing. Wash well in at least 4 washings.

2. Place spinach in a heavy-based, *large* saucepan with 1 tablespoon oil well mixed into the leaves before you start. Cook over a medium heat for 4 minutes. Stir and toss. Pour off any excess water in the bottom and remove cooked leaves.

3. Place spinach in blender and blend until smooth. Pour into a hand sieve and press out all surplus moisture. Add arrowroot and add back the removed moisture gradually, together with the milk.

4. Season this mixture highly with pepper, nutmeg, and a trace of salt. Add 3 egg yolks, stir in well, and let cool on a plate. Fold in 4 stiffly beaten egg whites.

5. Place spinach filling into rice crust. On the top of the pie make a lattice work of Swiss cheese using very thin slices ¼-½ inch wide. Bake at 400° F. for 20 minutes.

1 slice of quiche has 220 calories (serving 6), or it can serve 2 as a main dish at 660 calories per serving.
Complementary protein sources are rice + milk products + egg white.

# Apple Custard Tart

### Serves 6

#### INGREDIENTS:

PASTRY:
1 cup flour
Pinch salt
1 tablespoon sugar
4 tablespoons butter (½ stick)
1 egg, separated
3 drops vanilla extract
Water
FILLING:
¼ cup instant milk powder
1 cup applesauce
3 eggs
1 teaspoon vanilla extract
1 teaspoon grated lemon rind
1 cup regular milk
Nutmeg

#### PREPARATION

1. Combine flour, salt, and sugar. Cut in butter. Stir in egg yolk, vanilla, and enough cold water to form pastry into a ball. Press into 9-inch pie plate lined with foil. Bake at 375⁰ F. for 12 minutes. Remove from oven and, while hot, brush with "egg wash" (page 131).

2. Combine instant milk powder, applesauce, eggs, vanilla, and lemon rind. Gradually beat in milk. Pour apple custard mixture into partially baked shell. Grate a little nutmeg over surface. Bake at 325⁰ F. for 50 minutes. Serve cold.

# Quiche Lorraine $

**Serves 6**

## INGREDIENTS:

PASTRY:
2 cups all-purpose flour
½ teaspoon salt
8 tablespoons butter (1 stick)
1 small egg
1½ tablespoons ice water
FILLING:
6 ounces bacon slices
3 ounces Gruyere cheese
3 eggs
1½ cups milk
Freshly ground salt
Freshly ground pepper
Nutmeg

## PREPARATION

PASTRY:

1. Sift flour with salt, form a well in center, and add softened butter and egg. Mix gently with fingertips. Stir in ice water until soft dough is formed. Knead dough a few times, then form into a ball. Refrigerate 30 minutes.

2. Roll out pastry and put in an 8-inch pie plate, fluting a high edge on pastry shell. Prick bottom with a fork. Place a piece of cheesecloth over the bottom and sides of pastry.

3. Fill with dried peas, or bread crumbs to keep shape of pastry and bake in 425° F. oven for 20 minutes. Remove cheesecloth and dried peas and allow pastry to cool.

FILLING:

1. Lightly fry bacon and cut into strips to fit pastry bottom.

2. Cut cheese into thin slices. Mix eggs with milk and season with salt, pepper, and nutmeg. Preheat oven to 400° F.

3. Place bacon strips on bottom of pastry shell. Sprinkle with thin slices of Gruyere cheese. Put on oven shelf. Pour in half of the milk and egg mixture, leave in the hot oven for 2 minutes to set, and then add remaining liquid.

4. Bake for 25-to-30 minutes. Remove from oven, place on serving dish, and serve hot or cold, cut into small wedges.

SPECIAL HINTS:

You can use bread crusts in lieu of peas. Allow a ¼-inch clearance between egg and milk mixture and the pastry shell lip.

# HINTS

# Pastry

Any form of pastry that needs to be rolled out must *relax* before it's used and trimmed. It is strange that this simple rule isn't used in more basic cookbooks. The fact is that when the pastry has been "stretched," it will hold itself in that shape while it is raw, but when subjected to heat, soon retreats with indecent speed. When the pastry is placed on top of a pie, its "retreat" is painfully obvious!

Just leave the pastry in its rolled-out form for 10 minutes at room temperature, and you've got it made. Quite literally, it will have relaxed!

*Sense Advantage* is one of visual benefit. One of the most obvious tests is the pastry top used on a treacle tart (see recipe on page 127).

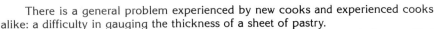

# Rolling Pin

There is a general problem experienced by new cooks and experienced cooks alike: a difficulty in gauging the thickness of a sheet of pastry.

Some dishes, such as the French Vol au Vent (a pastry case made from puffed pastry), call for the pastry to be ¼-inch to ⅜-inch thick, while some pies specify ⅛-inch, and some recipes even go down to nearly "zero" for pasta.

The experts simply run their fingers under the edge and feel the distance with their thumbs. For the inexperienced, that's a little hard. Now we have a wooden rolling pin based on a French design that has round rolling discs at each end to raise or lower the rolling surface of the pin at will. It works.

Easy to adjust;
Remove ends and insert interchangeable discs

# Pastry Pies

Many pies, tarts, flans, quiche — call them what you may — suffer from soggy bottoms. All manner of techniques have been developed to deal with them, but two seem worthy of attention.

The first — to be used only for sweet pastries — is apricot jam melted and brushed lukewarm over the partly cooked pastry base.

The second is to use an egg wash, made up of 1 whole egg, ½ teaspoon salt, and 1 tablespoon light salad oil. This is completely combined and brushed over the precooked pastry case before it is filled.

*Sense Advantage* is primarily a textural one, but clearly there is a benefit to the digestion (at least in my case).

# Custard Pies

Many attempts at such dishes as pumpkin pie and Quiche Lorraine are doomed to failure because of the "one-hit" filling technique where all the mix is added at one time and the pie is carried with trembling hands to the oven. The filling expands as it heats and pours over the lip of the pie plate.

To avoid this, place the pastry-lined pie plate or mold (filled with any non-liquid garnish) on the oven shelf and then add *half* the liquid. Put to bake at 400° F. for 2 minutes, then add the rest — taking care to leave a ¼-inch clearance from "custard" to top edge of pastry (which shrinks!).

*Nutritional benefit* is found from making possible a new variety of easily prepared, low-cost, high-protein open pies such as Quiche Lorraine (per slice): 570 calories; 15.5 g. protein; 32.2 g. carbohydrate; 41.8 g. fat. The fat can be reduced by replacing the bacon with lean ham, thinly sliced.

*Sense advantage.* This method provides good visual appearance and helps to keep the base free from "sog" (see above) which occurs because the overfilled mix can boil up to the rim and float underneath (since the crust shrinks away from the side of the pie plate).

# Raised Pies $

### INGREDIENTS:

5 ounces lard
¾ cup water
1 lb. flour
½ teaspoon salt
6 1-inch cubes of meat
Salt to season
Ground black peppercorn to season
1 beaten egg
Jelly stock to fill
Beef stock — simmer 4 hours
1 veal knuckle

*This is another one of those methods that needs ample illustration. The method of molding took me three days of testing to develop. I hope it works as well for you — first time!*

**Step 1.** Boil lard with ¾ cup water. Place 1 pound of sifted flour and salt into a basin. Stand the basin in warm water.

**Step 2.** Add the boiling lard and water to the flour, mixing in well. Note that the bowl is still in the hot water.

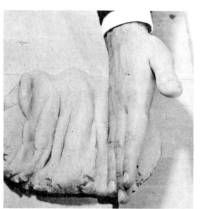

**Step 3.** Blend the dough on the board by using "poor man's karate" technique! When it is smooth and pliable (and still hot), roll it into a loaf shape.

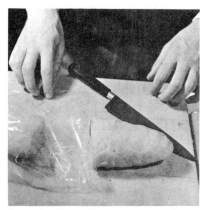

**Step 4.** Cut off a quarter of the dough and put it into a plastic bag to keep it moist. This will be used for the tops.

# Raised Pies | *continued*

**Step 5.** Upend a 2-pound bottling jar and dust it well with flour. Also dust the piece of dough.

**Step 6.** Place the dough onto the jar and mold it carefully so that it is roughly ¼-inch thick — no less. Cut a cross on top. This helps to release the dough from the jar.

**Step 7.** Clip a piece of double-folded paper around the paste and then upend and pour hot water into the jar. The dough shell will slide off easily.

**Step 8.** Fill the pie with 1-inch cubes of meat. Season well and half fill with water or stock. Cover with reserved dough and seal the top securely. Brush with egg before baking. Make a steam hole in the crust and bake at 350° F. for 1½ hours. After 1 hour remove the paper. When cooked, remove and pour in some jelly stock through the steam hole. Cool and then serve.

# eggs & pancakes

# eggs & pancakes

# eggs & pancakes

# eggs & pancakes

# Boiled Eggs

*I have two great ambitions in life. One is to be the Brigade of Guards officer who actually troops the Colour at the famous Horseguards' Parade ceremony. The other is to eat my daily breakfast of two boiled eggs in a heavily encrusted, elegant silver egg cup — with a long, slender, silver egg spoon. As I am unlikely to achieve the former, have you by chance got such an egg cup to spare?*

**Step 1.** No matter which way you like to cook eggs, they should *always* be taken from the refrigerator the night before. *Cold eggs don't cook well.* Prick the "blunt end" of the egg with a pin. This helps equalize pressure and stops shell from cracking.

**Step 2.** Bring water to the boil. Place eggs in a wire basket. By doing this you run less risk of cracking, and they all get the same time. Take the pan from the heat and add the eggs. Return pan to heat and boil. DO NOT ADD VINEGAR TO WATER — PLEASE.

**Step 3.** The egg on the extreme right has had 3 minutes — it is still very runny. The next has had 3½ minutes — the white has just set. The last opened has received 4½ minutes and the yolk is just soft but not runny. On the left is my method of opening an egg.

**Step 4.** In our family we eat the egg before the cereal. In this way the eggs are eaten at their best, and we can all sit down together. It makes a refreshing change, actually, and we think it's sensible.

# Dilled Eggs

**Serves 1**

### INGREDIENTS:

1 boiled egg
1 lettuce leaf
Light mayonnaise (page 214)
Dill weed to season
Cayenne pepper to season
4 anchovy fillets

### PREPARATION

1. Halve the egg; lay both sides yolk down on a crisp leaf of lettuce, and coat with Light Mayonnaise seasoned with dill and cayenne.

2. This can be garnished with two anchovy fillets crisscrossed over the top of each half. An excellent light salad meal that fills the mouth full of flavor.

# Poached-Egg Sandwich

**Serves 1**

### INGREDIENTS:

1 English muffin
1 slice cooked Canadian Bacon
1 slice Swiss cheese
1 poached egg
Parsley to garnish
Paprika to garnish

### PREPARATION

1. Toast the English muffin, cover with Canadian bacon, and melt Swiss cheese on top under the broiler.

2. Slip a good poached egg on top and dust with parsley and paprika. Serve as a hearty breakfast or lunch dish.

# HINTS

## Eggs — Size Fixation?

A quick look at the egg counter in a supermarket will be enough to at least raise a question in your mind. What is the real difference between Extra Large, Medium Grade "A", and Small? We made two identical sponge cakes in the same oven at the same time — the only difference was that one was made with Extra Large eggs and the other with the same number of Medium Grade "A". At the time of writing the gap between these eggs was about 16¢ to 20¢ per dozen. An identical test on soufflés was then run. Both the cake and the soufflé worked just fine with no discernable difference. We now buy only Medium for every purpose, from the breakfast egg to the test sponge cake.

*Nutritional advantage:* by using only "Mediums" we do get a small reduction in cholesterol over Large and Extra Large.

Sense advantage does appear to be a little negative, but in actual fact you get used to it very soon. I'm really talking about the "straight egg" (poached, fried, boiled) problem of size fixation. We feel we should have a "big egg", because it looks like all is right with the world. Well, this kind of size fixation, when we don't *need* that extra food, means that all is *not* right with the world!

*Buying notes on grades:*

"AA"  Covers small area; white is thick and stands high, yolk is firm and high. These are good for frying and poaching.

"A"  Covers medium area; white is reasonably thick.

"B"  Used for general cooking and baking.

## Boiled Eggs That Don't Crack

Various techniques exist to produce a perfectly boiled egg but none so inexpensive and yet so technically perfect as...the pin. The idea is simply to equalize the pressure inside the shell when the temperature starts to expand the trapped air. Puncture the blunt end of the eggs (where the air is), put them in a wire basket, and lower them all into water that has just been taken off the boil.

Nutritional advantage comes, in my opinion, from the fact that the egg has exceptionally high quality protein — so high that it is used as a model for other foods. You get 6 grams of protein per egg, and it's a complete protein. When you boil the egg, you get nothing else added; it's just as God made it.

## Hard-Boiled Eggs That Shell with No Fuss

Whatever way you cook eggs, they are better when started at room temperature. Take them out ahead of time or at least warm them for 5 minutes in hot tap water if you forget. One of the finicky jobs in the kitchen is to peel hard boiled eggs. This way it is simple.

Boil water, remove from heat, lower eggs into water in a wire basket or with a slotted spoon, return to heat, and boil gently for 5 minutes. Strain water from the pan and *rustle* the eggs from side to side gently until the shells are cracked all over. Cover with ice cold water (a couple of ice cubes help) for 5 minutes. Then simply twist off the shells. If you cut them open, you will notice that there is no darkened green ring around the yolk — we cured that one by cooling the egg quickly.

# Poached Eggs

*In one of my parents' hotels we kept chickens (not in the hotel, you understand). When their eggs were poached, they were perfectly formed. To get a perfect poached egg you really need a very fresh egg. I have found a way to reproduce this shape using the average egg.*

*It is given below. As a matter of interest, I haven't broken one yolk since I adopted this technique, and, best of all, there is no salt or vinegar added to the water.*

**Step 1.** Leave the eggs out of the refrigerator overnight. Place a frying pan on low heat and brush on a little melted butter.

**Step 2.** Bring water to the boil and lower the eggs into the water in a basket. Boil for 10 or even 20 seconds if the eggs are very "old", and then remove them. Pour the boiling water into the buttered pan.

**Step 3.** Break and add the eggs in a clockwise fashion — this keeps them in length-of-cooking-time order. Shake the pan gently after adding each egg. Cook at a low heat (just before simmer). Allow 3-to-4 minutes per egg until the white is fully set.

**Step 4.** Lift the eggs with a perforated spoon. Where the eggs are required for a made-up dish, they can be slipped into a bowl of cold water (on left) and reheated later. For normal use, however, I don't recommend this precookery, as it does tend to reduce some of the egg's fabulous food value.

# Jena Eggs

**Serves 1**

**INGREDIENTS:**

1 fluid ounce cream
Peppercorns to season
Salt to season
Enough salmon or liver sausage or
creamed shrimp or mushrooms
for 1 serving

*This is an unusual method of cooking eggs, but I hope it will catch on. They can be cooked only in a special container called an Eierkocher made by the Jenaer Glaswerk Schott & Gen., Mainz, Germany. As you will see, the possibilities for variety are unlimited, but my favorite is the one used here to describe the basic method—just cream, seasoning, and a touch of parsley — perfection. I'm delighted that I can write, rather than talk, about the container; you try to pronounce it!*

**Step 1.** Place cream in bottom of the container. Add some freshly ground black peppercorns and a little salt. For variety you can add a little salmon, liver sausage, creamed shrimp, or mushrooms, etc. Break an egg on top.

**Step 2.** Hold the container firmly and fix the spring clip.

**Step 3.** Place in boiling water, the level of which just comes to the base of the clips. Cover with a lid. Cook for 4 minutes soft or 5 minutes medium.

**Step 4.** Serve in the glass with a sprinkle of fresh, chopped parsley.

# Jena Eggs with Salmon

**Serves 4**

**INGREDIENTS:**

½ cup salmon
4 teaspoons lemon juice
4 teaspoons parsley stalks
White peppercorns to season
4 tablespoons cream
4 eggs
Parsley to garnish
Paprika to garnish

**PREPARATION**

1. Set out 4 single-egg-size Jena containers. Put a pan of water on to boil.

2. Measure the cream; chop the parsley stalks, and the parsley garnish.

3. Cream the salmon with lemon juice, parsley stalks, and ground pepper. Do not add salt.

4. Place equal amounts in the bottom of each Jena container and add 1 tablespoon of cream per container.

5. Drop an egg into each on top of the cream. Seal and place in the boiling water.

6. Cook for seven minutes, take the containers from the water, and remove the tops. Dust with paprika and chopped celery.

# Jena Eggs with Bacon and Mushrooms

**Serves 4**

**INGREDIENTS:**

4 bacon slices
4 mushrooms
1 tablespoon lemon juice
4 tablespoons cream
4 eggs
1 tablespoon chopped chives

**PREPARATION**

1. Set out 4 double-egg-size Jena containers. Put a pan of water on to boil.

2. Finely slice bacon slices and very finely slice mushrooms. Chop the chives.

3. Fry the bacon slices until crisp, then remove from the pan.

4. Fry the mushrooms lightly in the bacon fat (1 minute) with the lemon juice. Remove and mix with the bacon.

5. Divide the bacon and mushroom mixture between the 4 containers and press it down. Don't add salt.

6. Add 1 tablespoon of cream per container and drop an egg on top. Seal and cook for 7 minutes.

7. Remove tops and serve dusted with chopped chives.

# Scrambled Eggs

### Serves 2

### INGREDIENTS:

2 tablespoons butter (½ oz.)
4 eggs
Salt to season
Pepper to season
¼ cup milk (1 tablespoon per egg)

> *When I first devised this recipe, my young son Andrew, had just started to cook. His first attempt was scrambled egg. He made it exactly as shown on this page — it was perfect, wonderfully soft, creamy, and seasoned fit for the gods.*

**Step 1.** Leave the eggs out of the refrigerator overnight so they will be at room temperature. Place ½ ounce butter into a small pan and melt.

**Step 2.** Cut up another ½ ounce butter into small pieces. Beat 4 eggs in a bowl; add salt and freshly ground white peppercorns.

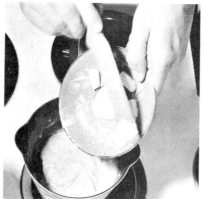

**Step 3.** Pour beaten eggs onto the melted butter and stir with a wooden spoon. Add the pieces of butter from time to time during setting period.

**Step 4.** When the eggs are just set, add ¼ cup milk and stir in well until the mixture is hot. By adding cold milk at the end, you arrest cookery at just the right moment, otherwise the eggs can rapidly become dry, even in the time they take to serve.

# Savory Omelets

### INGREDIENTS:

1 tablespoon butter (½ oz.)
2 eggs
2 tablespoons cream
Garlic salt to season
Ground white peppercorns
to season

*The omelet is the perfect instant meal for the do-it-yourselfer. You can add virtually anything that happens to be lying around, and the result is filling and extremely good for you. Some people are scared of omelets. I hope these instructions will cure this lack of confidence and that you will share in this "instant gastronomy."*

**Step 1.** Break eggs into a small bowl. Heat a 7-inch frying pan and add butter. Note the plates sitting on top of the saucepan of boiling water on the right of the picture. This is the best way to keep them hot and at hand when each omelet is cooked.

**Step 2.** Beat the eggs gently with the cream so that it blends with the yolks. Don't beat to a froth. Season with garlic salt and freshly ground white peppercorns.

**Step 3.** When the butter in the pan starts to go a very light brown, add the eggs and stir vigorously with a fork, moving the pan at the same time. Fold both edges into the center when the top of the mixture is still runny.

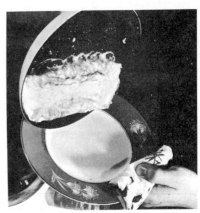

**Step 4.** If the bottom of the omelet should stick, then run a little butter along the edge (as shown above) and slip a spatula underneath to loosen. Turn onto hot plate and brush with a little butter. Serve and insist that it is eaten — immediately!

# Sweet Omelets

**Serves 2**

### INGREDIENTS:

4 eggs, separated
1 tablespoon water
¼ teaspoon salt
2 tablespoons fruit syrup
2 tablespoons superfine granulated sugar
½ tablespoon butter
Sugar to sprinkle

*There are very few classical exceptions to the rule that "savory omelets are solid in texture and sweet omelets are fluffy." If there is anything that I really detest, it is fluffy savory omelets. Hence I dedicate this recipe to that grand array of luxurious edibles — "afters."*

*Fillings can include fresh peaches, fresh strawberries, or plumped raisins and blanched almonds. You can fill lychee nuts with raspberries or use other fresh fruits in a low-fat yogurt binding. Steer clear of the regular canned syruped fruits and preserves, though. Their sugar content undoes the benefit.*

**Step 1.** Whip egg whites in a basin, adding water and salt. Add your choice of fruit syrup and superfine granulated sugar to the yolks, and beat together. When the whites are very stiff, fold in the yolk mixture gently. Add a small piece of butter to a heated pan and wait until the edges of the butter froth. Add mixture all at once and stir quickly using a spatula.

**Step 2.** Bang the pan onto the element a couple of times to settle the mixture. Smooth the surface with a knife.

**Step 3.** Place immediately under a moderate heat broiler and lightly cook surface until small bubbles or blisters appear and the level has risen.

**Step 4.** After the mixture leaves the broiler you can add your filling to the center of the omelet. Loosen the edges and carefully fold it out of the pan with the spatula. Serve sprinkled with sugar.

# HINTS

## Scrambled Egg Variations

Add some finely chopped small chilis to the pan just before you add the eggs. One level tablespoon per person is fine. They are very hot and obvious, so be sure that everyone likes the idea.

Another idea is to stir in very small cubes of mild cheese when the eggs have set (just before adding the milk); they *just melt* when being served — delicious!

## Omelet Pan Cured of Rust and Sticking

It is quite easy nowadays to buy a generally low cost pan made of steel or cast iron with an attached handle of the same material. They are heavy, spread the heat well, but, unfortunately, they rust. This needs to be taken into consideration when caring for them. The handles also get dangerously hot.

We advise buying an omelet/crepe pan 7 inches in diameter, of plain iron metal. This type is seldom, if ever, washed. Washing creates moisture and moisture means rust whereas constant absorption of fat means a non-stick finish.

In order to prepare such a pan for use, you must "cure" it with 1 cup inexpensive cooking oil. First *wash the pan* in plenty of boiling hot, soapy water and rinse thoroughly; *place it wet* on the stove to dry. When completely dry, add 2 tablespoons (⅛ cup) oil and leave at medium high heat for 5 minutes. Add enough salt to absorb all the oil and rub it into the pan with paper towels or newspaper. Repeat this action 8 times until the cup of oil has been used. Then lightly oil the pan all over and use when you need it, cleaning with oil and salt after each use.

# Soufflés $ ⅋

## INGREDIENTS:

4 tablespoons butter
5 tablespoons flour
1¼ cups milk
Salt to season
Ground white peppercorns to season
6 egg yolks
1 cup cheddar cheese, finely shredded
7 egg whites

> *I had the honor once to attend a luncheon given for me by the Home Science class of Te Puke High School in the Bay of Plenty, New Zealand. The students decided that I should be served with a cheese soufflé. The Te Puke Soufflé was so good that I asked one Maori student if I might have the recipe. She immediately brought me back a second helping — a happy mistake on her part. I got the recipe later.*

**Step 1.** Make a basic white sauce with butter, plain flour, and milk (see page 217). Season highly with salt and freshly ground white peppercorns. Cool the sauce and then mix in the yolks of 6 eggs. Finally, add 1 cup finely shredded cheddar cheese. Beat until very smooth.

**Step 2.** Very gently add the sauce to the whipped whites of 7 eggs. Do not overdo this mixing — many a soufflé is ruined at this point.

**Step 3.** Butter a soufflé dish and fix a band of foil about the dish, raised 3 inches from the rim. Scrape the mixture into the dish and smooth the surface.

**Step 4.** Place on the bottom shelf of an oven preheated to 350º F. with a solid baking sheet. Place soufflé on this sheet and bake undisturbed for 30 minutes. To test doneness, give the baking sheet a sharp tug. If the soufflé top wobbles, give it a little longer.

# Skillet Soufflé

**Serves 4**

### INGREDIENTS:

1 tablespoon butter
6 eggs
1½ cups grated cheese
(¼ cup per egg)
Salt to season
Pepper to season

### PREPARATION

1. Separate eggs and beat the whites.

2. Add grated cheese to egg yolks, season, and fold in whites (see technique in basic recipe).

3. Preheat broiler. Take large omelet pan, melt butter, and pour in egg-and-cheese mixture. Fold for 2 minutes with a spatula, then place under broiler to brown. Serve immediately.

# Apple-Lemon Soufflé

**Serves 6-8**

### INGREDIENTS:

2 envelopes unflavored gelatin
2 cups cold water
4 teaspoons grated lemon peel
3 tablespoons sugar
Pinch of salt
2 apples, pared, cored, and grated (Granny Smiths are good)
Juice of 1 lemon (¼ cup)
4 egg whites
1 cup plain yogurt (8 oz.)
2 tablespoons wheat germ

Use a regular soufflé dish or a 7 in. or smaller springform pan.

### PREPARATION

1. Assemble all ingredients; do not grate apples until the last possible moment. Bring egg whites to room temperature.

2. Sprinkle gelatin over ½ cup cold water in a small saucepan. Stir over low heat to dissolve.

3. Remove saucepan from heat. Stir in grated lemon peel, sugar, salt, and remaining 1½ cups cold water.

4. Chill gelatin until syrupy. Then beat gelatin until foamy.

5. Grate apples, cover, and toss well with lemon juice. Fold grated apples into gelatin.

6. Beat egg whites until stiff but not dry. Fold egg whites into gelatin mixture and pour into greased, prepared pan. Refrigerate 3 hours or until firm.

7. Just before serving, unmold and frost with 8 ounces plain yogurt. Dust with 2 tablespoons wheat germ. Serve immediately.

If 8 servings, then 71 calories/serving. If 6 servings, then 95 calories/serving.

*Desserts are of real value following a meal only if they delight and freshen, not saturate and make heavy. This soufflé is definitely a freshener!*

# Spinach Soufflé

## INGREDIENTS:

1 lb. trimmed fresh spinach or
2 8-ounce packages frozen spinach
1 tablespoon sesame/safflower oil
(page 186)
1 tablespoon arrowroot
¼ cup whole milk
Black pepper
Nutmeg
Salt
3 egg yolks
4 egg whites

*Soufflés tend to worry some folks, but this one isn't the kind that needs to rear up out of the dish like a status-seeking monster. It is basically a lightened, creamed spinach that is easy to fix and earns many compliments.*

## PREPARATION

1. Weigh 1 lb. trimmed spinach or defrost 2 packages of frozen spinach. Cut off heavy stalks before weighing. Wash fresh spinach well in at least 4 rinse-waters.

2. Place in a heavy-based large saucepan with 1 tablespoon sesame/safflower oil well-mixed into the leaves before you start. Cook over medium heat, lid on, for 4 minutes. Stir and toss. Pour off any water in the bottom and remove cooked leaves.

3. Blend until smooth in blender/chopper at medium speed. Pour into a hand sieve and press out all surplus moisture. Retain this juice.

4. Turn chopped spinach into a small saucepan and cook over medium heat to remove the excess moisture.

5. Add the arrowroot and pour in the reserved juice gradually, together with the milk. Season this mix highly with black pepper, nutmeg, and a *touch* of salt.

6. Add the egg yolks, stir in well, and let cool on a plate. Beat egg whites very stiff and fold in.

7. Bake in a 7-in. soufflé dish at 400° F. for 20 minutes.

Serve immediately. This can also be sent to the table in individual small dishes.

# HINTS

## Egg Whites

Essential to the success of so many dishes — cakes, souffle's, some special sauces — is the correct whipping of egg white.

I have found a dramatic advantage in using a copper bowl with a loop ring, a wet cloth under the bowl to hold it steady, a little cold water, a pinch of salt, and a large flexible hand whisk.

Simply add 1 tablespoon cold water and 1 level teaspoon salt to each 4 egg whites to be whipped, and beat in a grease-free bowl *just before they are needed.* You get better volume, it takes less time than the electric machine, and the whites *perform* better.

Caution: I must caution you about copper bowls. They look nifty, but they have one real problem. If the food being placed in a copper bowl is acidic and if the bowl is tarnished, then copper ions will migrate into the food at a level considered unsafe. Accordingly, be *absolutely certain that all your copper is kept tarnish-free!* I wipe out my bowl with salt and lemon skin until it is burnished bright. I then rinse it very well and dry it before use.

*Nutritional advantage* comes from the fact that egg white provides visual bulk for only 15 calories per egg white. Obviously, the better the eggs are beaten the better they will hold up and work in souffle's, cakes, sauces — in so many different ways. A skillet souffle' is one excellent use because here you avoid the necessity of the sauce base called for in other souffle's and thus reduce the fat and calories.

## Egg Whites Folded in

After carefully beating egg whites until they are peaked but not dry, many people then proceed to reduce their "spacious" effect by overmixing into the basic flavor base.

The best way to avoid overmixing is to add 25 percent of the whites to the base sauce and whip it lightly but *well.* This lightened sauce is then poured into the egg white bowl, and the mix is incorporated by turning the bowl counterclockwise and stirring clockwise with a spoon, lifting the mix up through the center. (See sketch.) Do this very lightly until just combined.

*P.S.* Don't forget to thoroughly season (over-season) the base sauce to compensate for the neutral egg white volume.

Nutritional advantage comes again from the use of egg whites (at only 15 calories each) to generate visual bulk, thereby cutting back on fats and calories. A large serving of a good cheese souffle' provides 471 calories (good); 27.8 g. protein (good); 15.1 g. carbohydrate (good); 15.4 g. saturated fat.

Budget advantage is very good with souffle's. They can and do provide complete satisfaction at only a fraction of the ordinary cost of fixing an adequate protein dinner.

1

2

3

# Pancakes

> *Pancakes can be made quite some time before they are served — in fact up to 12 hours in advance, providing they are prepared and kept in the way shown below. I think they are a very valuable asset in any repertoire of recipes, and can be used for sweet and savory purposes.*

**Step 1.** Make up a batter mixture (page 151). Allow to stand. Melt 2 tablespoons butter in the pancake pan and add this to the batter, mixing it in well. This provides each pancake with its own buttering and saves repeated greasing of the pan. It also helps to keep the pancake if it is prepared ahead of time.

**Step 2.** Pour the mixture into the heated pan and roll it around so that it covers the pan base. Do not allow it to creep up the sides, otherwise you will get hard crisp edges.

**Step 3.** Cook until small waxy bubbles appear on the surface. Then push a spatula under the pancake in one smooth movement; lift the pancake and turn it over. This is a much less demanding technique than trying to toss the beastly thing!

**Step 4.** When the second side is cooked, slide it out onto a hot plate, and brush the surface with a little melted butter. Cover with a clean cloth. You can keep them covered in the refrigerator for up to 12 hours. Reheat in the warming oven and serve.

# Egg Batter

**Yields 8 8-inch pancakes**

### INGREDIENTS:

1 cup flour
1 pinch salt
1 pinch white pepper
1 egg yolk
1 egg
1¼ cups milk
1 tablespoon butter

### PREPARATION

1. Combine flour, salt, and pepper, and make a well in the center of the mixture. Separate the yolk of 1 egg, and add it to another whole egg and the milk; now pour gradually into the well in the dry ingredients, beating all the time.

2. Melt butter, allow to cool slightly, and add to the mixture, beating well. Leave covered for at least 4 hours to allow starch cells to swell and absorb liquid.

This batter can be used for frying fish, fritters, sweetbreads, brains, or making pancakes.

# Crepes Antonin Careme

## ("Reformed" from the original)

**Serves 8**

### INGREDIENTS:

1 2¾-lb. whole fryer
1 onion, chopped
1 medium carrot, chopped
1 cup sliced celery
1 stick butter (¼ lb.)
¾ cup flour
1 cup milk
Salt
Pepper
Nutmeg
1½ cups chicken stock
½ cup white grape juice
2 teaspoons rice vinegar
4 tablespoons grated Parmesan cheese
Cayenne
Finely chopped parsley
CREPE BATTER:
¾ cup flour
1 whole egg
1 egg yolk
1⅛ cups milk
½ teaspoon salt
2 tablespoons butter, melted, for batter
1 tablespoon butter, melted, for skillet

### PREPARATION

1. Make crepe batter — mix flour, egg, egg yolk, milk, and salt together until smooth. Allow to stand 4 hours.

2. Meanwhile cut chicken into quarters; place in large saucepan with onion and carrot. Cover with water, bring to boil, and simmer 45 minutes or until tender.

3. Remove chicken from bone; cut meat into small pieces. Reduce chicken stock to 1½ cups. Strain. Cook celery in boiling salted water for 5 minutes, drain, and add to chicken.

4. Make crepes by melting 1 tablespoon butter in 8-inch skillet. Place small amount of batter in pan and roll around so that it covers bottom evenly. Cook until waxy bubbles appear on surface, turn with spatula and cook on other side. Remove to plate and continue until 8 crepes are made.

5. Melt butter in saucepan and stir in flour. Whisk in milk gradually to make thick sauce. Season with salt, pepper, and nutmeg. Stir in chicken stock and simmer 10 minutes. Stir in grape juice and vinegar and simmer 5 minutes longer.

6. Mix 1 cup of sauce with chicken-celery mixture. Stir 3 tablespoons Parmesan cheese into remaining sauce.

7. Place a heaping tablespoon of chicken-celery mixture in center of each crepe. Fold and turn over. Spoon cheese sauce over crepes. Sprinkle with remaining cheese and slide under broiler to brown (about 5 minutes). Dust with cayenne and parsley to serve.

# Sourdough, Homemade

### INGREDIENTS:

1 cup whole milk
1-1½ cups flour
Water

> ❝ *I'm not a sourdough fan, but I know many who are so here is the basic starter recipe.* ❞

### PREPARATION

1. Place the whole milk in a glass jar with a loose lid. Allow to stand at room temperature for 24 hours. Then stir in the flour and cover loosely for 2-5 days at room temperature (80° F. is excellent for 2 days, or winter "work" at 60° F. could take 5 days).

2. Reserve ¼ cup to use as a base for the next batch. To the remainder, add water at the rate of ½ cup water to 1 cup flour-and-milk mixture (an extra ¼ cup may be needed if the mixture is too firm). Let it bubble another 6-8 hours.

   Refrigerate starter between uses. It will keep 2-3 weeks undisturbed, but is better if used and refreshed more frequently. This starter can also be frozen for 4-6 months.

## HINTS

# A Filled Crepe

There appears to be a feeling that the crepe is a real diet villain. But when compared to the typical hamburger bun, the crepe has only 15 more calories.

That's hardly villainous, especially when you consider the variety plus factors.

*Sense advantage:* a filled crepe (thin pancake) has much more appeal than a hamburger bun (for me at least!)

*Budget advantage* comes from a small but satisfactory amount of protein (meat, poultry, or seafood) being combined with low-calorie sauces to provide a large attractive serving.

# potatoes, rice & pasta

# potatoes, rice & pasta

# potatoes, rice & pasta

# potatoes, rice & pasta

# Boiled Potatoes

*Surprising as it may seem, the leading chefs in London test their potential cooks by asking them either to cook a plain omelet or to boil potatoes. It isn't as easy as some people think to boil the humble spud, and this probably accounts for the fact that it is, in my opinion, the perfect way of cooking potatoes.*

**Step 1.** Select potatoes of even size and scrub well. Place in a saucepan and, in the case of new potatoes, cover them with boiling water. Old potatoes should still be boiled with skins on unless very badly marked, but they should be put in cold water.

**Step 2.** Add salt and a sprig each of parsley and mint. Make sure that the water level covers the potatoes, and then cover with a close-fitting lid. Boil for 20-25 minutes according to size.

**Step 3.** To see if potato is done, drive a thin knife or skewer into it. When lifted, it should slide off. With old potatoes, place under cold running water and peel off the skin with a knife. For new potatoes, place under cold running water and rub between your hands to remove skin. Put back into the dry saucepan, cover with a clean cloth, and "steam" for 3 minutes on a low heat (if gas, use heat pad to avoid direct contact).

**Step 4.** After the potatoes have dried out they will be floury on the outside. Add butter and a small handful of mixed chopped mint and parsley. Turn gently until coated with buttered herbs, then serve immediately.

# Plated Cabbage

**Serves 4**

### INGREDIENTS:

4 potatoes (¼ lb. each)
1 medium cabbage
2 medium onions
1 tablespoon safflower oil
1 tablespoon soy sauce
1 tablespoon chopped parsley
½ teaspoon dill weed
1 teaspoon white pepper
Salt to season
Pepper to season
2 tablespoons melted butter
1 medium tomato

### PREPARATION

1. Boil potatoes in their skins for 20 minutes and dry out in a covered, warm, dry saucepan (see basic recipe, page 154 for technique).

2. Strip off a dozen, dark green outer leaves from the cabbage and cut from them the heavy, white center veins. Boil the leaves rapidly for 2 minutes until bright green; strain and cool in a bowl of iced water.

3. Peel and finely slice the onions; fry in a large, deep pan with the safflower oil. Add 1 pound finely sliced cabbage (¼-inch thick strips). Cover and cook over medium heat for 4 minutes, then add soy sauce, chopped parsley, dill weed, and white pepper. Stir together thoroughly and cover for 2 minutes.

4. Grease (or oil) a large tart or pie dish and cover with the 6 best green cabbage leaves. Slice the potatoes and lay them over the entire surface. Season with salt and pepper, and coat with 2 tablespoons of melted butter.

5. Then slice tomato into very thin slices. Make a layer of these over the potatoes; season with salt and pepper.

6. Now heap on top the chopped seasoned cabbage, cover with the remaining green leaves, and press down tightly with another plate. Reheat by placing the dish *over* a boiling saucepan. Serve on the plate cut up into four like a green pie!

P.S. Sliced and fried bacon can be added for extra flavor.

This dish is high in Vitamin C from cabbage, potato, and tomato; it also has significant Vitamin A from tomato and cabbage. Cooking the potatoes in their skins and the cabbage for only a short time preserves maximum Vitamin C.

# HINTS

## Potato

Fad dietmongers frequently fall upon the potato as a starch/carbohydrate/calorie-filled no-no! In truth it only becomes a villain because of what you put on it. Look at this potato (which, incidentally, weighs 100 grams or 3½ ounces).
- Raw, it has only 76 calories, the same as parsnip and sweet corn, and it contains 20 mg. of Vitamin C, about one-third the daily recommended allowance of 55-60 milligrams.
- Baked in its jacket, the potato has 90 calories (due to moisture loss) and the same 20 mg. Vitamin C.
- Baked in its jacket, with 2 tablespoons butter added, it is now 290 calories and 20 mg. Vitamin C.
- Baked in its jacket, plus 3 tablespoons sour cream/chives, it has 165 calories and 20 mg. Vitamin C.
- Boiled in its skin but with the skin removed after cooking, it has 77 calories, which is same as it had raw *(but more if steam dried,* see page 154) and 16 mg. Vitamin C.
- Skinned and then boiled, it has 65 calories and 16 mg.* Vitamin C.
- Boiled, skinned, and buttered (2 tablespoons per serving), it has 277 calories and 16 mg. Vitamin C.
- Mashed with milk added, a ½-cup serving has 63 calories; plus 1 teaspoon of butter, 94 calories — and 9 mg. Vitamin C.
- French fries (100 g. or 20 pieces), 310 calories and 21 mg. Vitamin C.

*Nutrition comment:* to help you with your estimate of the effect of the additive, let's just give you a list of the enemies.
- 1 teaspoon butter (1 pat)          35 calories
- 1 tablespoon butter          100 calories
- ¼ cup milk for mashed potatoes          40 calories (about 10 calories per serving)

- 2 tablespoons sour cream          50 calories
- 1 teaspoon blue cheese          18 calories
- 2 tablespoons skim milk, yogurt          16 calories
- ¼ teaspoon dill weed          1–?

The recipe idea after all this information is really up to you!

*Only 4 mg. are lost when skinned — this proves that the major Vitamin C content is *not* in the skin.

# Baked Potatoes

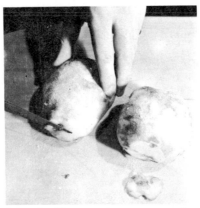

**Step 1.** Choose large, even-size, good-quality potatoes; scrub well and dust thoroughly with salt. This saves the outer skin from being scorched. Trim off a thin slice from one end. If you have ever experienced an exploded potato, you will understand the reason for this!

**Step 2.** Place the potatoes in an oven set at 350° F. and bake for 1½ hours. It is only economical to use this method when some other food requires the oven to be operated as in this case.

**Step 3.** Fold a cloth so that it can be slipped like a noose around the potato and cut deeply into the center to form a cross.

**Step 4.** Squeeze the cloth, gently at first, and then harder. The object is to fracture the potato flesh without damaging the skin. Gradually the cut will open out as shown above. A dab of butter, a touch of cream, a sprinkle of chives, and you can eat.

# Special Baked Potatoes

**Serves 1**

### INGREDIENTS:

4 slices bacon
1 baked potato
Milk to mix
Salt to season
White pepper to season
1 tablespoon chopped,
pickled walnuts
Parsley to garnish

### PREPARATION

1. Purchase a jar of pickled walnuts from a gourmet shop.

2. Cut bacon into 1-inch sections and fry until crisp.

3. Open the baked potato and spoon out all the flesh. Beat this smooth with a little milk, season with salt and pepper.

4. Now add chopped pickled walnuts, bacon, and top with freshly chopped parsley. Serve.

It looks and tastes wonderful! You can use the bacon alone, but the walnuts add a special touch.

# Reformed Baked Potato

**Serves 1**

### INGREDIENTS:

1 large Idaho potato
(10-12 ounces)
Salt to season
1 tablespoon grated
Parmesan cheese

### PREPARATION

1. Scrub the potato, preferably a Burbank Russet from Idaho, (which can be cut in half for good size portions). While the potato is still wet, roll it in a *little* salt. Trim a penny-sized piece from one end to allow steam to escape, and bake on the oven rack at 375° F. for 1 hour 15 minutes.

2. Before cutting open, wrap a towel about the potato and squeeze it carefully to break up the inside flesh; then cut and dust with grated parmesan cheese, brown under the broiler, and serve dusted with parsley.

*Sense advantage* is in a wonderfully crisp exterior (which is usually steamed soggy by its foil coating) and a light floury fragrant interior topped and crusted with cheese.

*Nutrition comment*: remember it's what goes *on* that is harder to take *off*, and the 30 calories of cheese (1 tablespoon) can replace the 100 or so represented by the usual butter or polyunsaturated spreads.

For another potato recipe, see Idaho Chili Pie on page 101.

# Reformed Sour Cream

### Yields 1¼ cups

#### INGREDIENTS:

1 cup low-fat cottage cheese
½ cup buttermilk
2 teaspoons lemon juice
¼ teaspoon salt (optional)

*" I'm ready to confess! The sour cream I've used in my old-style recipes would have been better measured by the bucket. Now I'm less free with your digestion (and mine), but I still like sour cream. So we set to work to take away some of its obvious problems — and we won. Please try it for yourself. "*

#### PREPARATION

1. Measure all ingredients; set up blender; have a rubber spatula ready to use.

2. Place all ingredients in the blender and whiz on the highest speed for about 1 minute total, but turn off every 15-20 seconds and push the mixture down with the spatula. It will firm up on sitting. Store in the refrigerator. Has the same consistency and appearance as sour cream. Takes 5 minutes to prepare.

At about 485 calories per cup for the commercial sour cream and 175 calories per cup for our sour cream, you would save about 310 calories per cup or about 20 calories per tablespoon.

# Creamed Potatoes

**Serves 4**

**INGREDIENTS:**

4 potatoes
Butter
Salt to season
White peppercorns to season
Grated nutmeg to season
Cream

*My grandmother used to live in Broadstairs, near Margate, in a house called Greenshutters. The things I remember most about her are her stories about The Gold and Silver Waltz and her creamed potatoes. She taught my Treena and me to do the quick waltz — and her creamed potatoes were a meteorologist's delight.*

**Step 1.** Creamed potatoes can be made from either well-boiled (and dried) potatoes (page 154) or from baked potatoes. I prefer the latter for quality, and there is very little waste.

**Step 2.** Scoop out the potato but do not throw away the skins. We butter these and slip them under the grill to get crisp and golden. They are always eaten with great relish — especially by our children.

**Step 3.** When you mash the potato, you will see the improved quality obtained from baking. The flesh isn't waterlogged, but dry and floury.

**Step 4.** Add butter, salt, freshly ground white peppercorns, and just a touch of grated nutmeg. Beat well with a wooden spoon over the heat and add very little cream.

# HINTS

## Phase Out Cardboard Foods

Firstly a definition is in order. What is a cardboard food? Well, I feel it is a food or collection of foods put together in a factory, which replaces a food that can be prepared at home by using an easily mastered, quickly executed skill.

Let's go a little further. The food is cardboard if it costs more, has less nutritive value, doesn't look, smell, or taste as good as the home-prepared food it replaces.

Of course, this doesn't include every food we buy in a can, or a jar, or a carton, or from the freezer, because a good many products do provide us with *time*. Even if the saving is pretty small on a unit basis, the sum total of them all is substantial.

So what do we do about it?

How's this for an idea?

Take out all your cardboard foods and put them on a kitchen counter.

Now, line them up in order of how much time they appear to save you.

Example: Instant tea. You need boiling water for both, so it's only going to save you the time it takes for the tea bag to steep — about sixty seconds in a cup and four to five minutes in a pot. The time is simply waiting time, there is no labor content. This would be a small time saver.

On the other hand, you could get a product that saves considerable non-creative, semi-skilled labor time.

Example: Instant potatoes. Here you have a compact product that requires only four to five minutes of cooking as compared with the bulky natural product, which requires washing, peeling, cooking, and mashing. You could save some thirty minutes of labor time. This would be a large time saver.

It really does help if you line them up from left to right, starting with the products that save you the least time and building to those that you know save you hours!

But it isn't really that simple. What about those instant products that save a mountain of labor but are fun to make from scratch? How about instant vegetable soup? The time saved can be up to an hour, but the pure pleasure *you* might get from assembling the soup could be time well spent.

To help with the decision, since we have all the products out, I suggest that you push those products that you feel have an attractive creative appeal (if made from scratch) back to form a second rank. You can then concentrate upon the front row.

Now, jot down a list of products that replace potentially creative skills in order of their time consumption, starting with the minor time savers.

Make a second list, this time of the products that save you from dull, repetitive labor, again in order from small to large.

It is important that you make up the list in your kitchen and by your rule of thumb — because it's your time/skill factors we are discussing.

Now — it's adventure time!

Undertake to master one cardboard food skill per week, starting off with the product that will take you the least time to replace.

Before long you will be making your own yogurt (page 239), buying bulk spinach (page 182), and using fresh vegetables and fruits. You will finally master the art of making real coffee and real tea. You will combine your own herbs and spices to make your own seasonings and more, much more.

Praise the Lord — *you* will be master of your own kitchen, rich in skills.

A word of warning! Do *not* try to defeat the enemy all at once. Go gradually down the list. Stop for a while to let the skills sink in and become perfected; then move on. Also, remember that there are some truly fine instant products that really do help you and give you more time to plow back into your creative kitchen.

# Fried Potatoes

*Surely French fries must be the most popular form of potato throughout the world. Yet, when you look at it, they are seldom made in the private home. I am a "French fry fanatic." My French fries have to be crisp and stay crisp until I get them down. This requires a very special process.*

**Step 1.** Part of my fanaticism for chips is that all chips should be the same size and shape. This obviously involves cutting loss, but, as you will see, I keep the peelings and trimmings in a plastic bag and use them up as flavor thickeners in soups.

**Step 2.** I find that chips are wonderful when they get an hour's soaking in warm water with a piece of lemon to keep their color. The warming oven is a good place to keep the water at the right temperature.

**Step 3.** Warm water helps to create a gradual conversion of some surface starches to a sugar, and this, when fried, goes crisp and stays crisp. After the hour, remove and dry thoroughly.

**Step 4.** Lower into fat or oil set at 350° F. for 10 minutes, then remove. This cooks the potatoes but doesn't brown them. Increase the heat to 450° F. and return the chips. Cook for a further 3 minutes or until a crisp golden brown.

# HINTS

## Squash Chips

French-fried potatoes are one of the least satisfactory foods we have, from the nutritional aspect — yet they flourish because of the primal taste additive of salt and their color and aroma. *All* of this can be improved upon with fewer calories and less fat absorbed by using squash in lieu of potato.

Cut butternut squash into chips 3 inches long by ½ inch thick. Cook in oil for 4 minutes at 320° F., drain, and serve dusted with salt and chopped parsley.

Just in case you should decide that this is for you, I give you below the actual saving involved — computed from an experiment conducted by the Department of Scientific and Industrial Research at my request in New Zealand.

*Nutritional advantage:* French-fried potatoes were cooked for 5 minutes at 300° F. in oil, and then for 6 minutes at 375° F. French-fried squash were cooked for 4 minutes at 320° F.

The French-fried potatoes contain approximately 272 calories per 100 grams (3½ ounces). The squash chips contain approximately 190 calories per 100 grams. The squash chips thus provide fewer calories per unit weight. This is quite obviously not an overnight miracle diet (as diets go this should still be a "watch-it" food), but if the French-fry urge overwhelms you, then go squash — not potato!

*Sense advantage* lies in a pretty broad coverage. The squash fries *look* better, *taste* better, *smell* better, and have a better *texture.*

Effort problem comes up due to the extreme toughness of the squash. You need a large French-chef's knife to handle it. On the other hand, there is a saving in cooking time.

# Boiled Rice

**Serves 4**

### INGREDIENTS:

⅝ cup long-grain rice
3 pints water
1 tablespoon salt
1½ cups water

❝ *When my first book came out, it created a good deal of favorable comment from people who wanted to cook rice dishes and succeed. The traditionalists, however, reacted against some of my techniques, saying, "He has taken too many short cuts. People who like cooking are prepared to spend all day doing so." Unfortunately, these people are few and far between, and the number is getting fewer every day. This method of boiling rice was criticized, but I have yet to find a better method. Even my Chinese greengrocer uses it now!* ❞

**Step 1.** The best rice for boiling is long grain — the short grain being the finest in the world for rice puddings. Wash the rice under cold running water until not a trace of white is left in the water.

**Step 2.** Add salt to water (3 pints), bring to vigorous boil, and rain in the rice. Boil for exactly 10 minutes.

**Step 3.** Pour rice into a colander and set it on top of the saucepan in which 1½ cups water have been added. Put a lid on top of the rice and steam for 8 minutes.

**Step 4.** The rice, as you can see, is separate, fluffy, and, I can promise, delicious. It will also keep well without becoming clods of sticky Turkish delight.

# Shelly Bay Rice

**Serves 4**

### INGREDIENTS:

½ cup sultana raisins
soaked in water before measuring
½ cup bamboo shoots; or the
center core of a fresh pineapple;
or the center core of a cabbage;
or the white of chard —
in all cases finely diced to the
size of a pea
2 tablespoons soy sauce
1 medium carrot, finely diced
1½ stalks celery, finely diced
½ small onion, finely diced
1 cup long-grain rice, well washed
1 teaspoon salt
3 pints water
Garnish: a few very green raw peas

### PREPARATION

1. Soak the sultanas and finely diced vegetables in the soy sauce for at least 15 minutes before cooking.

2. Wash the rice very thoroughly. Salt the water, bring to the boil, and add the rice. Stir and leave simmering for 10 minutes.

3. Drain the rice in a colander — but please do *not* run it under either cold or hot tap water.

4. Place the colander on top of a saucepan of 1 to 1½ cups of boiling water, and add the vegetables, sultanas, and soy sauce to the rice, mixing them in well.

5. Place the saucepan lid on top of the rice and steam in this way for 5 minutes. The water level in the saucepan should not reach the bottom of the colander when it boils.

6. Turn the now perfect rice out into a warmed serving dish and serve immediately, garnished with the raw green peas.

# Cumin Rice

**Serves 4**

### INGREDIENTS:

⅔ cup long-grain rice
1 cup water
2 teaspoons ground cumin
1 tablespoon oil
2 tablespoons slivered almonds
4 tablespoons plumped raisins
Freshly ground salt and pepper
to taste

### PREPARATION

1. Measure all ingredients. Plump raisins as follows: place in a small saucepan with ½ cup water, bring to a boil, remove from heat, and allow to sit for 15-20 minutes.

2. Boil the rice gently in ½ cup water together with the cumin and a dash of salt for 10 minutes. Then put the rice in a colander and return to the same pot, cover, and steam over the lowest heat for 5 more minutes.

3. Place 1 tablespoon oil in a frying pan, add the rice, almonds, and raisins; salt and pepper to taste. Stir to warm the rice and mix the ingredients. Serve immediately.

There are 171 calories per serving.

Rice can also be used as a crust for quiche (page 128) or as a dessert (page 234).

> *We wanted to create a mild but aromatic rice dish that could be laced with bits and pieces of meat, poultry, or fish leftovers and make a democratic backdrop for them all. We found that cumin answered our need. Its delicacy reminds one of curry, without curry's heat.*

# Savory Rice Pilaf

**Serves 4**

### INGREDIENTS:

1 small onion
1½ tablespoons sesame/safflower
oil (page 186)
1 cup long-grain rice
1 sprig thyme
6 parsley stalks
1 3-inch celery stalk
1 bay leaf
2½ cups stock
Salt to season
Pepper to season

*This is my favorite rice dish — favorite because it always works and because it is as versatile as an omelet for a quick, cheap meal. It can also be done in bulk. We served it to the cast of **Who's Afraid of Virginia Woolf** after their opening night in Wellington.*

**Step 1.** Finely slice onion and shallow fry in a flameproof dish in sesame/safflower oil until softened but not colored. Wash rice well under cold running water and dry thoroughly.

**Step 2.** Add rice to onions and fry 3 minutes. Add bunch of herbs. Pour in stock. The type of stock depends on whether you have fish, chicken, beef, lamb, vegetables, etc.

**Step 3.** Add salt and freshly ground peppercorns and set in an oven preheated to 450° F. Do not cover. You can add special fillings at this stage or cook them separately and mix in at Step 4.

**Step 4.** Bake for 20 minutes, then remove herbs. You will see that all the liquid has been absorbed by the rice. This is the most wonderful rice dish I know.

# Fried Rice

**Serves 4**

### INGREDIENTS:

1 pork chop, loin cut (10 oz.)
½ green pepper (2½ oz.)
4 green onion tops (1 oz.)
4-6 radishes (2 oz.)
1 tablespoon pork grease
1 garlic clove
2 teaspoons soy sauce
¼ teaspoon fresh ginger
1 can red kidney beans (15 oz.)
2 cups cooked, dry long-grain rice

### PREPARATION

1. Cook rice only 8 minutes and spread out to steam cold. Vegetable pieces must be cut very small and symmetrically.

2. Remove excess fat from pork chop. Chop green onion tops and cut radishes into eighths; thinly slice green pepper; measure out remaining ingredients.

3. Gently fry pork chop until done (keep moist). Remove meat from pan, cut into small pieces, discard bone and fat.

4. Leave 1 tablespoon grease in skillet. Add garlic, soy sauce, and ginger. Brown the green onions and pepper, add radishes, meat, rice, and beans. Heat through and serve immediately.

*Chinese Fried Rice is an excellent vehicle for stretching one pork chop to feed three or four people. It weighs heavy in the caloric scales, but it's easy and most fragrant and attractive.*

# Pasta

**INGREDIENTS:**

1 lb. pasta
1 gallon water
1 tablespoon salt

*Pasta is wonderful when used for variety, but it should never rule the roost in famous meat-producing nations.*

**Step 1.** Bring the seasoned water to the boil and place the ends into the pot, bending the strips around as they soften. When all are covered, make sure that the pieces are separate by prodding around gently with a fork.

**Step 2.** Boil until when you bite a piece, there is resistance to the teeth. *Al dente,* this is called. It should not be so soft that it melts in the mouth. Spaghetti needs 8-12 minutes; vermicelli 6-10 minutes; macaroni 10-12 minutes; noodles (egg-made) 6-9 minutes.

**Step 3.** Once the right texture has been achieved, pour a pint of iced water, into the saucepan, stir rapidly, and pour into a colander. DO NOT RINSE UNDER RUNNING WATER.

**Step 4.** You can serve the plain pasta straight from the colander, or you can drain it well, then put it back into a pot with some clarified butter and toss it well over the heat before you serve. (I prefer butter to oil and so do a great many Italians.)

# Noodles in Stock

**Serves 4**

### INGREDIENTS:

1 tablespoon soy sauce
1 cup meat stock
½ lb. noodles
1 teaspoon arrowroot
1 tablespoon chopped parsley
Water to mix

### PREPARATION

1. Add soy sauce to good, dark, meat stock (see Stock Cubes, page 35). Bring to the boil and add dried noodles (preferably the bundled Chinese egg noodles).

2. Cook according to the package directions until "al dente" — just firm to the bite. Then turn out, retain the stock, bring it to the boil.

3. Mix arrowroot and freshly chopped parsley with a little cold water to a cream-like consistency and pour this into the boiling stock. Stir briskly, adjust the seasoning to taste, and pour over the noodles. Serve immediately.

# Spaghetti Carbonara

**Serves 4**

### INGREDIENTS:

⅔ cup ham hock "bacon meat" (or bacon slices*)
2½ cups ice water
½ cup grated Parmesan cheese
3 eggs
Black pepper to season
Salt to season
10 ounces spaghetti
1 tablespoon safflower oil
1 tablespoon fresh chopped parsley

### PREPARATION

1. Finely dice bacon into ¼-inch cubes. Place pot of salted water on high heat. Have 2½ cups of ice water ready in refrigerator.

2. Finely grate the Parmesan cheese. Beat the whole eggs in a bowl with a fork and season with black pepper and a *little* salt.

3. "Curl" spaghetti into boiling salted water and cook for approximately 8 minutes until *al dente* (just tender).

4. Take pan from the heat and add the iced water. Stir and pour into a colander. *Do not rinse.*

5. In a large saucepan, fry the finely cubed meat in the oil until lightly crisped.

6. Add the drained spaghetti and toss until completely coated in the oil and bacon fat.

7. Pour in the beaten eggs and fold over and over in order to cook the eggs completely.

8. You can add half the cheese and toss again or serve the cheese separately if some members of your family prefer the taste of uncooked cheese.

9. Turn onto a dark platter or into a pottery casserole dish. Dust with parsley and serve immediately.

*Hock bacon can reduce the cost.

# HINTS

## Spaghetti Al Dente

The best cooked spaghetti is firm to the teeth ("al dente") and doesn't stick to itself! To achieve this we cook the spaghetti in vigorously boiling salted water for about 8 minutes (varies according to the manufacturer). When cooked, for every ½ lb. of spaghetti, add 1 pint of *ice* cold water to the pan, stir twice, and turn the pasta out into a colander ready for use. When it is drained, toss it in a little oil or butter or mixture of the two, season, sauce, or garnish according to the recipe, and serve *instantly* — it should never sit and steam itself flaccid!

## Bulk Parmesan

And now here we are with a good, tangible saving that also delivers on the emotional front: the purchase a good local Parmesan in its dry "block" condition as against the local or imported pregrated and packaged variety. The disadvantage is that you will have heavy rind on the bulk; on the other hand you will get a stale soapy taste with the pregrated. All in all we found the local bulk Parmesan best for price and flavor, with imported bulk a close runner-up. The worst buy was the local grated — it tastes awful and costs about twice as much as the bulk!

*Effort Advantage:* I suggest you use either a small rotary hand grater available in all good gourmet departments, or a plain metal grater which is cheap and works very well if you watch your fingers!

*Other ideas:* add it to pasta, such as spaghetti (see page 169); use over Baked Potatoes (page 157); put it on filled Crepes (page 152). Or improve a mixed vegetable soup by adding fresh grated cheese. Just grate it right in. The taste addition is fantastic.

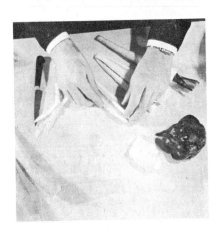

# vegetables

# vegetables

# vegetables

# vegetables

# Vegetables: The Unexploded Bomb

**❝** *Vegetables should be approached like an unexploded bomb, so fragile and so vitally important to our health is their locked-in goodness.*

*Our family has moved the star, animal protein, into the chorus and given vegetables the starring role. To do this we now eat lamb, veal, chicken, or fish on every other day (Monday, Wednesday, Friday) with an omelet on Sunday. This leaves Tuesday, Thursday, and Saturday for the vegetable. Even on meat days we still rely upon vegetable-centered meals and have only small portions of meat — about four ounces.*

*In order to plan for variety, which is essential to embracing this concept, we need to divide vegetables into groups that will provide seven different types. One meal can then be made with one vegetable of each type, with a minimum of four types represented in a meal. In this way we can get both variety and adequate nutrition.* **❞**

*TYPES OF VEGETABLES*

> *Roots: Beets, carrots, parsnips.*
> *Tubers: Potatoes, (Jerusalem) artichokes.*
> *Stems: Celery, asparagus.*
> *Leaves: Lettuce, spinach.*
> *Flowers and Heads: (French) artichokes, broccoli, cauliflower.*
> *Fruits:\* Tomatoes, watermelon, cucumber, squash.*
> *Seeds: Peas, sweet corn, beans.*

*Many true fruits which are not sweet, such as tomatoes, beans, and green peppers, are popularly called vegetables.

BUYING: If it is impossible to convert any part of your environment into a vegetable plot, then you will have to purchase your food some days after it has been picked. Here are some points to consider. Buy by type (the seven listed above). Remember, you combine at least 4 of the types for one meal. Your approximate needs for a family of four are:

| | | | |
|---|---|---|---|
| Roots | 8 oz. per person | = 2 | lbs. |
| Tubers | 8 oz. per person | = 2 | lbs. |
| Stems | 6 oz. per person | = 1½ | lbs. |
| Leaves | 10 oz. per person | = 2½ | lbs. |
| Flowers | 10 oz. per person | = 2½ | lbs. |
| Fruits | 6 oz. per person | = 1½ | lbs. |
| Seeds | ½ oz. per person | = 2 | oz. |

These are all raw, before-preparation weights and reduce by an average of 10 percent when ready for cooking and a further 10-15 percent in cooking.

Thus a meal consisting of

> 8 oz. carrots
> 6 oz. celery
> 10 oz. broccoli
> 6 oz. zucchini
>
> Total  1 lb. 14 oz.

can be reduced to about 1½ lbs. on the plate.

Obviously, in our profit-conscious society, the farmer is interested in developing hybrids that can stand mechanized methods of distribution. The tomato is bred for a tough skin and plenty of flesh. It is picked green and ripens on the truck, or is sprayed with ethylene gas to hasten the ripening process so that you and I might be pleased with its nice even color!

I need hardly add that all this is designed for profit and not nutrition. We need to be alert to this problem. To exert the greatest pressure on the businessman to provide good food, simply avoid *dull, lackluster foods, withered leaves or beans,* and *unnaturally colored fruits and vegetables.* Buy the best available by *type.* This means we stop buying celery because celery is on our list; we now write, for example,

> 2½ lbs. *stem*
> 2½ lbs. *flowers*
> 1½ lbs. *tuber*

and get the best!

But the best has already been dead for several days, so it should be treated carefully.

## PRE-PREPARATION

Since all store-purchased nonorganic fruits and vegetables are treated with some kind of chemical, we should get into the habit of washing our purchases before we store them.

The best method is to measure two tablespoons of hydrochloric acid to each gallon of cold water in your sink and thoroughly rinse *everything* you have purchased. Allow to drain and, in the case of leaves, dry them with a soft cloth or paper toweling.

Potatoes and hard squash can be kept without refrigeration, but all the rest are better held at 43°-45° F. in plastic bags or large glass jars.

## PREPARATION

The moment we lay hands upon a vegetable with a knife or grater, we rupture cells and expose valuable vitamins to both light and oxygen. As we do this, the nutrients are destroyed. The longer we leave cut food exposed, the less of its nutrients we will receive.

It is true that some vitamins are not readily harmed by light and heat, but since they do not *gain* by different handling, I prefer to treat all vegetables the same when it comes to preparation before cooking.

There is a catering practice of soaking prepared and sliced vegetables in cold water before cooking. This stops ugly browning from taking place. It's a poor method and has no justification in the home, since it severely depletes water-soluble vitamins and gives free reign to enzyme action. If you must prepare ahead of time, then put the vegetables in plastic, exhaust as much air as possible from the bag, and put it back into the refrigerator.

## BAD COOKING

I shall begin by sharply reducing the use of two well-known methods:
1. Shallow frying, as in the case of the Chinese wok or French *sauté*.
2. Boiling.

*Shallow frying* does two things. It exposes the cut surfaces to light, heat, and air and adds unnecessary fat to a consumption rate already known to be excessive. For example, in the case of vitamin A, it has been stated that "the combined effects of heat and the free access of air may completely destroy the vitamin A.*

*Boiling* — that is, covering food with water and raising the temperature to 212° F. — is a totally destructive method, especially when the food is raised to that temperature while sitting in the water.

Here I must tell you about vitamins and minerals. Vitamins are designed to control the body's use of minerals. They are the "highway police" in our system, but if we have less than our quota of minerals, the vitamins have nothing to do.

To this, then, I need to add the startling fact that the average mineral loss from vegetables through boiling is:

| | |
|---|---|
| Iron | 48% |
| Phosphorus | 46% |
| Calcium | 32% |
| Magnesium | 44% |
| Sodium | 42% |

These are hefty figures, a reminder that the foods we handle are fragile and need our care. There is no point in nourishing our drains!

*Stanley Davidson et al., *Human Nutrition and Dietetics* (6th rev. ed.; New York: Churchill, 1975), page 212.

## GOOD COOKING

Stove top and oven can be used effectively: the oven for the tubers, some roots and squash (fruits), and for casseroled vegetables. All the rest can be treated to steam, low-moisture, or pressure cooking.

*Oven baking.* 300° F. temperature should be used and all foods cut down to the size and shape that cooks quickest — usually no more than 1½ inches thick.

*On-Shelf baking.* This covers such foods as potatoes and hard squash. In all cases the root, tuber, or squash should be cut evenly to present no more than 1½ inches of dense flesh. We brush a light coating of safflower oil on the cut surfaces. This helps to retain the natural juices and keeps the food moist.

*Casserole baking.* This is defined as placing a mixture of vegetables in one container that has a tightly fitted lid and evenly distributes the heat. The *dofu* pan made of enameled cast iron does this handily. So do the clay pots we see in "earthy" stores, but you must check whether the lid fits.

Large lettuce leaves are put in first and can be used to separate the various vegetables added. Then the harder vegetables are grated and the softer textured are sliced, cubed, or even left whole. The whole affair is then seasoned with herbs appropriate to each vegetable (see list below), covered, and baked for 30 minutes. Tremendous stuff, especially without butter and salt!

*Steaming.* The object is to cook swiftly without leaching out the nutrients. The food is cut into thin pieces and placed into perforated steamer baskets. Three different segment baskets to one large pot is a good idea, as each can be added according to the time necessary. Here is an example for parsnips, Swiss chard, and fresh lima beans.

The water would be boiled and the lima beans added (they need 15 minutes). Follow this with the parsnips, which, when sliced, need 10 minutes. Then the Swiss chard, which takes only 8 minutes. After a total of 15 minutes' watching and care you have a marvelously cooked medley of fresh vegetables all in one pot! Please be careful to cover tightly after each addition in order to exclude oxygen and retain the steam and heat.

*Pressure cooking.* Vegetables can be cooked in one pressure cooker provided they have equal cooking times, since obviously you cannot keep on releasing pressure to add another batch. The pressure cooker is effective because, even though the heat is greater, it cuts down the exposure time, and that is a decided advantage (see page 36 for further information on the pressure cooker).

*Low moisture.* This technique is often called *waterless*, which is not strictly accurate. There is just enough water added to kick up some steam and stop the vegetables from scorching. Frankly, it doesn't make much sense when you compare the concept with steaming. Low moisture also means low heat, and low heat means longer exposure. Also, the direct contact between pan base and vegetable does cause uneven cooking. The argument is that the vegetable juices are totally saved, but I'm not impressed because the liquids used in steaming are equally rich and valuable as vegetable drinks or future broths, stocks, or soups.

*Bag boil.* Thinly sliced vegetables seasoned with the right herb or spice *but no salt* are placed into heavy, plastic, boil-proof bags. These can be added to boiling water by the bagful without any risk of losing anything. They can be added one at a time as with the steamer, and the exposure to oxygen is minimal. The bags can be rinsed and used again, so the idea is quite practical. It also reduces the washing up! Times are slightly longer than with steaming.

Now here are some methods for you. They are designed to *under-* rather than *over-*cook because heat is retained during service, and even on our plates this stored heat continues the cooking process.

In this next section you will find a table that you may wish to copy and to keep constantly displayed near your cooking top or range.

*Let there be no substitute for real love!*

TABLE 2
# Cooking Times for Vegetables By Types
(Let There Be No Substitute for Real Love!)

| | Cooking Methods – Times in Minutes Steam – Pressure – Bagboil – Casserole (350° F.) | | | | Suitable Herbs & Spices or Garnishes. | Calories | Protein per 100 Gram (3½ oz.) serving |
|---|---|---|---|---|---|---|---|
| **Heads and Flowers** | | | | | | | |
| Artichoke, French | 30 | 10 | 35 | — | Lemon and Butter Sauce Dip. | 70 | 2.2 |
| Broccoli | 10 | 2 | 10 | — | Crumbled Hardboiled Egg, Chives. | 29 | 3.3 |
| Brussels sprouts | 10 | 3 | 12 | — | Soy "Bacon" Bits, Buttered. | 47 | 4.4 |
| Cauliflower | 30 | 5 (whole) | 20 (pieces) | — | Grated Cheese, Paprika, Parsley. | 25 | 2.4 |
| Garlic | — | Seasoning | | — | — | 90 | 4.0 |
| Mushrooms | 5 | Raw in salads | | — | Dill Weed, Lemon Juice, Cayenne. | 16 | 2.4 |
| Onions | 15 | 6 | 20 | 60 | Dill Weed, Parsley. | 45 | 1.4 |
| **Stems** | | | | | | | |
| Asparagus | 10 | 2 | 12 | — | Unsalted Butter, Lemon Wedge. | 21 | 2.2 |
| Bean sprouts | 3 | — | 5 | — | Soy Sauce, Fine Sliced Ginger Root. | 35 | 3.8 |
| Celeriac | 20 | 3 | 25 | 60 | Chives, Parsley. | 38 | 1.7 |
| Celery | 20 | 3 | 25 | 60 | Dill Weed. | 18 | 1.3 |
| Green onions | 5 | — | — | — | Soy Sauce, Garlic. | 46 | 1.0 |
| Leek | 15 | 5 | 20 | 45 | Light Cream Sauce with Parsley & Tarragon. | 40 | 2.5 |
| **Leaves** | | | | | | | |
| Beet greens | 20 | 3 | 20 | — | Fine Sliced Onions, Soy "Bacon" Bits. Touch of Nutmeg. | 27 | 2.0 |
| Cabbage | 8 | 8 | 10 | — | Fine Sliced Onions, Soy "Bacon" Bits. | 24 | 1.4 |
| Cabbage, Chinese | 6 | 3 | 8 | — | Soy Sauce, Ginger Root, Garlic, Parsley. | 9 | 1.5 |
| Chard | 20 | 2 | 20 | — | Nutmeg (slight), Butter. | 21 | 1.4 |
| Collards | 20 | 3 | 20 | — | Marjoram, Thyme (slight), Soy "Bacon" Bits. | 40 | 3.9 |
| Cress, garden | — | Salads | | — | — | 40 | 4.0 |
| Cress, water | — | Salads | | — | Oil & Vinegar Dressing. | 20 | 2.0 |
| Dandelion greens | 3 | — | — | — | — | 44 | 2.7 |
| Endive | — | Salads | | — | — | 20 | 1.6 |
| Kale | 25 | 3 | 25 | — | Marjoram, Thyme (slight), Soy "Bacon" Bits. | 40 | 3.9 |
| Lettuce | — | Salads | | — | — | 15 | 2.9 |

| | | | | | Seasonings | | |
|---|---|---|---|---|---|---|---|
| Mustard greens | 3 | — | — | — | Marjoram, Thyme (slight), Soy "Bacon" Bits. | 22 | 2.3 |
| Spinach | 8 | — | 10 | — | Touch of Nutmeg, Soy "Bacon" Bits. | 20 | 2.3 |
| Turnip greens | 20 | 3 | 20 | — | Marjoram, Thyme (slight), Soy "Bacon" Bits. | 30 | 2.9 |
| **Seeds** | | | | | | | |
| Corn | 8 | 5 | 10 | 25 | Mustard Powder, Butter Sauce, Dill Weed | 92 | 3.7 |
| Lima beans (fresh) | 25 | 3 | 30 | — | Parsley | 128 | 7.5 |
| Pumpkin seeds | — | Added raw to dishes | — | | — | 547 | 30.3 |
| Sunflower seeds | — | Added raw to dishes | — | | — | 615 | 19.1 |
| Sesame seeds | — | Added raw to dishes | — | | — | 584 | 17.6 |
| **Roots** | | | | | | | |
| Beets | 30 | 14 | 35 | 45 | Bayleaves in Cooking, Basil as garnish. | 42 | 1.6 |
| Carrots | 20 | 6 (whole) 3 (sliced) | 25 | 90 | Nutmeg (touch), Honey butter Glaze, Parsley. | 42 | 1.2 |
| Parsnip | 25 | 8 | 27 | 60 | Nutmeg, Parsley, Paprika. | 78 | 1.5 |
| Radish | — | Salads | | — | — | 20 | 0.10 |
| Rutabaga | 20 | 5 | 25 | 60 | Paprika, Parsley, Basil. | 38 | 1.1 |
| Kohlrabi | 20 | 6 | 25 | — | Paprika, Parsley, Basil. | 30 | 2.1 |
| Turnip | 20 | 5 | 25 | 60 | Paprika, Parsley, Basil. | 32 | 1.1 |
| Salsify | 40 | 16 | 45 | 60 | — | 89 | 1.4 |
| Water chestnut (canned) | 5 | — | 5 | — | Soy Sauce, Ginger, Celeryseed. | 79 | 1.4 |
| **Fruit** | | | | | | | |
| Avocado | — | Salads | | — | Lemon Juice or Lime Juice, Black Pepper. | 185 | 2.0 |
| Breadfruit | — | — | — | 45 | Curry Powder, Butter Sauce, Coconut Cream. | 185 | 2.0 |
| Beans, green | 15 | 3 | 18 | 30 | Nutmeg, Garlic, Butter, Parsley. | 35 | 2.4 |
| Beans, wax yellow | 15 | 3 | 18 | 30 | Nutmeg, Garlic, Butter, Parsley. | 35 | 2.4 |
| Peas | 12 | 2 | 16 | 30 | Bayleaf, Thyme, Celeryseed, Honey. | 98 | 6.7 |
| Pea pods | 5 | 2 | 7 | — | Soy Sauce, Fine Sliced Onion. | 27 | 2.4 |
| Cucumber | — | Salads | | — | Chives, Sour Cream, Chili Powder. | 12 | 0.7 |

| | | | | | | | |
|---|---|---|---|---|---|---|---|
| Eggplant | — | — | 15 | 45 | Marjoram, Fine Sliced Tomatoes, Basil. | 24 | 1.1 |
| Okra | 15 | — | — | — | Mild Curry Powder, Parsley Garnish, File. | 32 | 1.8 |
| Pepper, green | 5 | — | 8 | 30 | — | 30 | 1.0 |
| Pumpkin | 25 | 10 | 30 | 60 | Mace or Touch of Cinnamon, Parsley. | 30 | 0.6 |
| Squash, summer | 15 | 5 | — | 45 | Marjoram, Basil, Thyme | 16 | 0.6 |
| Squash, winter | — | 10 | — | 75 | Mace or Touch of Cinnamon, Parsley. | 38 | 1.5 |
| Tomato | — | — | — | 20 | Basil, Black Pepper, Garlic (touch). | 20 | 1.0 |
| Watermelon | — | — | — | — | — | 28 | 0.5 |

### Tubers

| | | | | | | | |
|---|---|---|---|---|---|---|---|
| Artichoke, Jerusalem | 25 | 3 | 30 | 45 | Lemon Juice, Butter, Parsley. | 70 | 2.2 |
| Potato | 25 | 10 | 28 | 90 | Parsley, Mint. | 83 | 2.0 |
| Potato, sweet | 20 | 10 | 22 | 60 | Nutmeg, Mace or Cinnamon. | 123 | 1.8 |

Bayleaf in all casseroles.

File in all casseroles.

# Green Vegetables

### INGREDIENTS:

1½ lbs. Swiss chard
4 tablespoons butter
Lemon

> *I have quite a thing about green vegetables, largely, I think, because my mother had more rows with our chefs over this point than any other. Why — if something is so beautifully colored by nature — does it have to be boiled into a gray pulpy mess? We should respect our vegetables.*

**Step 1.** I have chosen Swiss chard because it contains a trap. The heavy, white stalks take twice as long as the green to cook, therefore either the stalks are undercooked or the green is overcooked. Obviously the best way is to strip off the green and cook each separately.

**Step 2.** Leave the leaves whole whenever possible; shredding only releases the natural vitamins. Wash the leaves very well — don't dry them (use same technique for all green leaf vegetables). Season with salt and freshly ground black peppercorns.

**Step 3.** Melt 4 tablespoons of butter to each 1½ pounds of leaf vegetable in a saucepan and add the leaves. Place a lid on top. *Add no water.*

**Step 4.** Shake the pot, holding the lid on firmly. This coats the leaves in butter. Allow 5 minutes at a low heat and then remove leaves direct to table. They should not be left to "stew in their own juice"!

The stalks are cooked in lemon-flavored water for 10 minutes.

# Beans in Garlic-Flavored Butter

**Serves 4**

### INGREDIENTS:

1 lb. fresh green beans
1 garlic clove
2 tablespoon butter
½ cup cold water
Freshly ground salt to season
Freshly ground white pepper
to season
Pinch of nutmeg

### PREPARATION

1. Trim and wash beans. Smash garlic. Measure butter. Put some ice in a bowl of cold water. Heat a vegetable dish in warming oven.

2. Place a small amount of water in a small saucepan and bring it to a boil.

3. Pop beans into boiling water and cook for 8 minutes.

4. Drain beans and immediately plunge them into iced water. Do not leave in the water once they are cool. This prevents their losing their beautiful color.

5. Return pan to heat, add garlic and butter, and allow to sizzle.

6. Drain beans and toss them in garlic butter. Add salt and pepper with a pinch of nutmeg. Heat through and toss to cover the now glistening beans in garlic butter. Serve in heated vegetable dish.

# Cabbage and Onions

**Serves 4**

### INGREDIENTS:

½ lb. onions, in ¼" slices
1½ lb. cabbage, in ¼" slices
1 tablespoon sesame/safflower oil
(page 186)
½ teaspoon salt
½ teaspoon white pepper
1 teaspoon dill weed
1 tablespoon parsley

### PREPARATION

1. Fry the sliced onions in the sesame/safflower oil until *just* softened but *not* colored.

2. Add the sliced cabbage, salt, and pepper, toss together, and cover tightly. Cook for 8 minutes over a medium heat, tossing from time to time.

3. When cooked but still crisp, add the dill weed and parsley, taste for other seasonings, turn into a dish, and serve (100 calories per serving).

# White Lima Beans

**Serves 4**

*Method A*

### INGREDIENTS:

½ lb. lima beans
4 cups water
1 cup ham stock
1 garlic clove
1 medium onion
4 cloves
1 bay leaf
¼ teaspoon thyme
1 piece celery (5 oz.)

### PREPARATION

1. Bring beans to a boil in water. Turn off heat, cover, and let stand for at least 2 hours (overnight is OK).

2. Drain and add ham stock, garlic, onion stuck with the 4 cloves, bay leaf, thyme, and celery. Cook slowly for 1½ hours.

*Method B (Pressure Cooker)*

### INGREDIENTS:

½ lb. lima beans
2 cups water
2 cups ham stock
1 garlic clove
1 medium onion
4 cloves
1 bay leaf
¼ teaspoon thyme
1 piece celery (5 oz.)

### PREPARATION

1. Place lima beans in mixture of water and ham stock. Bring to a boil uncovered. Add garlic, the onion stuck with the cloves, bay leaf, thyme, and celery.

2. Cover and let pressure rise to 15 psi. Then time 25 minutes, take off heat, and let pressure drop naturally (10 minutes).

3. Remove lid and serve with freshly sliced tomatoes and finely shredded raw spinach folded carefully into the steaming broth. Dust with grated cheese for a complete protein.

*Dried lima beans have always impressed me as being a super budget food with little gourmet interest. How wrong I was, and how wrong are the odd recipes given here and there for their preparation. No wonder they have a poor reputation.*

*This is how we set about preparing them:*

# Cauliflower and Cheese

**Serves 4**

### INGREDIENTS:

1 head cauliflower
1 teaspoon Parmesan cheese, grated
½ cup Parmesan Cheese Sauce (see below)
Paprika
Parsley

### PREPARATION

1. Clean the cauliflower, by trimming off the outer leaves and hollowing out the heavy stem; leave whole.

2. Boil covered in water for 10-15 minutes, no longer, just until tender. Pour off water.

3. Cover with Parmesan Cheese Sauce (see page 219), and grated Parmesan cheese, and place under the broiler for 4 minutes until lightly browned. Dust with paprika and parsley, and serve.

*❝ I have always liked cauliflower and cheese, the head smothered in a rich sauce Mornay (cheese sauce) laden with calories and saturated fats. We have now reformed this elegant vegetable and have discovered to our glee a light, delicious vegetable with a new flavor — this time you can actually taste the vegetable!* ❞

# Braised Celery

**Serves 4**

### INGREDIENTS:

2 cups Pressure Beef Stock (see page 31)
1 tablespoon tomato paste
¼ teaspoon oil
2 tablespoons arrowroot
1 celery heart

### PREPARATION

1. Make up Pressure Beef Stock. Remove all fat and season properly. Place tomato paste in oil in pan and brown the mixture thoroughly over medium heat. Add stock and stir in to color. Thicken with arrowroot and cold water mixed (2 tablespoons arrowroot).

2. Precook the celery heart (cut 4 inches long and sliced once, in half lengthways). Trim the root end, clean, and place in cold water, raise to the boil and cook for 10 minutes. Drain and place in a shallow baking dish half covered with the thickened stock.

3. Bake at 325° F. (with the roast) covered for 1 hour and uncovered for the second hour. Baste with the stock occasionally.

Serve the braising liquid as a sauce with the meat.

*❝ Braised celery hearts are a great favorite of ours. They take a long time to cook, and they are a fuss, but in my search for a low-calorie, delicious vegetable I found no close competitor.*
*We suggest you only do this dish if you have a long, slow roast to cook and thus can use the oven more effectively.* ❞

# HINTS

## Broccoli

Some green leaf and "bud" vegetables have heavy stalks and light fragile leaves. If the *whole* plant is cooked until the stalk is tender, then the leaves are frequently overcooked. A little ingenuity easily solves this problem. Using broccoli as an example: Cut off the bud tops and slice the stalks in half lengthwise. Cook the latter in a little tomato juice, garlic, and basil. This makes a "red" vegetable. The tops can be cooked later in very little water in a covered pot, making an excellent lightly steamed green vegetable from the same source.

*Nutritional advantage* comes from retained Vitamin C (lost when the tops are overcooked).

*Effort advantage* is produced by getting two vegetables from the one source.

*Budget advantage* results from the elimination of the excessive trimming that people do to the otherwise hard-to-cook stalks.

*Senses* are jingled visually by the bright green of the buds and texturally by the crisp goodness of "both" vegetables.

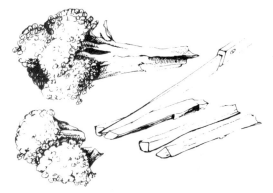

## Spinach

It's good that at least one excellent green leaf vegetable should be enjoying volume sales. Spinach is one of the current superstars and, as with all superstars, part of the new image is the packaging.

Spinach is sold in a variety of ways, but the keenest competition is between packaged in a plastic bag, and the loose and fresh. We conducted a test by buying 1 pound of loose spinach and 10 ounces in a plastic bag. We kept both in the refrigerator for 2 days, and then picked over, trimmed, washed, and weighed the result. We found it took 2 minutes 26 seconds to pick over and trim the 16 ounces of loose leaves and that this produced 10 ounces. The bagged variety actually weighed 8 ounces when trimmed and took 2 minutes 12 seconds to prepare (only saving 14 seconds).

The price of the loose spinach per pound should be cheaper than the packaged variety (this is not always so — check in your locale), and it's better looking.

*Nutritional advantage:* spinach is 90.7 percent water. For each 3½ ounces you have this profile: 26 calories (good) 3.2 g. protein; 4.3 g. carbohydrate (good); 8,000 I.U. Vitamin A (good); 51 mg. Vitamin C (good). It's a thoroughly satisfactory vegetable which, I think, makes a great salad green.

*Sense advantage:* spinach left as nature made it (not squashed in a plastic bag) looks better as a salad; it just seems fresher, larger, and crisper.

# HINTS

## Blanching Vegetables

What is the best way to cook vegetables? Some think it is better to blanch green vegetables such as snap beans, broccoli, peas, broad beans, and corn by boiling rapidly for a few minutes (number of minutes varies according to the vegetable) to establish the bright color. Then (saving the cooking liquid) the vegetables are turned into a little iced water to instantly stop the cooking. When cold, drain, and cool-store ready for reheating. Just before service, the original cooking liquid is brought to the boil to simply reheat the vegetable. The question is — in the *average home* would this result in better-cooked vegetables than the normal "cook until tender" method? At present the vegetables compete with the main dish for last-moment attention and are frequently decidedly overcooked.

We would like to let you decide this one for yourself. There is loss of Vitamin C in this new method, but since Vitamin C can be fairly easily found from our other daily foods, would we not be more excited by beautifully prepared vegetables?

# Root Vegetables

> *I am basically against the use of water with vegetables, but I do appreciate that, for strict dietary reasons, there may be no alternative. I have given below two methods of cooking root vegetables. The main thing to remember with all vegetable cookery is to "keep it short and eat it crisp." There is such an abundance of vitamins in our vegetables that it is ridiculous to compensate for bad cooking by buying pills.*

**Step 1.** One pound of root vegetables, if carefully peeled, usually serves 4 people. I like to mix roots. My favorite combination is kumera (the Maori sweet potato), parsnip (with center core removed, and tender juicy carrots. If you have space *always* keep them in the refrigerator and cut them immediately before cookery. *Don't* cut and leave in cold water. Keep the peelings for soups.

**Step 2.** Add just enough cold water to cover and some salt. Cover and boil until just tender.

**Step 3.** The water should boil away almost completely. Strain off the excess (if any). Add butter (I use the foam and sediment from the making of clarified butter — page 77) just before you serve. Taste for seasoning. A little sugar can also be added if you want a high gloss finish.

**Step 4.** Root vegetables can also be shallow fried very gently in butter in a frying pan with a close-fitting lid. Stir from time to time to keep from scorching.

# Carrots

**Serves 4**

## INGREDIENTS:

Julienne cut 2-3 large carrots
into 4"x ¼" strips
1 tablespoon butter
Salt to season
Pepper to season
½ teaspoon sugar
⅛ teaspoon freshly
grated nutmeg

## PREPARATION

1. Blanch carrots 10 minutes. Cool quickly and store in refrigerator until ready to serve.

2. Place butter in frying pan, add carrots, and stir-fry to rapidly heat through. Season with salt, pepper, sugar, and, finally, freshly grated nutmeg. Serve immediately — 40 calories/serving.

# Braised Onions

## INGREDIENTS:

2 cups Pressue Beef Stock
1 tablespoon tomato paste
¼ teaspoon oil
2 tablespoons arrowroot
4 onions, 3 inches in diameter
3 cups water
2 finely chopped mushrooms
2 teaspoons sesame/safflower oil
(page 186)
1 tablespoon lemon juice
1 garlic clove, crushed
1-2 slices bacon, uncooked

## PREPARATION

1. Make up Pressure Beef Stock (page 31). Remove all fat and season properly. Place tomato paste in oil in pan and brown the mixture thoroughly over medium heat. Add stock and stir in to color. Thicken with arrowroot and cold water mixed to make braising sauce.

2. Place onions in cold water and bring to the boil, then boil for 20 minutes.

3. Fry the finely chopped mushrooms in sesame/safflower oil and add the lemon juice.

4. Remove onions from water and take out the centers by cutting off the top and easing the core out with a fork.

5. Chop the center "leaves" finely with the crushed garlic mixed with the fried mushrooms. Fill the empty centers of the onions with this mixture and top each off with a small piece of bacon.

6. Place in a *small* oven-proof baking dish, half cover with braising sauce, and bake uncovered at 325° F. for 1½ hours or until tender. Serve the sauce on the side as gravy for a roast.

*Another excellent vegetable, when braised, is the onion. We use exactly the same braise liquid as we do with celery (see page 181), but the onions take more time and are a little more complicated. Once again, this dish should only be made when the oven will be in use for 1-1½ hours at 325° F.*

# The Glazed Look

### INGREDIENTS:

½ cup safflower oil
2 cloves garlic, crushed
½ teaspoon thyme
4 bay leaves
Peel of ¼ lemon, unblanched
2 teaspoons grated fresh ginger
½ teaspoon salt

### PREPARATION

1. Measure or prepare all ingredients first.

2. Gently boil all ingredients in a small saucepan, except the salt, for 30 minutes, uncovered.

3. Strain through a cheesecloth, add salt, and stir to dissolve.

4. Place in a spray atomizer and spray over a cooked, unseasoned steak just before serving.

Nutrition profile — One squirt of about ¼ teaspoon equals 10.4 calories (1 teaspoon butter equals 33.3 calories).

*" Now that the "pump" has largely replaced the aerosol can, we can thoroughly clean the unit and use it for a wild idea — a low-calorie, highly flavored mist of seasoned oil that gives a surface sparkle to your food, bringing out the highlights without stirring in gobs of butter. "*

# HINTS

# Home-Seasoned Oil

Since the frying pan or skillet is, in our Western culture, the most-used piece of culinary equipment, it follows that we should give more than a passing thought to the shallow-frying oil.

As a *standard,* we have suggested 1 part sesame seed oil to 20 parts of safflower oil — but how about a real "house oil," special to your home and personal likes. I tried one that has worked so well we are almost addicted to the taste! To each cup of safflower oil, add 2 large cloves of fresh garlic (crushed), 1 teaspoon rosemary, and 1 teaspoon oregano. Simmer together, without blackening the herbs, for 10 minutes with lid on. Cool, then strain carefully and bottle. Use this with fish, chicken, or steak. It's a wonderful general seasoning all your very own!

We prefer standard processed sesame seed oil to that referred to as *cold pressed.* The impact of severe heat upon certain nutritive elements of oil-bearing seeds has been determined, as has the effect upon the seeds of cold pressing. The process of cold pressing also involves very high heats, high enough to scorch the residue. For my part, I see the potential spoilage of cold pressed, coupled with its higher cost, as edging out the slight nutritive advantage it has over the standard processed oil.

# HINTS

## Mixed Root Vegetables

A good example of the kind of dish you can create for yourself would be to cook a combination of carrots, parsnips, rutabagas, and sweet potatoes in a very little clarified butter (see page 77) in a flameproof casserole covered with a tightly fitting lid. Toss well in the butter and season with salt and pepper. Cook slowly for approximately 25 minutes. Add *no* water or liquid — just let them cook in their own steam — then serve dusted with finely chopped fresh parsley.

## Knifework

The right knife for chopping light vegetables and fruits such as onions, cucumbers, green peppers, tomatoes, green onions, green beans, asparagus, celery, zucchini, radishes, mushrooms, pineapples, avocados, apples, oranges, melons, pears, bananas, peaches, nectarines, etc., is the 8-inch French chef's knife. This blade is designed to be used in a specific manner by being guided by the curled-under first joints of the fingers. Thus the blade side must be completely smooth so that it can run up and down without cutting the fingers (hollow ground blades cannot be used this way). I call this the "Fingernail chop."

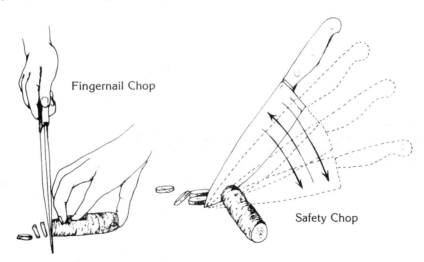

Fingernail Chop

Safety Chop

You can move on to the tip-down *Safety Chop*. Here you must be able to *roll the blade* from tip to heel for best results while holding the tip to the board. This is an excellent way to finish a *fine chopping* procedure as for parsley and can be done with any blade that has a rounded edge.

*Nutritional advantage:* the correct use of the French chef's knife will encourage use of fresh produce — it's so easy. Many people stick to processed, dried, or powdered products because they fear the use of a sharp knife.

*Equipment note:* I feel that a stainless steel blade has several advantages over straight carbon steel; it is less likely to rust and stain food, *and* it will also hold its shape much longer. *Shape* is vital as you can see from the above techniques.

# Cabbage Casserole

**Serves 4**

### INGREDIENTS:

1 tablespoon butter
1½ lbs. white cabbage, sliced
into ¼ inch strips
1 tablespoon chopped parsley
2 teaspoons fresh chopped mint
(if not available then leave
the recipe until it is)
Salt and white pepper
to season
3 stalks celery, finely sliced
2 medium carrots, grated
1 teaspoon dill weed, dried
2 large tomatoes, cut in halves
and broiled lightly
1½ cups Dutch Gouda or Edam
or U.S. Cheddar (order of
preference), cut into ½-inch
cubes — no larger (6 oz.)

### PREPARATION

1. Melt butter in a large deep pan over medium heat. Add cabbage, season, and toss well (lid on!). Cook 4 minutes only.

2. Add celery, carrot, herbs, salt, and pepper. Toss well, cover, and cook 4 minutes.

3. Cut lightly broiled tomatoes in cubes and add with the cubed cheese, stir carefully, and serve immediately.

A low-calorie meal (241 calories/serving with Edam and 279 with Cheddar), good source of protein, and Vitamins A and C.

**❝** *Incredibly quick with few ingredients — these are the classic advantages of this vegetable "Super Dish."* **❞**

# Vegetable Pilaf

**Serves 4**

## INGREDIENTS:

2 tablespoons safflower oil
2 carrots, diced
2 medium onions, diced
1 cup long-grain rice
1 stalk celery
1 bay leaf
¼ teaspoon powdered thyme
2½ cups Ham Hock Stock
(page 34)
¼ lb. small mushrooms
½ cup snap beans (2 oz.)
¼ lb. lima beans
3 tablespoons raisins
2 tablespoons split almonds
¼ lb. peas
1 large tomato
Salt
½ teaspoon basil
(Tabasco and soy sauce on
the side)

## PREPARATION

1. Heat oil in an ovenproof casserole (4-quart size). Shallow-fry carrots, onions, rice, and celery, in the order given, over a medium heat, stirring often, for approximately 10 minutes.

2. Add bay leaf, thyme, and stock, cover and place in 425° F. oven for 25 minutes.

3. After 10 minutes, stir in mushrooms and snap beans.

4. After 5 more minutes, stir in lima beans, raisins, almonds, and peas.

5. Slice tomato into thin rings, salt, and dust with basil. Remove from oven, cover the vegetables with the tomato as a topping, and serve immediately.

This one-dish meal is relatively low calorie (443 per serving), and a good source of Vitamin A. Protein is of good quality since you're combining 2 "incompletes" (legume-type and rice), which complement each other to produce a "complete."

**❝** *Another vegetable dinner fully prepared in one dish.* **❞**

# Casserole in Cream Sauce

**Serves 4**

### INGREDIENTS:

1 tablespoon safflower oil
2 medium carrots, diced
8 small onions
¼ lb. snap beans
1½ cups sliced green onion
¼ lb. cauliflower "tops"
(flowerettes)
¼ lb. small mushrooms
1 cup Ham Hock Stock
(page 34)
2 tablespoons arrowroot or fecule,*
mixed to a thin paste with a
little milk
1 cup milk
1 heaped tablespoon chopped
parsley
1 cup frozen peas, thawed
1 cup frozen lima beans, thawed
¼ cup grated cheese

*Fecule — refined potato starch — is also
called Kartopfel Meal; imported by Holly
Woods, Inc.,
Colorado Springs, Colorado 80901.

### PREPARATION

1. Pour oil into a large skillet. Add carrots, onions, snap beans, green onion, cauliflower, and mushrooms *in order given* and fry over medium heat with lid on for 10 minutes. Do not season.

2. Add stock, cover, and cook at a barely moving simmer for 10 minutes.

3. Add arrowroot paste, boil, and add milk.

4. Stir in parsley, peas, and lima beans. Turn into a flameproof casserole, dust with cheese, and broil for 5 minutes, until just browned.
Serve very hot, preferably on brown earthenware plates.

This casserole is high in Vitamin A (carrots) and Vitamin C (cauliflower and other vegetables); it has some high-quality protein as well as calcium from milk and cheese. Stock made with ham hocks supplies small quantities of thiamine, as ham is high in this B vitamin. There are small amounts of iron from vegetables, particularly lima beans and peas, but overall iron content is not high. This is a low-calorie dish at 296 per serving.

❝ *This is an excellent 25-minute vegetable casserole that takes only about 10 minutes' preparation time. It's a one-dish effort and tastes super.* ❞

# "New Testament" Pottage

**Serves 4**

### INGREDIENTS:

2 cups lentils (½ lb.)
2 garlic cloves, crushed
1 tablespoon sesame/safflower oil
(page 186)
¼ teaspoon cumin
¼ teaspoon coriander
2 ham hocks
¼ teaspoon celery salt
2 bay leaves
1 quart water
Nonfat dried milk (to taste)
Parsley
1 cup chopped onions (4 oz.)

### PREPARATION

1. Cover lentils with 2 cups boiling water, cool, and drain.

2. Fry garlic with onions in oil. Add cumin and coriander.

3. Add drained lentils, stir in well, and add ham hocks and celery salt plus bay leaves. Cover with 1 quart (4 cups) water and simmer for 2 hours tightly covered.

4. Remove ham hocks. Cut off rind (outer skin), finely chop meat, and put into the lentils.

5. Add nonfat dried milk to taste. This makes a complete protein dish. (For our taste we added ⅓ cup + 1 tablespoon nonfat dried milk powder with 1 cup water.)

Even before I became a Christian I was fascinated by Esau's "mess of pottage." How could a man be tempted to give up his birthright for a dried grain stew?

As we wanted to look closely at lentils as a good food at a low price, we thought it would be fun to look at this famous biblical dish. Our first efforts were awful until we got nonscriptural and produced a "New Testament" pottage!

# HINTS

# Vegetable Flavor Oils $

Root vegetables and vegetables with a high degree of volatile oils, such as celery, will "give up" these oils when heated. At moist heat temperatures up to and including boiling point, a degree of "release" takes place, but at a frying heat of 320° F., the flavor generation is much greater. The old "Professional Chef Schools" talk about "sweating off" the vegetables; the word *sweat* describes beads of volatile oils that are driven to the surface by the heat and exploded as aroma. We have focused on an interesting point here: If good flavor release is achieved, do we need less root vegetables as a flavor base? The normal ratio is roughly 1 pound of vegetables for 2 pounds of meat. In our test we reduced vegetables to 10 ounces (6 ounces saved) with no real flavor loss. The initial root vegetable base is thrown away in our stews and casseroles anyway.

One way of testing this on your family is to shallow-fry some root vegetables instead of just boiling them. If that works, then I would urgently suggest you consider frying or "sweating off" all your root vegetables used in casseroles and stews.

*Sense Advantage:* this method gives excellent flavor and aroma — plus factors to all casseroles, stews, and sauces. In fact, I find it an indispensable step in the correct use of vegetables.

# Stir-Fried Western Vegetables

**Serves 2 Complete Dinners**

### INGREDIENTS:

1 garlic clove
5 scallions (white ends)
8 Brussels sprouts
2 celery sticks
2 medium carrots (4 oz.)
¼ lb. cauliflower
1 cup mushrooms
¼ teaspoon ginger root
5 green scallion tops
4 tablespoons sesame/safflower oil (page 186)
1 tablespoon soy sauce

*Stir-fried vegetables are known as a part of Far Eastern cookery. For its proper execution you need a wok or wo (the right spelling) and a special gas fire with large flame jets. It is possible, however, to borrow their technique and translate it into our simple skillet and regular range use.*

*Caution. This technique can become a stumbling block to those who believe it is the only way to cook vegetables. The fact is that it isn't without blame in the list of damaging methods. It exposes cut surfaces to light, heat, and air while adding unnecessary fat to a consumption rate already known to be excessive.*

### PREPARATION

Cutting the vegetables correctly for quick cooking is vital. We have found that following the cutting techniques below helps to hasten cooking and preserves an attractive finished appearance. The ingredients list is given in the order in which the vegetables are to be cooked, from toughness to delicacy, so that an *even* degree of doneness is achieved at the end.

All vegetables must be cut and ready *before* you begin to cook.

1. Partly crush the garlic clove.

2. Cut off the white ends of the scallions. These will be added first.

3. Cut the Brussels sprouts in quarters lengthways.

4. Slice the celery sticks in ¼-inch thick slices diagonally with the round side up.

5. Peel the carrots and slice them diagonally to a thickness of ⅛ of an inch.

6. Use only the tops of the cauliflower. Cut these into small "flowers" the size of a 25¢ piece.

7. Use only the mushroom caps; the stalks can be reserved for use in a soup stock.

8. Grate the ginger from a fresh or dried whole root.

9. Cut the green scallion tops into 1-inch-long pieces.

10. Heat the oil in a 10-inch pan over a medium-high flame and add the vegetables in quick succession in the order listed.

11. At the last moment add the soy sauce, cover the pan with a lid, toss well, and serve.

# Eggplant

**Serves 4**

## INGREDIENTS:

1 eggplant, peeled and
sliced into ⅓-inch strips
2 eggs
½ cup flour (2 oz.)
¼ cup tonic water
Pinch of salt
¼ teaspoon dill weed
1 lemon
1½ teaspoons Parmesan cheese

> ❝ We are delighted with this way of fixing eggplant. So often the problem with this bulbous purple vegetable is the way it blackens and becomes bitter. We use the salt press method and coat the strips in tonic water batter. They are a real treat. ❞

## PREPARATION

1. Eggplant can be prepared in either of 2 ways:
   a. Place slices in salt water for ½-1 hour (1 tablespoon salt to 1 or 1½ cups water), *or*
   b. Place slices in a bowl, but lightly salt both sides of each slice first, and put a plate with something heavy on top of the eggplant ½-1 hour ahead of time.

   Allow to stand for at least 30 minutes. Pour off liquid, rinse very well, and pat dry.

2. Beat eggs well. Add flour, tonic water, salt, and dill weed. Beat well until all lumps are gone. Cover and let stand 1-2 hours so that batter will go flat.

3. Dip dried eggplant in batter, and fry in hot oil 2-3 minutes or until lightly brown on both sides. Drain on a paper towel. Sprinkle 1½ teaspoons Parmesan cheese on top and serve. A 1-lb. eggplant makes about 20-25 slices. Squeeze lemon on top immediately before serving.

There was no appreciable difference in bitterness for either technique. For method "b", one must be careful not to use too much salt and to wash all of it off. Coarse (kosher) salt is too strong and does not wash off very well. This dish is expensive in the winter but cheap in the summer.

At 20 slices per eggplant, you have about 26 calories per slice.

# HINTS

## Mushrooms

This simple "vegetable" goes a long way to help our daily meals. It has a look of luxury, yet when you see the quantity you get in one pound you have some idea of their advantage. They are also low in calories and take little effort or time to prepare and cook.

*But,* there are a couple of tricks (aren't there always!). If the mushrooms are cultivated, they won't need to be peeled, only washed. The washing should only be done *just before* they are cooked because a damp mushroom rots easily and gets discolored and slimy.

If you are frying them, simply place the mushroom tops in a lightly buttered pan, cap side down (gills up), and squeeze fresh lemon juice into the cap. Cook gently for 4 to 5 minutes, then turn over and cook briefly. Dust them with parsley and a *very little* cayenne and serve instantly.

*Note:* The stalks of cultivated mushrooms can be used in stock — don't just chuck them out!

*Sense advantage:* The well-known greasy 'finish' of fried mushrooms is sidestepped — the lemon *stops* the fat from begin absorbed by the gills. Therefore both taste and texture are helped.

*Nutrition comment:* Mushrooms are a great eating *reform* tool. 10 small mushrooms (or 4 large ones) raw have only 28 calories. If you add 1 teaspoon of butter for each 10, then the total will be 61 calories, and that's a gourmet's mouthful of flavor for the reformer who wants to lose weight and smile doing it!

*VOLUME / WEIGHT / PRICE\* COMPARISON*

|  | VOLUME | | PRICE/POUND | PRICE/1 CUP |
|---|---|---|---|---|
| 8 oz. tomatoes | 1 | cup | 79¢ | 39.5¢ |
| 8 oz. carrots | 1 | cup | 39¢ | 19.5¢ |
| 8 oz. mushrooms | 1¾ | cup | $1.32 | 37.5¢ |
| 8 oz. peas | 1 | cup | 89¢ | 44.5¢ |

\*Prices at time of writing. Prices may vary according to locale.

# HINTS

## Water-Bath Processing $

One commonly used food preservation technique is the water bath. Jars of food are sealed with special lids and boiled for various lengths of time, then cooled and kept in a cellar ready for out-of-season use. In order to launch yourself into this rewarding skill you will need space and patience; you might do without the former, but pray for the latter and it *will* be yours.

Equipment needed: a large deep boiler pan, a perforated disk to keep the jars from direct contact with the bottom, the jars themselves with lids and screw tops, and a pair of jar tongs to lift the processed jars from the container.

If you have an electric stove or flat cooking top, you will have to buy a perfectly flat-based heavy utensil. If you want to process non-acid fruits and vegetables, then a large pressure canner is a wise dovetail investment.

The size depends upon the type of jar you want to use. The jar we have selected for our family is the 6 in. (1 pt.) size. So we need 1 in. at the bottom, 6 in. for the jar, 1 in. for water coverage, and 2 in. for the water to boil. This means we need a container with at least 10 in. total depth.

### SOME TIPS ON WATER-BATH PROCESSING

1. Water-bath processing is used only for *acid* foods: fruits, juices, tomatoes, pickles, relishes, rhubarb, etc.

2. Nonacid foods (most meats and vegetables) *must* have pressure canning at temperatures of 240°-260° F. to kill any possible botulism spores. Boiling water is *not* hot enough. Remember that botulism is usually fatal!

3. Water-bath processing means heating the water to almost boiling. Prepare, fill, and seal jars, place in the water, and cover with 1-2 inches water over the top of the lids (fill with preheated water).

4. Bring water back to a boil and begin timing then.

5. When processing is completed, remove jars from rack, and place in a draft-free area on a towel to cool 12-14 hours. Remove outer rims, wipe, and store in a dry, dark place. Contents will remain good for several years.

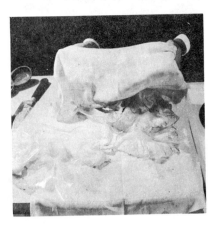

# salads & dressings

## salads & dressings

## salads & dressings

## salads & dressings

# Salads

*I eat salads with practically anything. We are "all in" salad eaters. We usually keep to one technique, but put in anything that is crisp and edible. On this page I have highlighted what I believe to be the most important elements in salad preparation.*

**Step 1.** Salads, if they must be kept, are best protected by peeling off the leaves, washing them gently, and then either drying with a cloth or spinning in one of those wire salad baskets. The leaves can then be put into polyethylene bags and kept in the crisper.

**Step 2.** Garlic is a delightful flavor for salad. I add it in three ways:

1. Rub the bowl around with a cut clove — finest flavor, very light.
2. Cook small bread pieces with cut cloves — slightly stronger.
3. Rub bread pieces with cut clove — stronger still — usually the bread is not eaten.

**Step 3.** Lettuce and other leaf salads should be torn apart, never sliced with a knife. Knife cuts mean greater loss of vitamin C. An exception can be made with cabbage for fine-shredded salads.

**Step 4.** If a dressing is used, add it to the salad at the last possible moment. In this photograph a little sugar, mustard, and cayenne pepper are mixed with oil, and then twice the quantity of good vinegar is added. It is then mixed well and scattered over the salad at the table. This is a very good piece of showmanship for the man of the house!

# Raft Salad

**Serves 4**

## INGREDIENTS:

½ lb. cooked, cleaned shrimp
¼ cup water
¼ cup cider vinegar
1 can pink grapefruit (8 oz.)
1 head iceberg lettuce
1 avocado
Salt and pepper to taste
Blender Mayonnaise (page 212)
(or ½ cup mayonnaise and I
beaten egg white)
⅛ teaspoon dry dill weed
⅛ teaspoon cayenne pepper
4 green Spanish olives
(with pimiento)

*Western iceberg lettuce, the large-hard-crisp one, is so tightly designed that it can be cut into a "raft" between ½ and 1 in. thick and usually halved once again for a moderate portion.*

*The raft can be used to hold all kinds of decorative saladry. We use avocado, shrimp, grapefruit, olives, and our light Blender Mayonnaise (page 212). The result looks impressive and tastes delicious.*

## PREPARATION

1. Steam shrimp in water and cider vinegar for 6 to 8 minutes or until a deep pink. Drain, cool, and clean, removing the shell and vein down the back.

2. Open and drain grapefruit, wash and drain lettuce, peel and slice avocado.

3. Measure out mayonnaise and seasonings. Separate egg white and allow to come to room temperature.

4. Slice 1 (½-1 inch thick) layer of lettuce per serving and place on a salad plate.

5. On the lettuce, alternate avocado slices with shrimp and grapefruit. Continue until you reach the edge of the raft.

6. In a small mixing bowl, fold together Blender Mayonnaise and beaten egg white, dill weed, cayenne pepper, salt, and pepper.

7. Slice up 4 olives; reserve for garnish. Spread 2 tablespoons of Blender Mayonnaise over the salad in a line and garnish with one whole sliced olive, laid in a row down the line.

Salad contains 192 calories per serving. Light, Blender Mayonnaise has 815 calories (58 calories/tablespoon).

# Avocado Salad

**Serves 4**

## INGREDIENTS:

1 avocado
Juice of 1 fresh lemon
4 tablespoons sour cream
1 tablespoon horseradish
Salt to season
Black pepper to season
4 romaine lettuce leaves

## PREPARATION

1. Cut the fruit into eighths and drench the slices in lemon juice.

2. Make a dressing with sour cream, horseradish, salt, and black pepper. Combine with the lemon juice, which is strained, *at the last moment,* from the avocado slices. Lay 2 slices on each romaine lettuce leaf, coat with the sauce, and serve.

# Little Patti Tomatoes

**Serves 4**

## INGREDIENTS:

¼ teaspoon dry mustard
½ teaspoon cayenne
1 medium onion, finely diced
1 garlic clove, well crushed
1 tablespoon sugar (this is added to suit the dressing to local taste and is not classical)
½ cup olive oil
1 cup rice, or apple cider vinegar
1 lb. medium tomatoes (8 per lb.), skins removed
Stalks of parsley, finely chopped (stalks only)
Leaves of lettuce heart, left whole for garnish
Very thin slices brown bread and butter, cut into quarters

## PREPARATION

1. Mix mustard, cayenne, onion, garlic, and sugar with olive oil. When sugar is dissolved, add vinegar; shake well.

2. Plunge tomatoes into boiling water, having first loosened the skin around the stem. Boil for 1 minute until you can see the skin begin to peel away from the stem area. But do not overcook, because the flesh becomes mushy.

3. Remove quickly, plunge into cold water, and strip off the skin.

4. Place the peeled tomatoes in a small bowl, scatter top with chopped parsley, and cover with the dressing; place in the refrigerator to keep overnight for best results.

5. Drain off the dressing. Slice tomatoes, lay them out on the lettuce, coat with a little dressing, and serve very cold with the bread slices as a first course.

> ❝ *The quantities for this sauce are more than adequate for the dish itself. This has been done on purpose in order to make available a surplus for the next time you serve, but please be careful not to "soak" green salads in the mixture as the result is slimy, to say the least!* ❞

# Bean and Black Olive Salad

**Serves 4**

### INGREDIENTS:

1 lb. fresh green beans
Freshly ground salt
Parsley
Chives
1 medium onion
Freshly ground black pepper
Nutmeg
Black olives
FRENCH DRESSING
(Note: only ¼ cup needed):
1 garlic clove
½ teaspoon dry mustard
½ teaspoon cayenne
1 to 2 tablespoons sugar
½ cup salad oil
1 cup rice vinegar
Yield: 1½ cups (12 fl. oz.)

### PREPARATION

1. Make French Dressing: Crush garlic and add with dry ingredients to oil. Add rice vinegar.

2. Wash and trim beans. Drop whole beans into salted boiling water and cook for 8 minutes. Drain. Finely chop parsley, chives, and onion.

3. While beans are still warm, season with salt, pepper, and nutmeg. Mix with onion. Chill in refrigerator.

4. Shake French Dressing well immediately before dressing salad so that oil and vinegar emulsify.

5. Toss beans with French Dressing and serve garnished with chopped parsley, chives, and a few black olives. Serve cool.

# Spinach Salad

**Serves 4**

### INGREDIENTS:

10 ounces of washed and trimmed spinach
1 cup finely sliced raw mushrooms (4 oz.)
1 tablespoon finely chopped green onions
¼ lb. fried bacon bits (optional)
FRENCH DRESSING
1 garlic clove
½ teaspoon dry mustard
½ teaspoon cayenne
1 to 2 tablespoons sugar
½ cup salad oil
1 cup rice vinegar
Yield: 1½ cups (12 fl. oz.)

### PREPARATION

1. Wash, trim, thoroughly dry, and tear up 10 ounces of fresh spinach leaves (requires about 1 lb. loose leaf or 12-14 ounces packaged).

2. Make up French Dressing. *Note:* The recipe makes more than you will need.

3. Add the mushrooms, green onions, and bacon bits to the spinach. The bacon bits are optional, but if added, they must have been fried crisp, and then well drained to remove the fat.

4. Toss the salad in the dressing at the last moment before service. Enjoy!

# Chilled Ratatouille Salad

**Serves 4**

### INGREDIENTS:

⅓ cup sesame/safflower oil
(page 186)
1 small onion, sliced
2 garlic cloves, minced
2 medium green peppers, sliced
½ medium eggplant, sliced
¼-inch thick, unpeeled
2 medium zucchini, thinly sliced
lengthwise
Salt and pepper
4 medium tomatoes, peeled
and sliced
4 lettuce leaves
DRESSING:
¼ cup sesame/safflower oil
½ cup rice vinegar
1 teaspoon sugar
½ teaspoon dry mustard
½ teaspoon salt
½ teaspoon ground black pepper
¼ teaspoon cayenne pepper

### PREPARATION

1. First prepare dressing.

2. Then heat oil in large skillet, add onion, and cook until golden.

3. Add garlic, peppers, eggplant, and zucchini. Fry vegetables gently. Season with salt and pepper. Cover pan tightly; simmer 30 minutes.

4. Add tomatoes, allow to heat through.

5. Transfer to bowl; chill. Serve cold on lettuce. Shake dressing well before adding to salad.

For another delightful salad idea, see Watercress Salad on page 211.

# Tomato in "New Wine" Aspic

### INGREDIENTS:

10 medium/large fresh summer
tomatoes (skinned)
2 packages unflavored gelatin
dissolved in 1½ cups water
1 cup red grape juice
2 tablespoons rice vinegar
¼ teaspoon ground black pepper
½ teaspoon salt
1 teaspoon basil

> *Ice cold and full of tomato, a rich red aspic can set people's appetites on the march on really humid summer days.*

### PREPARATION

1. Skin (page 207) and cut tomatoes into quarters, removing all the seeds but leaving the other flesh. Reserve quarters. Reserve inner pulp minus the seeds.

2. Combine gelatin, grape juice, vinegar, and spices in a bowl and chill to an egg-white consistency.

3. Chill 2-quart mold thoroughly in the deep freeze. When gelatin mixture is ready, remove mold from deep freeze and rinse quickly in ice-cold water. Immediately add 1 cup of the gelatin mixture and roll it around the mold to set about ¼ in. thick. Lay the reserved tomato quarters into the mold like leaves overlapping upward to the rim.

4. Combine the reserved inner pulp with the remaining gelatin mixture and add more vinegar or salt according to your taste. Pour into the mold. Set to chill and turn out when thoroughly cold (see page 209 on how to successfully unmold an aspic).

# Shrimp Salad

### Yield 2-2½ cups

### INGREDIENTS:

½ lb. cooked medium shrimp
⅓ cup cider vinegar
1 cup mung bean sprouts (4 oz.)
½ teaspoon dill weed
1 tablespoon capers
Dash of Tabasco sauce
⅓ cup Blender Mayonnaise
(see page 212)

**❝** *Choux pastry shells may be found in many recipe books, or they can be purchased boxed by the two dozen at good bakeries. We recommend the 1-1½-in. diameter "mouth size" for this salad.*
*The dish is served cold as an appetizer before sitting down to a party dinner or as a covered dish at a buffet evening. At less than 30 calories each, the stuffed choux are a delicious, nourishing alternative to many dangerously fattening starters.* **❞**

### PREPARATION

1. Steam shrimp in ⅓ cup water and ⅓ cup vinegar for 10 minutes or until all shrimp are very red. Drain and remove the shell and veins. (Be sure to start with 1 lb. raw in order to have enough.) Cut shrimp in long threads (1 in. x ¼ in.).

2. Weigh or measure out bean sprouts (may need to be cut in half, if they are too long.). Measure out dill weed and capers.

3. Prepare Blender Mayonnaise and measure out ⅓ cup.

4. Combine all ingredients and fill shells, or refrigerate and let the flavors mingle before serving. 1 level tablespoon is enough to fill the shells.

This amount fills 38 small choux pastry shells. Mung beans are a good source of vitamin K and of the B vitamins.

# Cucumber Salad

### Serves 4-6

### INGREDIENTS:

2 cucumbers, sliced
Juice of 1 lemon
½ teaspoon freshly ground salt
1 egg white, beaten
1 tablespoon sour cream
Dill weed

**❝** *A light salad before dinner at any time of the year is no surprise; it was popularized by restaurants eager to gain time to fix your order. But this one is unique. A salad that weighs in at 30 calories with dressing is for anyone — but making it taste as good as this does is something else!* **❞**

### PREPARATION

1. Skin the cucumbers, if not freshly picked (commercial ones are waxed), and squeeze the lemon.

2. Combine the first 3 ingredients and allow to sit several hours or overnight. Drain off the juice.

3. Allow egg to come to room temperature. Beat egg white until stiff but not dry.

4. Stir sour cream into the cucumbers and, at the last minute, gently fold in the egg white. Sprinkle dill weed over the top and serve.

Serves 4 at 30 calories/serving. Serves 6 at 20 calories /serving.

# Raw Fish in Quick Pickle

**Serves 4**

### INGREDIENTS:

1 lb. fresh fish (not frozen)
¼ lb. onions
4 lemons
½ cup each (2 oz.) diced carrots, celery and cucumber for each lb. of fish
⅞ cup Blender Mayonnaise for each lb. of fish (see page 212)
Lettuce leaves

### PREPARATION

1. The fish is boned, skinned, and cut into ½-inch pieces. Cut the onion into fine rings. Mix these with the fish and add the juice of 4 lemons.

2. Set this simple pickle to mature in a covered glass bowl or jar for at least 8 hours (we have left it for 24 hours without harm).

3. The flesh will now be white. Drain, throw out onions and lemon juice, and add finely diced (¼ in.) carrots, celery, and cucumber. Combine this salad with our Blender Mayonnaise. Serve well-chilled on lettuce leaves.

> We first had this dish when we lived in New Zealand. It is a favorite in Tahiti, where one version is called Poisson Cru and is laced with coconut cream before serving.
>
> This recipe turns the concept into a distinguished "tuna salad" alternative. We suggest you await your guests' inquiries and respond after they have eaten! By then they may be persuaded to try making it themselves.
>
> Perfectly fresh fish is the key to this dish. We believe, after comparing the two, that frozen fish does not work.

# Winter Salad

### Serves 8

### INGREDIENTS:

3 apples, grated (9-10 oz.)
Lemon juice
2 carrots, grated (4 oz.)
½ cup chopped almonds
⅓ cup dried apricots, chopped
(2 oz.)
⅓ cup pitted dates, chopped
(2 oz.)
⅓ cup raisins
½ cup yogurt

### PREPARATION

1. Grate apples (don't cut) and cover with lemon juice; grate carrots, chop almonds, apricots, and dates. (Dates cut better if knife is dipped in flour before every second or third cut.) Measure out raisins and yogurt.

2. Combine all ingredients in a large bowl. Serve immediately or chill before serving — delicious either way!

*" Even though salad makings are available year round, we feel it's a neat idea to serve a special salad in the winter when snow is about.*
*This is a splendid contribution that you may find equally suited to hot days. It's rather high in calories (146 / serving), but it's all good stuff — and it's variety! The yogurt really brings out the flavor of the fruits and the carrots. "*

# Tomato and Basil Salad

### Serves 4

### INGREDIENTS:

5 tomatoes
1 teaspoon basil
6 tablespoons plain yogurt
Freshly ground pepper
Salt
Romaine lettuce
4 ripe olives

### PREPARATION

1. Choose 4 blemish-free tomatoes and, leaving the skin on, make a basket out of each. Scoop out the tomato pulp, leaving the shell. Make the basket edges jagged.

2. Skin and finely dice the fifth tomato along with the scooped-out parts of the other 4. Mix tomato dicings with the yogurt, pepper, and basil.

3. Salt and pepper the inside of the tomatoes. Cut the lettuce to make 2 "leaves" per tomato. Peel the edible part away from the olive seeds, making 3 segments per olive.

4. To assemble: place 2 lettuce "leaves" halfway inside each tomato; spoon mixture into the tomatoes. Add the finishing touch of 3 olive segments per tomato for garnish. Serve on a lettuce leaf — 65 calories/serving.

*" This dish "happened" one day at lunchtime. When I was working on* The New Seasoning, *Ann Collier, my food researcher, came in with a comment that there just wasn't anything in the icebox. So she "sloshed up" this little salad. It is wonderful — and it was all hers! Now it's yours. "*

# HINTS

## Cress Salad

As a child I was given special, very small, very thin brown-bread sandwiches filled with a wonderful, spicy, crisp green salad. We called it "Mustard and Cress," but more correctly it is harvest or garden cress. Mustard is a different seed, which takes a little longer to grow, and therefore I am doubtful that they would be combined.

We purchase garden cress seeds from a wholesale seed house. This is much less expensive than the regular mini-pack available at health foods stores.

We lay out 4 thicknesses of cheesecloth in a glass dish and cover it with cold water; pour the water off and scatter on the seeds. Scatter them thickly, touching each other.

Water with a household mist sprayer several times a day. At night cover with a large plastic bag and seal to keep the moisture in. When the green tops break out, give the dish plenty of sunshine in a protected place or put under fluorescent grow-lights. Keep watering until the seedlings reach just over 2 in. high. Then harvest with scissors and build wonderful *ultrathin* cress sandwiches.

## Split Salad

The Split-Salad technique involves dividing those salad ingredients that can absorb a powerfully astringent dressing without wilting from those that can't. Let the former "soak" for several hours (24 hours doesn't hurt, but 4 is enough to do the job.) You then serve perfectly dried, chilled leaves with the marinated mixture on the side.

We find that these hard salad ingredients should be handled as follows:

*Carrot* — cut in very fine sticks.

*Radish* — cut in thin, "penny" rounds.

*Tomato* — skin (page 207) and slice thinly; select firm tomatoes for preference.

*Onion* — peel, slice in thick ½-inch rings, put in cold water, and bring slowly to the boil. Throw out water and allow rings to cool slowly.

*Green pepper* — slice in very thin strips like carrots.

*Cucumber* — peel and slice fine.

*Zucchini* — slice fine, skin on, and drop into boiling water for just 30 seconds. Remove and put into the bowl with other ingredients.

# Split Salad Dressing

## INGREDIENTS:

½ cup white wine vinegar (4 oz.)
¼ cup sesame/safflower oil (page 186) (2 oz.)
1 teaspoon sugar
½ teaspoon dry mustard
½ teaspoon salt
½ teaspoon black ground pepper
¼ teaspoon cayenne pepper

## PREPARATION

Shake dressing well and pour over the prepared hard salads. Marinate in a cool place or refrigerate. This salad can be served in two ways: 1) the marinated mixture can be added to the salad greens immediately before they are served just as a dressing would be, or, 2) they can be served in separate bowls on the table.

# HINTS

## Storage

A rather simplistic message reads,

*If mold won't grow on it,*
*Neither will you!*

Your whole foods are going to be more easily spoiled than those you have hitherto purchased. Keep a waste list on your refrigerator door. Actually admit to all that you have to throw out *before* it is cooked. In a study conducted in Arizona, it was conjectured that if the local figures were a reflection of the national scene, then each year we waste some eight billion dollars on foods that never get to the pan, let alone the plate!

What, we wonder, is this costing you?
Keep a list and you'll know!

## Avocado

Avocado *in season* is a good buy, especially near or in the growing areas. Select fruit that when held in cupped hands and pressed gently will "give" a little. (You can rapidly mature a hard avocado by placing it in a plastic bag with an apple and leaving it out of the refrigerator for a day.)

Cutting is best achieved by cutting into halves, then into quarters, and then running a knife round just under the skin as you would remove the flesh from a melon slice. Once you've cut into an avocado, it is vital that you smoother the cut slices with lemon juice the instant they are exposed to the air; otherwise the flesh discolors badly. As a matter of fact, the lemon juice also helps the otherwise rather bland flavor of the fruit.

*Appearance advantage* is the greatest asset: there is a quality of luxury about a salad containing avocado slices. The gold and green coloring of the slices can add wonderfully to a mixed green salad.

*Nutrition advantage* lies mainly in its being a good source of Vitamin A — one-half of a good-sized fruit provides 290 I.U. (about one-third of the daily recommended allowance). A word of caution: One half has 167 calories, and this places it quite high on the list of avoidables for anyone on a strict diet. So decide on a quarter of a fruit at 83.5 calories for salad use. Remember a little of even the "fattening" things will bring you variety, and variety is vital for your daily health.

## Skinned Tomatoes

The outer skin of the tomato is ultra-thin but practically indestructible in normal cooking processes. When a tomato is chopped or sliced and then cooked, the skin toughens and remains long after the soft tissue has dissolved. These rolls or flakes of skin are unsightly and indicate a lack of care. They can be removed easily by plunging tomatoes into boiling water for 60 seconds (or less), and then simply plunging them into cold or iced water. The skin just slips off without effort.

*Sense advantage* is the main benefit. I'm frankly of the opinion that "scruffy is as scruffy does", and that sloppy food preparation means a thoughtless cook. Those little rolls of tomato skin are a dead giveaway.

# HINTS

## Homegrown Bean Sprouts

Bean sprouts are usually made from either mung beans, soy beans, or alfalfa seeds. The technique is tedious to read about but easier to do! First measure ¼ cup of beans (quite adequate for a first effort). Now rinse them thoroughly in tepid water, drain, and place in an opaque (not clear glass) bowl with a lid firmly on top. Each evening add more tepid water until the bowl is full, pour off, and repeat. Scoop off any little green husks that float to the surface. Leave by the stoveside in the winter. Change the water twice each day, and continue for 7 days until the bean sprouts are at least 1-inch long, overall. They are best to eat in salads at this length. You will find the mung beans are best for cooking purposes. As the mung grows to approximately 8 to 10 times its original weight, this means that by growing your own you wind up with 8 to 10 pounds of sprouts from 1 lb. of beans.

*Nutritional advantage:* includes low calories (only 35 for 3½ ounces) as well as contributions of iron and vitamin C.

*Budget advantage:* Certainly cheaper (and better nutrition) to sprout your own rather than buy packaged sprouts.

Bean sprout suggestions: One simple idea is to add 1 teaspoon sesame/safflower oil (page 186) to a large skillet. Throw in 2 cups of bean sprouts, dash with 1 tablespoon of naturally brewed soy sauce, stir rapidly for *60 seconds* — just long enough to heat through — and serve to four people. A really delicious vegetable.

Another idea is to use them in your next salad — they add an exotic touch at such a low cost.

## Western Iceberg Lettuce

When buying Western Iceberg Lettuce, note that the head should "give" slightly when squeezed. To make the best use of this green, strip off the outer leaves to use in sandwiches or in a cream of lettuce soup. Bang the core end of the lettuce hard onto the counter and twist out the heavy core. This avoids the use of a knife, which would discolor the cut surfaces.

Hold the head under the faucet with the cavity up and let a strong jet of cold, running water flow into the lettuce. Turn it upside down and let it drain out thoroughly (this replaces some of the moisture lost in transit). When drained, put into a plastic bag, refrigerate, and use as required.

*Nutritional advantage* is found almost exclusively in its really low calorie yield: 3½ ounces equals only 14 calories!

*Sense advantage* is textural: the crisp finish to this lettuce, when kept washed, drained, and chilled like this, is *fabulous.* What it lacks in flavor it certainly makes up for in texture.

*Budget advantage* is also good, especialy when using a thick (1-inch) slice of lettuce as a "raft." Be careful to cut only at the last moment. Top the raft with slices of hard-boiled egg, one slice of ham, and coat with our Light Mayonnaise (page 214) — you've got a real plateful of emotion for next to nothing!

# HINTS

## Unmolding an Aspic

Unmolding an aspic can often be a real pain. We have devised what we think is a really nifty idea. We call it the "rubber plug and hot towel technique"! The idea is to drive a hole in the top center of your mold (it's better to have a friendly repair shop do it for you). Get a small rubber plug from a hardware store and fit it snugly in the bottom.

Fill the mold with your favorite recipe (having rinsed it first with iced water) and then chill.

To release, all you do is turn the mold upside down on a plate, remove the rubber to release the vacuum, wrap a hot towel about the mold, and count to 5. You'll hear it release itself. Perfect — every time.

## Growing Garlic Leaves

You can derive enormous satisfaction as a kitchen gardener by growing your own garlic tops. These tender green shoots will give you a mild, delicious seasoning quite unlike the robust bite of the bulb.

This is how we grew ours:

1. Clean small plastic or clay pots (be sure they have a drainage hole).
2. Cover the bottom with small stones.
3. Combine potting soil and enough water to make up a damp (not wet) mixture. Fill the pot ⅔ full with soil, then push 2 garlic bulbs into the soil round side down, pointed end up, and cover the bulbs with soil to within ½ inch of the top of the pot. Be sure to put something under the pot for proper drainage.

Progress should be seen after 3-4 days as a little green speck. After 6 more days the shoot will be about 2 inches high and showing the start of the second leaf. After another 2 days you can begin to trim off the outside leaf down to, but not below, the secondary leaves. We put the tops in our sesame/safflower oil (page 186) and use it as a normal frying oil. It adds a unique and excellent taste.

# Mayonnaise Salad Dressing

## INGREDIENTS:

White of 2 eggs, whipped
2 egg yolks
½ teaspoon dry mustard
Salt
1 cup oil
1 tablespoon boiling water

*When the famous author and gourmet, André Simon, dined at my home (I was terrified!), I gave him a hideous meal, but he did ask for a second portion of my mayonnaise. This pleased me immensely because I have taken some trouble to develop a good recipe. Here it is.*

**Step 1.** It is essential to start off by warming everything that you need to use to make mayonnaise. You will also note a bowl full of whipped white of egg. This is insurance against curdling. If the mayonnaise does separate, a spoonful of egg white whipped in will solve the problem.

**Step 2.** Place egg yolks in the warmed basin with dry mustard and a pinch of salt. Beat together thoroughly.

**Step 3.** Add oil (and you can please yourself which you buy — the flavors vary considerably — my favorite is corn oil). Add the warmed oil drop by drop at first and then in a light steady stream. Keep the egg white nearby.

**Step 4.** When the mayonnaise is thick and creamy, add 1 tablespoon boiling water. This helps to keep the sauce. You can fold in the beaten white and make a very light-textured mayonnaise, but be sure to add more seasoning when you do.

# Watercress Salad

### INGREDIENTS:

¼ cup sesame/safflower oil
(page 186)
½ cup rice vinegar
1 teaspoon dry mustard powder
Freshly ground salt
Freshly ground black pepper
Sugar to taste (not more than
1 tablespoon)

### PREPARATION

Combine all ingredients and shake until sugar has dissolved. Always shake well immediately before using.

> *Dip freshly rinsed and dried watercress in this recipe.*

# Reformed Sour Cream

### Yields 1¼ cups

### INGREDIENTS:

1 cup low-fat cottage cheese
½ cup buttermilk
2 teaspoons lemon juice
¼ teaspoon salt (optional)

### PREPARATION

1. Measure all ingredients; set up blender; have a rubber spatula ready to use.

2. Place all ingredients in the blender and whiz on the highest speed for about 1 minute total, but turn off every 15-20 seconds and push the mixture down with the spatula. It will firm up on sitting. Store in the refrigerator. Has the same consistency and appearance as sour cream — delicious with baked potatoes (page 157).

Takes 5 minutes to prepare.

> *I'm ready to confess! The sour cream I've used in my old-style recipes would have been better measured by the bucket. Now I'm less free with your digestion (and mine), but I still like sour cream. So we set to work to take away some of its obvious problems — and we won. Please try it for yourself.*

# Blender Mayonnaise

## INGREDIENTS:

1 cup polyunsaturated
vegetable oil
1 whole medium egg
½ teaspoon salt
2 tablespoons rice vinegar
½ teaspoon dry mustard
1 teaspoon sugar

*Add just before serving:*
1 beaten egg white per cup
mayonnaise
¼ teaspoon dill weed
Pinch cayenne pepper

## PREPARATION

1. Place egg, salt, rice vinegar, dry mustard, and sugar in blender with ¼ cup of the oil. Blend at lowest speed and add a slow, steady stream of the remaining ¾ cup oil through the feeder cap, the slower the stiffer.

2. Just before serving, add the beaten egg white, dill weed, and cayenne pepper. This increases the volume by about 35 percent, but must be added only just before the mayonnaise is used; otherwise it will fall.

**"** *One of the greatest pieces of social status nonsense I know is beating mayonnaise by hand when the blender is available. This great kitchen-aid can take the often difficult-to-make, time-consuming mayonnaise and make it in less than 1 minute. This is how it's done.* **"**

# Homemade Cheese Spread

**Yields 2 cups**

### INGREDIENTS:

¾ lb. grated cheddar cheese
1 cup milk
1 egg, beaten
½ teaspoon dry mustard
½-1 teaspoon optionals:
onion, garlic, chives, dill weed,
bacon bits, pimiento, olives, etc.

### PREPARATION

1. Grate cheese. Measure other ingredients. Beat egg. Plan and prepare optionals for special flavors.

2. Heat milk in a double boiler over hot water. Combine egg, grated cheese, and seasonings. Add slowly to the hot milk, stirring constantly.

3. Cook, stirring, for 15 minutes after the cheese has melted.

4. Cool completely, then store in a covered jar in the refrigerator.

5. Will keep for 2 weeks. Be sure to have at room temperature before serving, because it spreads better and has better flavor.

One cup of the spread has about 775 calories; a tablespoon has about 48.

# Reformed Blue Cheese Dressing

### INGREDIENTS:

3 tablespoons local blue cheese, crumbled
6 tablespoons plain yogurt
3 tablespoons cottage cheese
2 tablespoons mayonnaise
¼ teaspoon dill weed
¼ teaspoon chopped garlic clove
2 tablespoons celery, chopped fine

### PREPARATION

1. Combine all ingredients in a blender, except the celery, which is neatly chopped by hand into very small dice and stirred in.

2. Refrigerate and serve cold over salad greens.

*Nutrition Comment:* The U.S. Department of Agriculture quotes blue cheese dressing at about 525 calories for 100 gm. (about 3½ oz.). Our value per 100 gm. = 145 calories.

**❝** *This fabulous dressing is unknown in Europe. We have been working to create a new American blue cheese dressing so that we can move it into the realm of cost and nutritional reality.*

*We note that imported Roquefort is about twice the price of local cheese. When used in this dressing there is not enough difference in quality to justify the imported-cheese purchase.* **❞**

## French Dressing Reformed!

Most French dressings served in the United States are tomato-mayonnaise style; in Europe French dressing is *Vinaigrette* — rather similar to our Italian dressing.

In France the ratio of oil to vinegar is 2:1. I prefer the reverse, 1:2 — using a rice vinegar and adding a little sugar and mustard powder to compensate for the acidity.

Nutritional advantage is high in both calorie reduction and fat reduction. Let's look at the comparative figures for 1 ounce of each:

|  | CALORIES | FAT | POLYUNSATURATED FAT |
|---|---|---|---|
| European French dressing | 192 | 21 g. | 11 g. |
| "New" French dressing | 86 | 9 g. | 5 g. |

As is clear from these figures, the "new" one is better for health.

## Light Mayonnaise

Mayonnaise is one of those sauces that find general use in our day-to-day kitchens, over salads, in sandwiches, combined with tuna. We decided that it was possible to create a light mayonnaise that would reduce calories and yet not limit taste, and that we could reduce the cost by increasing the volume.

By adding the beaten white of one egg we increased ½ cup mayonnaise to ⅞ cup, an increase of ⅜ cup. We added ¼ teaspoon of dill weed and a dash of cayenne to fill in the taste vacuum. It pours well, looks good, tastes excellent, and has a fringe benefit. If you make your own mayonnaise and *curdle it,* you can repair the curdle by adding the whipped egg white slowly.

*Nutrition comment:* Mayonnaise has 100 calories per tablespoon; therefore ½ cup (8 tablespoons) has 800 calories. Since an egg white contains only 15 calories, you then get ⅞ cup for 815 calories and that reduces the new Light Mayonnaise to only 466 calories for ½ cup — and with the new seasoning we don't suffer.

*Budget advantage* is apparent by looking at the volume — a 75 percent increase with the addition of only an egg white. A pretty clear advantage even taking the dill and cayenne into consideration at less than a penny.

Simple recipes exist everywhere for regular mayonnaise. A tuna salad is especially good with this mixture. Have fun!

# batter & sauces

# batter & sauces

# batter & sauces

# batter & sauces

# Yeast Batter

### INGREDIENTS:

1 cup flour
¼ teaspoon salt
1 teaspoon active dry yeast
5 tablespoons fish stock
5 tablespoons flat beer
1 tablespoon olive oil
½ white of one egg, whipped

*This is not a basic batter as all the other illustrated basic methods are. But yeast batter is, in my humble opinion, the only batter to use with fish. It is fantastic! This recipe was supposed to have originated at Madame Prunier's restaurant in London.*

**Step 1.** First warm the mixing bowl. Now add 1 cup flour sifted with ¼ teaspoon salt. Make a well in the center.

**Step 2.** Place the active dry yeast in the well and add the warmed fish stock made from fish bones (or water if you are in a rush, which you shouldn't be if you are making this gastronomic batter!). Dissolve the yeast and incorporate the flour. Add the flat beer and olive oil.

**Step 3.** Put the mixture in the warming oven for at least 2 hours, preferably 4. Cover with a clean cloth.

**Step 4.** Add the whipped white of egg — half an egg white is enough — immediately before you use the batter. See page 42 for fish frying method.

# White Sauce

Yields just under 1 pint

INGREDIENTS:

3 tablespoons butter
7 tablespoons gluten-reduced flour
2 cups milk
1 clove
2 slices from medium onion
1 bay leaf
2 parsley stalks, chopped
Salt
White peppercorns, freshly ground

*Escoffier really set the culinary world twittering in 1907 when he released his famous A Guide to Modern Cookery. In this work he commented upon the use of pure starch in the preparation of a roux for sauces. He said, "It is only habit that causes flour to be still used as the cohering element of roux...with a roux made from the purest starch...a sauce Espagnol may be made in one hour...and be clearer...and better than that of the old processes, which needed three days at least to despumate." In this recipe I have used the new gluten-reduced flour, a flour specially processed to remove the gluten content. It is not the pure starch to which Escoffier refers, but it does do the job that he specified sixty odd years ago when this modern flour process could not have been anticipated.*

**Step 1.** Melt butter over a moderate heat and add flour. Stir well until sandy in texture.

**Step 2.** This step shows the roux in the making. Always use a wooden spoon and keep the roux constantly moving while it cooks together. About 2 minutes should be sufficient for a white sauce.

**Step 3.** Remove saucepan from element and add milk in three equal lots. When the first third has been added, stir and bring back onto heat to combine. Take off the heat again to add the second third, and so on. Stir well each time so that the sauce remains perfectly smooth.

**Step 4.** Place clove, onion, bay leaf, and chopped parsley stalks into a muslin bag. Beat the bag with a rolling pin (to bruise items to release flavor). Place bag in the sauce and leave on low heat for 15 minutes. Taste, season with salt and freshly ground white peppercorns. Remove herbs and serve.

# Dill Weed Fish Sauce

**Yields 1¼ cups**

### INGREDIENTS:

2½ cups fish stock (20 oz.)
(page 34)
4 6-oz. fish fillets
1 teaspoon soy sauce
1 tablespoon arrowroot
¼ cup milk or light cream
¼ teaspoon dill weed

**""** *The French once said that they had a thousand sauces and one religion, whereas the English appeared to have a thousand religions and only one sauce — and that was parsley! In an effort to undo this slur, we have added another sauce while seriously praying for a reduction in the number of denominations!* **""**

### PREPARATION

1. Make up a fish stock in a saucepan, or melt enough frozen cubes (page 35).

2. Place fish fillets in a shallow pan, such as a frying pan, that has a lid. Pour stock through a strainer and measure. Pour over the fillets in the pan. Cover and poach for 8 minutes, only.

3. Remove fish to a heated plate, cover, and keep hot.

4. Cook stock down to 1 cup. Mix soy sauce, arrowroot, and milk. Remove stock from heat and add most, but not all, the arrowroot, stirring constantly.

5. Return to the heat and continue stirring. Add the rest of the arrowroot, if needed, but wait until the sauce boils before adding the remainder.

6. Stir in the dill weed at the last minute. Pour over heated fish and serve. Gives 41 calories per serving.

# Homemade Mustard Sauce

**Yields 2 cups**

### INGREDIENTS:

⅓ cup dry mustard (2 oz.)
⅓ cup rice vinegar
⅓ cup horseradish sauce
1 tablespoon arrowroot
1 teaspoon turmeric
1⅓ cup cold water

**""** *This is a small sauce technique that can be made in an infinite number of ways, according to your taste. The saving over bought mustard is substantial, and it gives you your very own "house" mustard. This pungent sauce is highly acceptable to those who like to know they are eating mustard and who like horseradish, as it combines both.* **""**

### PREPARATION

1. Measure all ingredients.

2. Boil the water; stir in the turmeric and arrowroot until thickened. Remove from the heat and add the vinegar, horseradish, and dry mustard; stir until smooth.

3. Place in small, sterilized bottles (baby food jars are great!) and keep refrigerated. Shake before serving.

# Cheese Sauce

### INGREDIENTS:

1 heaping tablespoon (¼ oz.) grated Parmesan
¼ cup milk (2%)
½ teaspoon arrowroot

### PREPARATION

Blend together and heat until almost boiling (190° F.), stirring constantly.

One way to reduce calories in sauces that use milk is to replace it with instant milk. See page 240.

❝ *This is a "reformed" cheese sauce, excellent with cauliflower (page 181).* ❞

# HINTS

# "Sauced" Chicken

Cook breasts of chicken in a little oil in a skillet at a low heat. When cooked, pour off the fat, lay thin slices of mozzarella cheese on the surface, and sprinkle with a few capers, anchovy fillets, and parsley. Cover the dish and cook 2 minutes. Serve the coated chicken breasts dusted with paprika.

# Coconut Milk $

A swift trip to the Polynesian or Indonesian Islands will give you ample justification to use coconut milk and cream. Both can be made from either the fresh, dried, or frozen/canned pre-prepared creams or liquids.

Most of the fully prepared liquids have sugar added. For meat cookery, this is a real disaster area as the sweetening ruins the flavor of the dishes. So make your own, avoid a ruined dish, and save some money!

The milk is made by placing 8 ounces of *grated*, not sweetened, white coconut flesh in a pan and covering it with 2½ cups vigorously boiling water — and allowing it to cool with a cover on it for 30 minutes. Then squeeze through muslin or cheesecloth. This produces 14 ounces of pressed coconut milk — quite enough to be used as a cooking liquid for, say, a neck of pork stew with green peppers and a light curry seasoning. The infused flesh can be infused once again, but it will be so weak that it can only be recommended for cooking vegetables.

*Nutritional advantage:* The food value profile is interesting. This is for 1¾ cups (14 ounces), enough to provide flavor for a 4-portion casserole: 504 calories (bad); 6.4 g. protein (poor); 49.8 g. saturated fat (bad); 200 mg. phosphorous (good).

Obviously you need to be very sure that you are not on a fat free diet when you try this one.

# HINTS

## Mozzarella as a "Sauce"

The traditional shape of mozzarella is like a pear. The shape makes it easy to slice into rings and use as a melted topping. The idea is to use the cheese in lieu of a sauce (see "sauced" chicken, page 219). To do this all you have to do is cook your piece of fish, poultry, veal, beef, lamb, or pork in a skillet, then drain off all the fat and cover the cooked food with the slice of cheese, sprinkle with a suitable "seasoning" such as sage for veal, tarragon for chicken, or capers for pork, and cover the dish for 2 minutes. Then remove the "sauced" items and serve.

*Effort advantage:* This saves the entire time it takes to make a sauce.

*Nutritional advantage:* Since only half as much cheese is needed per serving to replace the white sauce, this results in a reduction in calories from 106 to 84. In addition, the cheese yields over twice as much protein in spite of being half of the amount.

## Arrowroot, a Super Thickener

Sauces that require a mixture of equal parts of flour and butter combined and cooked (called a roux) will absorb six times their total weight in liquid. A 3-ounce roux will therefore absorb 18 fluid ounces of liquid to make 20 fluid ounces (2½ cups) of sauce.

The same 18 ounces can be thickened with 1 ounce of arrowroot. Arrowroot thickens without adding a taste of its own, it *clears* completely without "cornstarch cloudiness," and it thickens instantly at 212°F. The arrowroot is measured, placed in a bowl, mixed with a little water to form a thin creamlike consistency, and then poured into a boiling liquid to thicken.

Nutritional advantage:

*Roux sauce base*

1½ ounces butter plus 1½ ounces flour = 455 calories

*Arrowroot sauce base*

1 ounce arrowroot = 68 calories

20 ounces sauce makes approx. 6 servings; therefore

Roux base* is 74.5 calories per serving.

Arrowroot base* is 11.3 calories per serving.

*Sense advantage:* There is some downgrading of the finished sauce, especially if it is white. There is a texture loss, a "lack of substance," but the flavor is usually enhanced. Brown sauces do not suffer from these drawbacks nearly as much, and they have the clarity plus factor.

*Effort advantage:* A considerable amount of time is saved.

*Budget advantage:* Buy the arrowroot in 1-pound bags from good health-food stores, *not* in the small glass jars sold by herb-and-spice concerns.

For your next casserole (or stew), try adding *no* flour or thickening at any stage. Just before you serve it, skim off all the fat, and strain off all the thin juices. Bring the juices to the boil and pour in the arrowroot, which has been mixed with a little water (about 1 tablespoon of arrowroot per cup of liquid to be thickened). Stir rapidly and return to the stew, fold in gently, and serve. It will look brilliant and glossy, just like a *McCall's* food page!

*Note that this is for the base only, not the liquid or garnish used.

# Double Boilers

The double boiler was first developed in China around 3,600 years ago for a method called *Huann,* in which the juices of ham and chicken are allowed to exit the flesh and form an essence unsullied by any added moisture.

Our kitchen practice uses the double boiler or "porringer" for foods that need to cook out over fairly long periods that might otherwise stick or "catch," such as cream of wheat or white sauce; it is also used for holding fricassees or sauce-based mixtures ready for serving without scorching. Finally, it is used for making egg-based sauces such as Hollandaise and for desserts. Select a clear glass unit in preference to the metal because you can *see the heat** and control it. The glass unit is generally cheaper.

*By concentration of water bubbles.

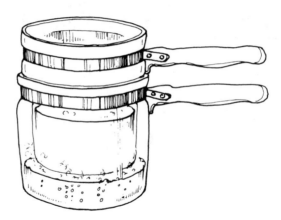

# Brown Sauce

**Yields 1 cup**

### INGREDIENTS:

2 tablespoons clarified butter
(page 77)
½ cup tomato
1 pint 30-Minute Beef Stock
3 teaspoons arrowroot
Salt to season
Freshly ground black peppercorns
to season

❝ *Bread and brown sauce — not really a gastronomic pair, but they have something in common in this modern day and age. We very seldom make our own bread — it is now conveniently baked for us. A good brown sauce, including the preparation of an excellent stock, can take up to 4 days to make. Some hotels and restaurants may still do this, but the modern homemaker doesn't have the time and has been forced to accept some processed product in lieu. I have developed this quick brown sauce, made in 1 hour maximum, as a possible alternative to the processed offering!* ❞

**Step 1.** Melt clarified butter in a saucepan and add ½ cup tomato that has been skinned and had the seeds removed. Fry at quite a high heat, scraping off the bottom all the time so that it darkens in color but does not actually burn.

**Step 2.** When the tomato is well colored, measure out 1 pint of 30-Minute Beef Stock (page 31). Mix in well.

**Step 3.** Measure the depth and make a mark on a spoon exactly halfway between top and bottom. This helps to record the exact level wanted for a reduction by half. Boil vigorously until the level is reduced to this mark, skimming off foam from time to time.

**Step 4.** Add arrowroot mixed with cold stock or water. As it enters the boiling sauce, stir rapidly with a wooden spoon. When the sauce thickens and becomes clear, adjust the seasoning with salt and freshly ground black peppercorns and serve.

# Meatless Spaghetti Sauce

### Serves 4

## INGREDIENTS:

2 garlic cloves, mashed
1 large onion, chopped
¼ lb. mushrooms, chopped
⅔ cup ground sunflower seeds
½ cup ground peanuts
1 tablespoon oil
¼ cup soy grits
1 teaspoon oregano
1 teaspoon basil
1 bay leaf
2 14-oz. cans Italian-style
tomatoes
1 tablespoon Parmesan cheese

## PREPARATION

1. Mash garlic, chop onion and mushrooms. Cover the mushrooms with a little lemon juice to keep from discoloring. Grind sunflower seeds and peanuts. Measure out the rest of the ingredients.

2. Saute' garlic and onions in a large skillet with the oil until slightly brown.

3. Add the grits, seeds, and nuts and stir over medium-low heat until thoroughly toasted (5 minutes). You may need to add a little more oil to keep the mixture from burning and to toast it well.

4. Add herbs, tomatoes, and mushrooms, and stir well to mix. Simmer with lid on for 10-15 minutes. Stir often. Serve over spaghetti or over zucchini for even fewer calories. Dust with the cheese. Makes 4½-5 cups sauce, or 4 servings at about 300 calories a serving.

**❝** *One of the most popular sauces used from day to day is the Italian meat sauce served over spaghetti, meat loaves, etc. Can we make such a sauce attractive and meatless, yet retain the complete protein of meat? And do it all at a reduced price and take less time? We achieved this by combining soy grits, sunflower seeds, and peanuts. The result is both delicious and less expensive than meat. The fat is severely reduced, and for this alone it would be worth the effort for your family.* **❞**

# Chicken Cobham Style

**Serves 4**

### INGREDIENTS:

1 3½-lb. roasting chicken,
plus its giblets
2 tablespoons sesame/safflower oil
(page 186)
6 stalks parsley
2 tablespoons naturally brewed
soy sauce
Ground ginger
Salt
Arrowroot

### PREPARATION

1. A good chicken will have its giblets and liver sold with it. Remove the liver and keep it frozen until you have a paté or a spaghetti bolognaise. It can be added to either and gives an excellent flavor boost.

2. Chop up the giblets and brown well in only 1 tablespoon of hot oil. Cover with 2 cups of water, add 6 stalks of parsley, and allow to simmer until the liquid is reduced to 1 cup. Then add soy sauce to taste, about 2 tablespoons.

3. Truss the chicken (a simple way is shown on page 104), having first seasoned the inside with ground ginger and salt.

4. Mix ½ teaspoon of ginger with 1 tablespoon of oil, and brush this mixture over the chicken until the bird is thoroughly coated.

5. Strain the prepared giblet stock into a roasting pan and add the chicken, laid on one side. Cover the bird with buttered paper or foil, and roast for 25 minutes on one side, then turn onto the other side for 25 minutes. The oven should remain at a steady 300° F. throughout cookery.

6. Remove the paper or foil, and raise the oven temperature to 425° F. to just brown the outer skin — for, say, 5 minutes only.

7. Skim the extra fat from the gravy, and serve the bird in a shallow casserole with gravy thickened by a little arrowroot (see page 220 for technique).

# Tomato Sauce

**Serves 4-6**

### INGREDIENTS:

¼ cup juice from meat loaf
¼ cup tomato juice
1 teaspoon lemon juice
1 teaspoon soy sauce
1 teaspoon arrowroot
1 teaspoon fresh parsley

### PREPARATION

1. Place meat juice in a small saucepan and add tomato juice, lemon juice, and soy sauce. Heat to almost boiling.

2. Dissolve arrowroot in a little water and stir into the hot mixture. Stir constantly, remove from the heat, and add parsley. Pour over turned-out Barley Meat Loaf (page 98).

Serves 4 at 395 calories per serving or 6 at 263 calories per serving.

# desserts

# desserts

# desserts

# desserts

# Baked Apples

**Serves 4**

### INGREDIENTS:

4 firm McIntosh apples
Juice of ½ lemon
4 tablespoons oatmeal, dry
Scant ¼ teaspoon ground allspice
16 pitted, plumped prunes

*So many of the dishes served as desserts are surrounded by a cloud of carbohydrate or smothered in cream! Here is a good recipe that traces almost all its calories to pure healthy fruit.*

**Step 1.** Core apples and score the skin all around the equator of the apple, about 1 inch up from the bottom.

**Step 2.** Rub lemon juice inside cut surface and set apples in a shallow baking dish.

**Step 3.** Place prunes in water that has been brought to a boil and simmer for 10 minutes to plump. Remove pits and mash prunes with a fork or spoon. Add allspice and mash; stir in oatmeal.

**Step 4.** Fill each apple just to the top with this mixture. Bake at 350º F. for 45 minutes. Serve immediately. One serving has 148 calories.

# No-Crust Apple Pie

**Serves 6**

### INGREDIENTS:

4 cooking apples
½ cup dry oatmeal
1 tablespoon coconut
2 tablespoons sliced almonds
1 tablespoon wheat germ
2 tablespoons brown sugar
1 teaspoon cinnamon
2 tablespoons melted butter

### PREPARATION

1. Melt butter. Measure out other ingredients, except apples, into a medium-sized mixing bowl. Pour butter over the mixture and stir to blend.

2. Peel and slice apples into a 9-inch pie plate. Sprinkle coarse mixture over the apples and bake at 375º F. for 25 minutes. Serve warm as is, or with skim milk, or a dollop of yogurt, or Papufa.

One serving is 117 calories.

> *This recipe takes much less time than a pastry-crust pie. The calories are greatly reduced and the taste is wonderful. The only negative is appearance. We find that a good blob of yogurt helps, or you could try Papufa Topping (page 234).*

# Apricots and Mace

**Yields 1½ cups**

### INGREDIENTS:

1 cup dried (sulfur-free) apricots*
1 cup water
½ teaspoon mace, grated

### PREPARATION

1. Measure out apricots and water; grate mace and measure ½ teaspoon.

2. Place fruit in a glass saucepan with an equal amount of water.

3. Bring fruit to a boil. Sprinkle grated mace on top, cover, and simmer gently for 10 minutes. Remove from heat and allow to cool. Most of the moisture should be absorbed.

*5 oz. dry equals 1 cup; 9 oz. cooked equals 1 cup.

> *Dried fruits plus spice and water only can be delicious. Try the recipe below and add whipped egg white for a low-calorie, sugar-free dessert. The sweet-tasting mace replaces the sugar.*

# Spiced Peaches

**Serves 4**

### INGREDIENTS:

1 lb. (drained wt.) water-packed, sliced peaches or peach halves
Reserved liquid from peaches
1¼ cups rice vinegar
½ teaspoon cloves
1 small cinnamon stick piece (½ x ¼ in.)
½ teaspoon allspice berries

### PREPARATION

1. Simmer last 4 ingredients together for 30 minutes in a covered small saucepan. Strain and pour hot over peaches. Soak for 10 minutes.

2. Pour off the vinegar mixture and re-cover peaches with the original juice from the can.

*The spiced fruit garnish is a splendid accompaniment to rich meat dishes, such as pork, spareribs, roast beef, or lamb. Here we have Spiced Peaches. You can start out with fresh peaches in season, or make up limited quantities as required using preserved fruit.*

# Broiled Grapefruit

**Serves 4**

### INGREDIENTS:

2 pink grapefruit
2 tablespoons white grape juice
1 teaspoon rice vinegar
Dash of ground cardamom

### PREPARATION

1. Cut grapefruit in half. Loosen and remove cores, and cut around each segment to loosen it.

2. Place grapefruit on a heat-proof plate, cut side up, and broil 4 inches away from heat for 5 minutes.

3. While the grapefruit are broiling, heat the grape juice and vinegar to almost boiling. Pour the liquid over the grapefruit; dust very gently with a little cardamom and serve immediately.

Each ½ grapefruit now has only 55 calories.

Pink grapefruit has much more vitamin A than white grapefruit (½ white grapefruit = 10 I.U. vitamin A; ½ pink grapefruit = 540 I.U. vitamin A).

*This is our lowest calorie dessert and I highly recommend it to you. The cardamom and grape juice will add enough "new" flavor interest to replace the usual kirsch or other liqueur.*

# Pineapple Dessert

**Serves 4**

### INGREDIENTS:

1 pineapple
1 cup low-fat yogurt
¼ cup sour cream
4 tablespoons wheat germ

### PREPARATION

1. Combine the diced flesh with 1 cup of plain low-fat yogurt mixed with ¼ cup sour cream and 4 tablespoons of wheat germ.

2. Stir all together well and serve from the chilled husk (see page 231 for technique).

# Pear Helene

**Serves 4**

### INGREDIENTS:

2 medium pears
¼ cup dark brown sugar
1 teaspoon vanilla
2 ounces semi-sweet chocolate
1½ teaspoons butter
1½ cups vanilla ice cream (¾ pint)

### PREPARATION

1. Peel and halve pears; do not remove cores.

2. Dissolve sugar in 2 cups water in skillet. Add vanilla. Place pears in syrup, and poach gently until just cooked.

3. Remove pears, scoop out seeds and core. Cover pears with syrup and allow to cool.

4. Make chocolate sauce as directed on page 232. Beat until smooth and glossy. Place scoop of ice cream in dish, cover with pear half and chocolate sauce.

# Fruit Curry

**Serves 4-6**

## INGREDIENTS:

2 lbs. mixed fruit (not citrus) cut into 1-in. pieces
1 tablespoon oil
½ cup onion, finely chopped (2 oz.)
2 teaspoons mild curry powder
1 teaspoon ground ginger or
1 tablespoon freshly grated ginger
1 pint veal stock
1 tablespoon arrowroot
Salt
⅜ cup desiccated coconut liquid (3 oz.)
Juice of 1 lemon
½ cup light cream

> **We offer this Fruit Curry to those with a taste for the unusual.**

## PREPARATION

1. Use pineapple, peaches, pears, plums, etc. If fruit is canned there is no need to cook it. Otherwise poach fruit until semi-cooked. Measure or otherwise prepare other ingredients.

2. Put oil in frying pan and lightly sauté onions, but do not let them get brown or hard (just to transparent stage).

3. Add curry powder and fry 1 minute longer. Add ginger and stir to mix. Add veal stock, bring to a boil, and reduce by half the original volume. Thicken with arrowroot dissolved in a little cold water.

4. Add salt to taste, but keep to an absolute minimum. Add fruit and boil for a few minutes.

5. Add the coconut liquid and lemon juice, mix well, but *do not boil,* and, finally, stir in the cream.

6. Serve with plain boiled rice — hot Fruit Curry in the winter and cold Fruit Curry in the summer.

Serves 4 generously at 292 calories per serving.

# HINTS

## Fresh Pineapple

When pineapples are plentiful, it's a good idea to make the most of the purchase and remove the flesh in such a way that the husk becomes a serving piece. You can make a dessert pineapple, with, say, yogurt on the side, into a serving visually larger than it really is.

A good pineapple is yellow-green in appearance, especially about the base. Beware of the golden-yellow color — it may be too ripe. Another test for ripeness is to pluck out a center leaf from the top and bend it. It should bend right back without cracking.

*Nutritional advantage:* Here you can see the relative effect that processing has upon the foods we eat. A 3½-ounce piece gives us a little over one-third the recommended daily allowance of vitamin C.

| | GRAMS | CALORIES | PROTEIN | FAT | CARBOHY-DRATE |
|---|---|---|---|---|---|
| Fresh | 100 | 123 | .9 g. | .5 g | 32.3 g. |
| Canned in Heavy Syrup | 100 | 336 | 1.4 g. | .5 g. | 88 g. |

| | CALCIUM | IRON | VITAMIN A | VITAMIN C |
|---|---|---|---|---|
| Fresh | 40 mg. | 1.2 mg. | 170 I.U. | 40 mg. |
| Canned in Heavy Syrup | 50 mg. | 1.4 mg. | 200 I.U. | 30 mg. |

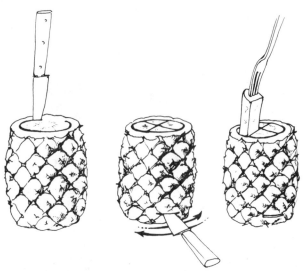

## Maturing Tree Fruit at Home

We have found that very hard fruit may be brought to edible maturity in 1-2 days by placing the fruit in a plastic bag with a green apple. Not only is maturity hastened, but the flavor is markedly improved.

Peaches, apricots, kiwis (Chinese gooseberry), and small plums were tested, and only the kiwi showed little change. The apricots may need only 8-10 hours, while the rest were perfect after 24 hours. It's really well worth the test.

# Reformed Zabaglione

**Serves 4**

### INGREDIENTS:

4 medium eggs, separated
¼ cup granulated sugar
¼ cup sweet white grape juice

### PREPARATION

1. Cream the egg yolks and sugar with a wooden spoon until very pale and creamlike.

2. Add the grape juice very gently, stirring all the time.

3. Pour the mixture into a double boiler over warm water; the water is heated slowly to a simmer but should never boil. From the moment the mixture is placed over the water it must be stirred with a wooden spoon. Be careful here — scrambled eggs are revolting with grape juice and sugar!

4. The mixture is cooked when it thickens; this should only take about 4 minutes for 4 servings.

5. Remove the double boiler from the heat and allow the mixture to cool.

6. Beat the egg whites stiffly and fold into the cooked yolks. The finished dish should look golden and fluffy.

7. Serve in previously chilled glasses.

If you want to serve this dessert hot, then you have to face up to the fact that into the kitchen you must go. This cannot be cooked in advance, though you can go through step two a good 2 hours beforehand.

# Chocolate Sauce

**Serves 4**

### INGREDIENTS:

1½ teaspoons butter
2 ounces chocolate

### PREPARATION

1. To melt chocolate, place the squares in a small saucepan and cover them with some hot water that is almost at the boil. Use semi-sweet cooking chocolate for best results. Allow to sit in the water on a cold stove until the chocolate is softened (about 1 to 2 minutes).

2. Pour off the water gently. To produce a high gloss, add 1½ teaspoons butter to 2 ounces chocolate for a topping suitable for 4 servings.

*Nutrition comment:* Be aware of the source of calories. You can only widen your net to include all the goodies when you know *exactly* what you are eating! Just remember that, where food is concerned, *ignorance can show!* This sauce has 86 calories per serving, it is delicious and fun to eat, but it doesn't take much extra to double the impact to: 1 tablespoon butter + 4 ounces chocolate — and you get *hit* with 172 calories per serving for the topping alone, and that is when it gets out of hand!

# Baby's Fruit Gelatin Dessert

**Yields 8 Servings**

### INGREDIENTS:

1⅓ cups fresh orange juice
(3 temple oranges were
just right)
¼ cup cold water
1 tablespoon unflavored gelatin
⅔ cup water
½ cup ripe banana, sliced (2 oz.)

### PREPARATION

1. Squeeze orange juice. Measure other ingredients.

2. Place cold water in a small saucepan. Add gelatin, stir, and heat gently to just dissolve gelatin granules.

3. Place orange juice, ⅔ cup water, banana slices, and gelatin mixture in a blender and blend for 15-25 seconds on the lowest speed.

4. Pour into small custard cups and refrigerate until used. Makes 8 servings of about ⅓ cup each. Do not store for longer than 1 week.

*Nutrition comment:* This could be fed to a baby starting at 3 or 4 months old. As the baby gets older, the ⅔ cup water can be replaced with all orange juice or other types of juices except fresh or frozen pineapple juice. This is much healthier for the child than artificially flavored and colored, oversweetened, premixed gelatin desserts.

# No-Cook Peach Jam

**Yields 2 cups**

### INGREDIENTS:

9 fresh peaches, peeled
Juice of 1 lemon
2 cups sugar
1 package (1¾ oz.) powdered
pectin in ½ cup water
1 envelope gelatin in
¼ cup warm water

### PREPARATION

1. Peel and pit peaches. Chop in blender at lowest speed (fruit will be lumpy). Add the lemon juice. Stir in the sugar and let stand for 10 minutes.

2. In a saucepan, stir the pectin into ½ cup water. Bring to a boil over medium heat, stir constantly for 1 minute, then add to fruit and stir for 3 minutes.

3. Dissolve the gelatin in ¼ cup warm water and stir until clear. Add to the fruit and stir well.

4. Pour into jars and place in the refrigerator for 8-12 hours to harden. The jam may be refrigerated up to 3 weeks or frozen for 6 months.

> ❝ *Jams and other sweetened preserves hit our bodies with a huge load of sugar at breakfast time — at 55 calories per level teaspoon. I set out to reduce the recipe for a No-Cook Peach Jam from 5 cups sugar (770 calories per cup = 3850 calories) to 2 cups sugar, a saving of 2310 calories.* ❞

# Papufa Whipped Topping

**Yields 3 cups**

### INGREDIENTS:

½ cup ice water
½ cup nonfat dried milk (1½ oz.)
3 tablespoons sugar
1 tablespoon safflower oil
½ teaspoon vanilla extract

### PREPARATION

1. Place mixing bowl in freezer. Fill a larger bowl ⅓ full with ice cubes and water. Measure out all ingredients.

2. Place ½ cup ice water and milk in chilled bowl and place this bowl in the larger bowl. Mix at high speed with an electric beater until stiff peaks form (7-10 minutes).

3. After peaks form, add the sugar, 1 tablespoon at a time, beating well after each addition. Add the oil slowly and beat well. Finally add the vanilla and beat only enough to mix.

Commercial toppings contain 175-230 calories per cup with 12-20 grams fat per cup. Ours weighs in at 109 calories per cup and 4.6 grams fat per cup.

❝ *The word* papufa *means Physiologically Active Polyunsaturated Fatty Acid. This topping is suited to low-cholesterol diets. It replaces artificial toppings and costs next to nothing.* ❞

# Rice Pudding

**Serves 4**

### INGREDIENTS:

½ cup dry rice (4 oz.)
4 cups 2% milk
2 pieces lemon peel (1x2 in.)
1 vanilla pod
2 tablespoons granulated sugar
1 medium egg

### PREPARATION

1. Place rice, milk, lemon peel, and vanilla in a medium-large saucepan. Raise to the boil and simmer for 20 minutes uncovered on very low heat.

2. Remove lemon peel, add sugar, stir in well, and let the mixture cool naturally. Then chill.

3. Beat egg white, stir into egg yolk, and fold this mixture into rice. Serve in parfait glasses with a colorful fruit topping.

❝ *Milk puddings provide a splendid dessert — filling, satisfying, inexpensive, and nutritious. One of the easiest is rice pudding. For this you need short-grain rice, such as Carolina; long-grain rice will not work.* ❞

# Blueberry and Strawberry Parfait

**Serves 4**

## INGREDIENTS:

⅔ cup well-drained strawberries
⅔ cup blueberries
2 tablespoons plus
2 teaspoons honey
4 8-oz. cartons plain yogurt
½ teaspoon vanilla extract
2 drops blue food coloring
4 teaspoons wheat germ

*This is a fun dessert originally developed to celebrate 1976. In addition to being fun and obviously patriotic (it is red, white, and blue), it is high in protein, low in fat, and "costs" only 236 calories for a giant feast!*

## PREPARATION

1. Mash berries in 2 separate bowls.

2. To the strawberries add 1 tablespoon honey and 1⅓ cups yogurt. Stir to mix. Set aside.

3. To the blueberries add 1 tablespoon honey and 1⅓ cups yogurt, and 2 drops blue food coloring. Stir to blend. Set aside.

4. To the final 1⅓ cups yogurt add 2 teaspoons honey and ½ teaspoon vanilla.

5. Layer the 3 fillings in 4 parfait glasses, starting with the blueberry, then the vanilla, and finally the strawberry layer. The second and third layers must be poured in very carefully, or they sink into the first layer. We bent a teaspoon upward to form an L at about a 100° angle, and poured the top 2 layers onto the spoon, allowing them to spill over and cover the first and second layers, respectively.

6. Garnish with 1 teaspoon wheat germ sprinkled over the top of each parfait.

One serving has 236 calories.

# Fruit Compote

**Serves 4**

## INGREDIENTS:

1 lb. fruit
2 cups water
3 tablespoons brown sugar (1 oz.)
2 tablespoons fresh lemon juice
2 pieces lemon peel

## PREPARATION

1. Cut away all bruised parts of fruit and add 2 tablespoons (1 ounce) water to each ounce of fresh fruit.

2. For each cup of water add 4 packed teaspoons brown sugar (½ ounce) and 1 tablespoon fresh lemon juice plus a small piece (1 by 2 inches) of lemon peel.

3. Bring to a boil slowly for 10 minutes, remove fruit pieces to bowl, and reduce liquid by boiling to only ¼ cup of syrup. Stir syrup into the fruit and cool.

*Nutritional advantage* comes exclusively from the fruit and therefore is big on Vitamin A. Whichever fruit you use, the one common factor is the syrup. This has a profile for 4 servings of: 56 calories, 14.6 grams carbohydrate, 3 I.U. Vitamin A.

Add this to the Vitamin A from the plain fruits, and that looks like really good news to me!

*Sense advantage:* Splendid taste and appearance.

*Budget advantage:* Bruised fruit should cost you half the price of the original and wind up, in volume, saving you 25 percent (after cutting away bruised parts). When compared with prepared foods, the sky gets to be the limit for your savings.

*For a "sweet 'n sour" dessert,* try a spoonful over ice cream.

*As a fruit base for homemade yogurt* (see page 239), it's delicious.

*For a spiced "dressing"* for roast "young" meats — pork, veal, lamb, poultry — add ¼ teaspoon allspice.

# Low-Calorie Cheesecake

**Serves 8**

### INGREDIENTS:

1¼ cups graham cracker crumbs
¼ cup melted butter
2 tablespoons cold water
2 tablespoons lemon juice
1 envelope unflavored gelatin
½ cup nonfat dried milk,
liquefied and heated to boiling
1 whole egg
⅓ cup sugar
2 cups low-fat cottage cheese
1 teaspoon vanilla flavoring

### PREPARATION

1. Place graham crackers in blender and whiz until fine. Melt margarine. Blend together and press into a 9-in. pie plate to make crust.

2. Place cold water with lemon juice and gelatin into blender, cover and process at low speed to soften gelatin.

3. Remove feeder cap and add boiling milk. When gelatin is dissolved, turn to highest speed.

4. Add remaining ingredients and continue to process until smooth. Pour mixture into graham cracker crust. Refrigerate 2-3 hours before serving.

Serves 8 at 198 calories per slice.

**"** *Cheesecake is one of those desserts I order when I'm in an extreme state of diet rebellion. Because of this we decided to produce a "low-impact cheesecake." We were excited about this project, and when we eventually discovered the method that gave us a 198-calorie slice against the regular 456-calorie slice, we rejoiced. I believe that much can be done by adding to this basic recipe, and I do urge you to experiment with adding raisins or chopped dates. You can also stir in a little blue cheese — you name it — it's a creative possibility!* **"**

# Tapioca Pudding

### Yields 3¼ cups

## INGREDIENTS:

⅓ cup pearl tapioca
2¼ cups milk
¼ teaspoon salt
1 tablespoon arrowroot
2 tablespoons milk
1 egg
¼ cup sugar
¼ teaspoon vanilla extract
Cinnamon

> " *Tapioca is made from the roots of the cassava or manioc plant. It is very digestible, recommended for babies and elderly persons.* "

## PREPARATION

1. Soak the pearl tapioca for 3 hours in ¾ cup water.

2. Pour off water from tapioca. Add 2¼ cups milk and salt, and place mixture in a 1½-quart saucepan (nonstick is best). Heat and stir until it boils. Simmer uncovered, stirring frequently, over lowest possible heat for 50 minutes.

3. Mix the arrowroot and 2 tablespoons milk, pour into the hot mixture, and bring to a boil, stirring constantly; reduce heat.

4. Beat the egg, sugar, and vanilla extract together. Mix about ½ to ¾ cup of the hot tapioca with the egg, then pour mixture back into the saucepan. Stir rapidly to mix. Remove from heat.

Serve hot or chilled, in small glasses, and dusted with cinnamon.

This recipe, at 124 calories per ½ cup serving, has somewhat fewer calories than regular tapioca (140 calories).

# Low-Calorie Reform Custard

### Yields 2 Cups

## INGREDIENTS:

1½ cups nonfat dried milk, liquefied
3½ cups water
1 tablespoon sugar
3 egg yolks
1 vanilla pod, uncut
2 teaspoons arrowroot

## PREPARATION

1. Reconstitute the dried milk at the rate of ⅓ cup plus 2 tablespoons per cup of water. Reserve 2 tablespoons liquefied milk to mix with the arrowroot.

2. To the remaining milk, add the sugar, egg yolks, and the vanilla pod (uncut, because otherwise the fine seeds would spill out and spoil the appearance of the custard).

3. Stir well and place in the top of a double boiler. Heat to 190° F. Cook 10 minutes over boiling water.

4. Add the arrowroot mixed with the reserved cold milk and stir into the hot mixture. Continue stirring until the custard thickens.

If served plain, you may need to add a little sugar (1 tablespoon maximum), or try 1 teaspoon decaffeinated instant coffee and no extra sugar. Serve ice cold. Served plain, with the added sugar, one ½ cup serving is 145 calories.

# Homemade Yogurt

**Yields 1 Quart**

### INGREDIENTS:

1 tablespoon plain,
natural yogurt
1 quart milk

### PREPARATION

1. Purchase the smallest-size plain, natural yogurt from your market (or purchase a package of dry starter from a health food store). Combine one tablespoon yogurt with 1 quart milk that has been heated to 100° F. (You can use "2 percent" skim milk for only 125 calories per 8 ounces.) Stir well, put in a glass bowl or 4 8-ounce preserving jars, cover with cloth or lids, and put into an oven preheated to 200° F. Turn oven *off* immediately and leave overnight or about 10 hours.

2. Remove, place in refrigerator, and use as required.

We suggest adding fresh fruit with a very little honey and wheat germ for sweetness and texture. Always keep one tablespoon of plain yogurt as a starter for the next batch. It will be necessary to start a new culture every 4 to 6 months, because the yogurt gets stronger and more acidic with time.

*Nutritional advantage* can be obtained by using non-fat dried milk in lieu of whole milk. The nourishment obtained in one cup of regular yogurt is the same as for one cup of whole milk. It is a complete protein and provides high amounts of calcium and riboflavin.

*Effort advantage* comes from there being almost no effort at all! The suggested use of smaller containers, 1-cup size, is due to the fact that a large quantity, when disturbed, tends to separate and look unsightly.

*Sense advantage* results in a slight effort expenditure being rewarded with your very own, uniquely flavored yogurt.

# HINTS

## "Instant" Milk

A large number of recipes, such as white sauce (page 217), call for *whole* milk. It's used in custards, sauces, puddings, and added to whipped potatoes, eggs, bread, and soups.

However, non-fat milk in the *instant* form provides an interesting economy — when we take careful steps to reduce fresh consumption accordingly.

For some dishes, however, the result, using nonfat milk, is somewhat *thin* and, as a rule, we would suggest using an extra 3 tablespoons (1½ oz.) to each quart of water. If you add a very little fresh grated nutmeg to "fill in the holes" left by the removal of the fat content, you can achieve a tastier product at realistic savings without any suffering.

*Nutritional advantage:* This is the profile comparison for various milks:

|  | CALORIES | PROTEIN | FAT | CALCIUM | RIBOFLAVIN |
|---|---|---|---|---|---|
| 1 cup whole | 160 | 9 g. | 8.6 g. (3.5%) | 288 mg. | 420 mg. |
| 1 cup "instant" per package directions | 90 | 9 g. | 0.2 g. | 298 mg. | 440 mg. |
| 1 cup "enriched instant" (see above) | 113.8 | 12 g. | 0.25 g. | 390 mg. | 453 mg. |

*Budget advantage:* For economy and also ease of doing this, we'd suggest buying bulk — not only are money savings greater, but it's also much easier to use the milk, since using 1 quart packages will necessitate opening another package when you want to add extra powder. For even greater ease and money saving, we suggest that you buy in bulk and transfer the powder into airtight jars. Don't store in the package. It can be messy, you may lose some, and it will go stale if exposed to the air for a period of time.

# Decaffeinated Coffee

## (made by the Cold-Water Method)

### INGREDIENTS:

1 lb. decaffeinated coffee
2 1-lb. coffee cans of water

*Coffee is now the six-letter dirty word and is likely to remain so. My family and I avoid any product that produces a craving when discontinued. If a withdrawal sensation is noticed, then we assume we are building a dependency, and our only dependency as Christians should be on our Lord Jesus. Here we have used decaffeinated coffee in a special way that eliminates the dependency but tastes good. It is also less expensive and quicker than perked coffee to make.*

### PREPARATION

1. Select a good decaffeinated ground coffee and measure 1 lb. coffee to two 1-lb. cans of water (use coffee can to measure).

2. Take a bowl holding 6 pts., add 1 lb. decaffeinated coffee, and cover with 2 lbs. *cold* water. *Don't stir.* * Cover the bowl and allow to stand for at least 12 hours.

3. Then strain through 8 thicknesses of cheesecloth. Use a colander at first, then gather the ends together and hang up over the bowl to drip. A good deal of the water will be absorbed by the coffee so that we should get approximately 5 cups (40 fl. oz.) coffee extract, sufficient for 53 6-oz. cups of regular coffee.

4. Allow the coffee to drip through slowly. Place the extract in a bottle and cork or seal it tightly.

To make coffee for breakfast, boil milk and serve hot milk with the cold coffee extract on the side in a small jug. Each person adds coffee to suit personal taste. For a "black" cup, pour 3 tablespoons into a cup and add 6 fluid ounces (¾ cup) boiling water, stir, and drink.

Keeps well for at least a week in the refrigerator.

*This is because decaffeinated coffee is super-fine and reassembled into ground bean form. When stirred, it breaks down into dust that clogs any filter.

# Hot Sippin' Cider

### Yields 8 Cups

### INGREDIENTS:

2 quarts fresh apple cider (unsweetened)
1 teaspoon allspice berries
¼ teaspoon whole cloves
3 inch stick cinnamon
Dash of nutmeg

*As I wrote this recipe I was looking out at Old Baldy, an 11,000-foot peak in Colorado. It's often at freezing or below outside in the winter, and it's a great comfort and pleasure to put aside the usual tea and coffee or hot chocolate, and brew up some spiced cider, equally good on a cool evening anywhere.*

### PREPARATION

1. Tie spices in a small piece of cheesecloth.

2. Measure cider and pour into a saucepan or heat-proof tea or coffee pot (if using the latter, be sure pot has no coffee odor, and spices can be put in the percolator part where ground coffee ordinarily would be placed). Cover container and simmer for 15 minutes.

3. Remove spices and serve with orange peel or plain in mugs.

One cup of cider has 120 calories and contains a small amount of B vitamins. Canned juice is a poor source of vitamin C.

# Iced Coffee for Four

**Yields 1 Pint**

### INGREDIENTS:

2 cups 2% milk
1 teaspoon vanilla extract
6 tablespoons coffee extract (3 oz.)
1 egg white
1 tablespoon confectioner's sugar
1 tablespoon nonfat dried milk powder
Fine-grated cinnamon

### PREPARATION

1. Make a good coffee (see page 241) double strength.

2. Heat the milk with the vanilla extract, and add the coffee extract.

3. Place in the refrigerator to get very cold (always make up well ahead of time). Never add ice cubes; they dilute and ruin the drink.

4. For each pint of coffee/milk mixture, whip 1 egg white with 1 tablespoon confectioner's sugar and 1 tablespoon nonfat dried milk powder, and place a blob atop the ice-cold coffee just before serving. This will look like a good "head" of whipped cream and it tastes good, too. Dust the top with a little fine-grated cinnamon for that extra touch.

# Old-Fashioned Lemonade

**Yields 5 cups**

### INGREDIENTS:

4 lemons
⅔ cup sugar
5 cups water
5 leaves fresh mint
4 thin slices of fresh lemon

### PREPARATION

1. Cut the lemons into small pieces, skin and all, reserving 4 thin slices. Mix the cut pieces with the sugar in a heat-proof bowl.

2. Boil water and pour it over the lemon/sugar mixture. Let stand for 10 minutes, no longer, or a bitter taste will develop.

3. Stamp down the mix with a potato masher, strain, and pour into a jug. Decorate with the mint leaves and the lemon slices. Makes 40 fluid ounces.

The cost of a lemonade mix will be about the same as the homemade, but the flavor of the homemade is superior. Furthermore, the manufactured product is overly sweetened to compel overconsumption.

> *There is something elegant, Old World, and loving about a large pitcher of ice-cold, homemade lemonade surrounded by tall thin glasses. How this homey image has been ruined by foil envelopes of this and that slung together under a tap!*

# New Wine Recipes

> *We used, for our tests, Welch's White and Red Grape juices. These are bottled pure grape juices and do not need reconstitution.*
>
> *We are sure that there must be many other companies that process what we call new wine (non-alcoholic grape juice), but we are equally certain that the degree of natural sweetness will differ in each case. Therefore we use this brand name only as a base for our recipe measurements and not as an endorsement of its superior qualities.*

# New Apple Wine

### Yields 2 cups

**INGREDIENTS:**

⅝ cup white grape juice (5 fl. oz.)
¼ cup clear apple juice (2 fl. oz.)
1 cup ice cubes

**PREPARATION**

1. Combine items at slow speed in a blender.

2. Serve garnished with a slice of red apple, coated with lemon juice to prevent browning, and a straw. Makes 16 fluid ounces of juice at 24 calories per 4-ounce wine glass.

# New Claret

**INGREDIENTS:**

3 cups red grape juice (24 fl. oz.)
¼ - ½ cup strong cold tea —
add gradually to taste (2-4 fl. oz.)

**PREPARATION**

1. Make tea by pouring ¾ cup *boiling* water onto a teabag. Press it thoroughly and let it steep until cold.

2. Remove the teabag and add the cold tea to the grape juice.

Serve *lightly* chilled. It has an interesting turn in flavor associated with some claret wines.

# New Sangria

### INGREDIENTS:

New Claret Wine (above)
1 orange
1 lemon
1 teaspoon Angustura Bitters

### PREPARATION

1. Make New Claret recipe (above).

2. Add 1 orange and 1 lemon, both finely sliced, and 1 teaspoon Angustura Bitters. Add ice and serve.

# New White Wine

### INGREDIENTS:

½ cup white grape juice (4 fl. oz.)
1 teaspoon rice vinegar

### PREPARATION

Combine and use immediately.

> *This can be used in place of dry white wine called for in recipe books.*

# New Red Wine

### INGREDIENTS:

½ cup red (or purple) grape juice (4 fl. oz.)
1 tablespoon strong cold tea
1 tablespoon rice vinegar

### PREPARATION

Combine and use immediately.

You will find that I separate the grape juice and tea from the vinegar in some recipes for specific effects.

> *Use in lieu of red wines called for in recipe books.*

# HINTS

## Tea

The making of tea could hardly be described as an earth-shattering event, yet so many errors take place that it is quite possibly our worst kitchen moment. Here are some pointers:

- Tea is a fragrant herb — *the bag is insufficient protection.* Keep loose or bagged tea in jars with tightly fitting lids.
- Water should be allowed to run cold to remove the "pipe tastes" before adding to the kettle. This is especially important when you have been away from home, even for a day, and the chlorine has had time to "work" on the pipes and become concentrated.
- Water must boil *freshly;* if it boils too long it reduces the oxygen content that helps to release the aroma.
- "Instant Hot" systems do not make a good cup of tea because the water is heated constantly.
- The kettle should have a flat heavy base for electric and flat top stoves and a large open top to permit easy cleaning. It should be "Teflon" if possible to prevent an aluminum flavor and pot discoloration. Just look inside an old alloy kettle and you will see what I mean!
- For the teapot, clear glass is best because it removes the steeping time guesswork; you can *see* that it's the right color for you.
- Preheat the teapot by pouring in boiling water; pour it out, add teabags, pour on the *just* boiling water, stir 5 times and leave for 5 minutes.
- Serve China tea with lemon. For other teas, you can have cream, which is added to the cup *after* the tea, otherwise the tea "cracks" the cream, giving an off taste; or milk, which is added to the cup before the tea; or lemon, if you prefer. We use 2% fat milk in preference to whole milk.
- When using tea bags in a pot, we suggest you detach the swing tags before making. They look ugly hanging out of the pot and also they can impart a paper taste to the tea if left *inside.*

*Budget considerations can be important due to the tea bag count.* This is the number packaged per pound and gives you a clue on the strength you can expect. We buy Red Rose Tea because it has 160 bags to the pound instead of the usual 200. We find that our family gets enough tea for 2 cups each (8 total cups) from only 2 teabags.

*Sense advantage* is almost entirely aromatic with some taste pluses. The vital thing to remember with tea is to regard it as a fragrant herb and treat it accordingly, for that is what it is!

P.S. We use leftover tea as iced tea, simply pouring the dregs into an old ½-gallon fruit juice jar with a screw cap.

# the daily diet walk

# A Postscipt From Treena
# The Daily Diet Walk

Warning: This postscript is not for you if you are thin or can keep healthy and trim through exercise and moderate dieting. Graham has asked me to write this short chapter for those of us who need more than just a standard diet to keep us from becoming overweight. I'm certainly familiar with the problem; I've dieted since I was sixteen years old.

All too often during the last twenty years I have stood in front of a mirror, looking at myself while sucking in my breath and stomach at the same time.

"I'm fat!" I have said over and over again. Then I have questioned Graham, standing sideways in front of him, my hands on my stomach and back. "Do I look fat?"

Gray has looked at me, hesitated a split second, and said, "No darling, you look lovely!"

"You're just saying that to make me feel good. Shall I wear the other dress...the loose gray one? Don't you think it makes me look thinner?"

"Well..." Graham has said tentatively, "the gray dress does look much nicer on you and..."

"I knew it! You think I'm fat, too! Why don't you go out by yourself!"

Sometimes this scene has been violent, angry, with floods of tears and loud screams of foul language. But those were the days before Jesus changed my whole life and outlook. The violence changed, but the scenario lingered on:

"Are you sure I look alright?"

"Yes, darling."

"Well, say it like you mean it!"

"I already have — five or six times!"

"Well...I still feel fat!" No wonder. I was fat. I had a good twenty-five pounds worth of surplus fat on my five-foot-four body. And I continued to be fat until I realized my self-deception. Oh yes, I certainly ate less than most people, but I'd forget the times I'd eat as I prepared a meal, the odd piece of cheese I'd snack on when I went to the fridge, and the three-or-four pieces of fruit I'd eat in an evening.

At every meal I had a small plate of food with everyone else, and then would say, "I didn't have as much as you did, so I'm going to have a little more now." The "little more" was as much as anyone else had eaten by the time I'd finished my second "little more." I was caught in self-deception, something I have to be aware of even now.

I've tried diet pills, both prescription and over-the-counter. I've drunk potions and gone on the latest fad diets. I've eaten nothing, and then drunk gallons of water — both tap and distilled — and swallowed thousands of tablets to shift water retention. All this has caused me to lose hundreds of pounds — and gain them all back again in a week, or a month, or, at best, in a year.

Being fat, plump, or overweight all equal that horrible word *obese!* But some people are content and perfectly happy being pleasingly plump. It suits their nature, and no matter what they do, they will always be the contoured figure of a Reubens painting. So if you are truly content and comfortable with your weight, you do not need to read any further.

This chapter is for people like me, who lose the whole joy of living by being fat, concentrating on ourselves instead of on the Lord of our lives.

Feeling fat can cause stress within our relationships, both heavenly and earthly. It also causes a deep-seated lack of self-worth. How I hated buying clothes! I always came home feeling fatter than when I went out to shop. I'd buy dark, loose clothing, which in truth just emphasized my plumpness.

One trick I devised over the years was to ask the salesgirl for clothes that were one size larger than I really was. This was alright when I said "Size sixteen," and I really was a fourteen. But then came the fatal day when I was a sixteen. I had nowhere to go. A size sixteen for my height and bone structure was just too fat! Going shopping became as unpleasant as going to the doctor's for a feminine examination. I would get irritable as I planned the excursion, and by the time I returned home I had been utterly debilitated.

Just before I was chosen by Jesus, I lost approximately sixteen pounds so that I could have cosmetic surgery (a dignified term for a face lift). I had to get down to a reasonable weight before the operation could be done, and with effort I weighed in at about 125 pounds, still a little overweight. But I was right for me. I felt thin, looked good in my clothes, and felt well and happy. These are the signs an individual has attained his or her proper weight.

Later, when I became a committed Christian, I was warned by my new sisters in the Lord to be careful. "Watch your weight. It's the first thing the enemy likes to attack so you'll stop thinking about the Lord and concentrate on yourself."

I didn't listen. I boasted about how easy it was for me to fast for the Lord — and that would keep me thin. However, fasting "for the Lord" soon became, "fasting for me." Over the next few years I shouted and pleaded with God to take my weight away or keep me from eating, but nothing happened. Instead I got fatter. Why? I'd get really angry at God and eat out of rebellion. Obviously this didn't hurt Him — just me.

"Why can't I lose weight, Gray?" I complained. "I eat so little — half of what other people eat!" (the first time round!).

I continued to deceive myself up to a large, but not so jolly, 150 pounds. Finally I cried out again to the Lord, but this time not in demand or anger, just in sorrow and despair. I had seen myself a few days earlier on a television program, and I really did look like the proverbial side of a house, a very lumpy house at that.

After my desperate prayer, I waited and listened for a reply. I have found that it really helps to listen after prayer, for as we wait, we truly hear. Father must get so sad when we ask and then put the receiver down, so to speak, before he has time to give us his answer. This night I waited and listened, hoping to hear an answer to my fleshy problem, and assuredly I got one. The Lord impressed upon me to go to a local exercise establishment, and do exactly what they told me to do. Exactly!

When I went to sign up for their three-month course, I replied truthfully when the receptionist asked, "Who recommended you to us?"

"The Lord," I replied, "while I was in prayer." What better recommendation could they have had!

I hate exercise. Graham, bless him, had tried over and over to scare me with every frightening statistic he knew to make me either jog, walk fast, bicycle, or even row. It had been to no avail. I would try out of obedience to his wishes, but my heart wasn't in it. But this time, I had felt the Lord's direction. I had to do his bidding.

To say that within six weeks I was down to 140 pounds will show you that I was obedient. I did all that the professionals at the exercise salon suggested, even to the vitamin pill intake, which I knew Graham disapproved of.

But Graham continually praised and encouraged me, even when I was eating my vitamin pills. After a few months he admitted, "Well, darling, it's not what I would have chosen for you, but it's working. It shows me that obedience to the Lord and self-discipline are the answer, whether I agree with the methodology or not."

I still dislike exercise. It takes a good two hours of my time, which I can ill afford. But due to the disciplined training of the professionals at the exercise establishment, I can exercise daily at home and walk with Jesus during the day. I ask him whether I can have this or that, and I get "Yes," "No," or "One only, today." It's not easy. I am in constant warfare with the enemy. But I know I can win if I'm obedient and disciplined and don't lie to myself.

Here is the diet that I followed. Maybe it will help you overcome your struggles with overweight:

*Day 1*  1 8-oz. glass of water every hour
1 B, C, and calcium tablet every 2 hours

*Day 2*  Breakfast — 1 boiled egg
Lunch    — 1 boiled egg
Dinner   — 1 poached egg on 6-oz. of spinach (steamed with lemon juice)

*Day 3*  Breakfast — 1 boiled egg
Lunch    — 1 boiled egg
Dinner   — Breast of steamed chicken with 6-oz. of spinach or asparagus

*Day 4*  Breakfast — 1 boiled egg
Lunch    — Fresh spinach salad with 1 boiled egg
Dinner   — Steamed fish and broccoli

*Day 5*  Breakfast — 2 scrambled eggs
Lunch    — Spinach salad
Dinner   — Steamed chicken or fish with green beans, asparagus, or spinach

I followed this menu for a few weeks, making sure that each day I drank eight 8-oz. glasses of water and had a one-hour physical workout.

Now the following diet forms the basics of my eating habit:

*Vitamins*  4 B-complex (B-1, B-2, B-6, B-12) with meals each day
4 C's with meals
2 E's, one in the morning, one at night
6 calcium tablets (2 at a time, 3 times a day)
3 zinc tablets (1 at a time, 3 times a day)
3 lecithin tablets (1 at a time, 3 times a day)
4 kelp and alfalfa tablets (1 at a time, 4 times a day)
4 apple cider vinegar tablets (1 at a time, 4 times a day)
(I also take 2 B-6 tablets, 3 times a day, because I need them as a diuretic).

*Meat*  Broiled beef steak, very occasionally
Steamed breast of chicken, no skin
Steamed breast of turkey
Steamed fresh fish
None of the following: ham, bacon, pork

*Eggs*  Boiled
Water-poached
Scrambled, without butter or milk (I put parsley in the eggs with a little sprinkle of bacon bits.)

*Fruit*  One piece of fruit a day. The following have the least calories and carbohydrates:
Strawberries (You can have a serving of 8, since it is rather difficult to have just one!)
Peaches
Nectarines

None of the following:  Salt
Potatoes
Soft drinks
Cookies
Pastry
Peas
Corn
Bananas
Bread (You may begin to have 1 piece a day after 6 weeks.)

There is no secret formula for losing weight and keeping it off except obedience, discipline, and a changed life-style of eating. For me it is a daily diet walk with Jesus. Without Him I would fall back into my old lazy ways.

It used to be a pain every time I went out to a restaurant, because I had to look for a nonsauce, non-fat dish. I'd eat, and still do, a salad mostly of alfalfa sprouts, fresh mushrooms, celery, tomatoes, and fresh spinach if possible. I always ask the waiter to make sure there was no fat or butter on my broiled fish. Instead you can ask the waiter for a garnish of sliced mushrooms. I used to be embarrassed to ask the waiter, but now it's becoming a habit. As for dessert, I have none — just a spoonful of Graham's, should he have one, or some fresh fruit with Sanka.

The continuing excuse that we have to eat what people prepare for us is a lie. We won't offend anyone if we eat around the sauce and leave no-no's on the plate. No one even notices if you eat just a little.

At the time of this writing I'm down to 131 pounds. I still need to lose another 6-to-7 pounds, and slowly I will — with the grace of disciplined obedience and a daily diet walk with Jesus.

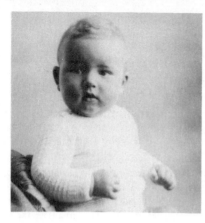

index

index

index

index